PUBLISHER'S NOTE:

on the back cover of this book, and also repro-
the plates, shows an original tape cassette on
sation with her friend James Colthurst, the
secretly recorded details of her life for Andrew
Her True Story. Colthurst smuggled the cassettes
Palace to Morton, who would then write up the
it back to the Princess for her comments and
shown are: correspondence from Diana to
at time, in which she expressed her appreciation
pport; a list of questions that Morton wanted
Diana; pages from the first draft of *Diana: Her*
th Diana marked her amendments; a page from
the Prince and Princess of Wales for the period
; a fax from Colthurst to 'The Mum Who
sent more than a year after the publication of
accompanying corrections the two men had
ech to the Centrepoint charity.

D

In

Dian
Moi

Nine For N

The photograph
duced as one of
which, in conver
Princess of Wales
Morton's *Diana: H*
out of Kensington
material and send
corrections. Also
Colthurst from th
of his help and su
Colthurst to put to
True Story, on whi
the official diary of
around publicatio
Should Be Proud',
Morton's book an
made to Diana's sp

DIANA

In Pursuit of Love

ANDREW MORTON

MICHAEL O'MARA BOOKS LIMITED

First published in Great Britain in 2004 by
Michael O'Mara Books Limited
9 Lion Yard, Tremadoc Road
London sw4 7nq

First published in the United States of America in 2004

ISBN 1-84317-084-1

Designed and typeset by Martin Bristow

Printed in the United States of America

Contents

Acknowledgements

O VER THE YEARS I have come to know some of those in whom Diana, Princess of Wales confided, and it will be apparent in my narrative that I have had numerous off-the-record conversations with people close to major events in her life. I would like to express my heartfelt gratitude to them for their insights and advice.

In the eighteen months it has taken to research and write this book I have enjoyed numerous convivial conversations with many others whose lives were also touched in some way by the late Princess. My thanks go to: Dickie Arbiter, LVO; Steven Bartlett; Carolan Brown; Dr James Colthurst; Paul Cooper; Mohamed Fayed; Debbie Frank; Philip Garvin, CEO Response International; Geordie Greig; Richard Greene; David Griffin; Robert Heindel; Soheir Khashoggi; Robert Lacey; Brian Lask; Ken Lennox; Keith Leverton; Thierry Meresse; Betty Palko; Vivienne Parry; Jean-Marie Pontaut; David Puttnam; Jenni Rivett; Ian Sparks; Raine, Countess Spencer; Chester Stern; Oonagh Shanley-Toffolo; Penny Thornton; Stephen Twigg; Matthias Wiessler; Ken Wharfe, and Hassan Yassin.

My thanks too to my researcher, Lily Williams, for her valiant efforts under continuous pressure. As ever I owe an immense debt to my editors Dominique Enright and Toby Buchan, as well as to the rest of the editorial team at Michael O'Mara Books for their fortitude, steadiness and support, in particular Helen Cumberbatch, Kate Gribble, Judith Palmer and Chris Maynard. My thanks too to Martin Bristow for designing the text, to Glen Saville for his jacket design, and to Andy Armitage for the index. Finally, from the walk along the beach to the trip down memory lane, Michael O'Mara has been, as he has always been, a great supporter and witness.

Photograph Acknowledgements

Alpha: 12 below right, 15, 18 below left, 19, 20 above, 22 above left, 26 below.
James Colthurst: 1 below.
Daily Mail/Solo Syndication: 1 above.
expresspictures.com: 9 above right.
By kind permission of Siân Frances: 31 above right.
Philip Garvin: 32 below left.
Getty Images: 24 below left.
Shelley Klein (© Michael O'Mara Books Ltd): 4 above.
Ken Lennox: 4 centre left and below, 5 above, 6 above, 10 main photo, 16, 20 below.
James McCauley/Capital Pictures: 24 right.
Michael O'Mara Books Ltd: 2, 3.
PA Photos: 9 above left, 18 above.
Rex Features: 5 below right, 6 below right, 7, 8, 9 below, 11, 12 above and below left, 13, 14, 17, 18 below right, 21, 22 below, 23, 25, 26 above left and right, 27, 28, 29, 30, 31 below, 32 above left and below right.
AboveFoto: 10 inset.

INTRODUCTION

Love Factually

O NE SATURDAY in March 2004 I was in my study adding the finishing touches to Chapter Eleven of this book when the front-door bell rang. It was a reporter from the tabloid *Sunday People* newspaper. She had been sent to get a quote from me about a story they were about to print. It concerned the contents of this book. They had learned, from the usual impeccable sources, that I was going to reveal in the book the identity of three of Diana's secret lovers. The actor Terence Stamp, a rich captain of industry and a British movie heart-throb, who was in his fifties, were on my list. I flatly denied the story and went back to work.

The next day I bought the *Sunday People* newspaper and discovered that the story occupied the front page and two inside pages with the headlines, 'Diana Sex Bombshell' and 'Named: Diana's Three Secret Lovers' (only one so-called lover was named). It went on to detail how the 'besotted' Princess had launched an 'astonishing stalking campaign to woo the three secret lovers', 'lovelorn' Diana bombarding the men with intimate letters. The authority for this story was my as yet unpublished 'explosive' new book. The article went on to suggest how the wealthy but unnamed captain of industry had consummated his affair with the Princess at the home of a mutual friend. The newspaper's source was quoted as saying, 'Some authors could be accused of picking names out of a hat but Morton has pored over thousands of

documents and interviewed hundreds of very well-placed people.'
All very flattering.

By Monday the story, which went round the world, was given a
further twist in the *Daily Mail* when they described the 'terrible
anguish' suffered by William and Harry over this new information. 'There seems to be no end to it,' noted a concerned royal
source. Then it was the turn of the columnists to weight in with
their five-cents' worth. In the *Daily Express* Vanessa Feltz was
delighted that the Princess had found 'tender, considerate
romance' with Terence Stamp, who, she was sure, would have
treated her with the 'utmost delicacy'. Not to be outdone, Diana's
former butler Paul Burrell – whose own book Diana's sons called a
'cold and overt' betrayal – joined the commentary. 'I think it's
disgusting, to be honest,' was Burrell's considered view of my
unpublished book. 'What goes on between two people behind
closed doors should be private. I've always respected people's
private lives and I have never talked about Diana's love life. What
he is doing is terrible.'

To round off the coverage, the *Sunday Times* published a full-
page profile of Stamp, who first made his name in the Swinging
Sixties and has followed a distinguished career ever since, not only
in the movies but as the author of a novel and an autobiography.

In consequence of all this media activity, within a matter of days,
a large number of people, in Britain and beyond, had some sort of
idea that Diana, obsessed and lovelorn, had pursued and had had
affairs with Terence Stamp and several other unnamed men.

There was only one problem with the story. It was utterly
untrue.

The bizarre episode reminded me of why I returned to the
subject of Diana, Princess of Wales in the first place, some twelve
years after my first biography, *Diana: Her True Story*, written with
her consent and cooperation, was published in 1992. This latest
work has its origins during a walk along St Petersburg beach in
Florida with my publisher Michael O'Mara one morning in
November 2002, when I was promoting a book called *Nine For
Nine* about the rescue of a group of Pennsylvania miners who had
been trapped below ground for three days.

At the time, the trial on charges of theft of Paul Burrell was taking place at the Old Bailey in London. During TV and radio interviews in America I would be asked about the miners but also about the significance of the evidence in the trial. As Mike and I discussed the trial and Diana during our morning stroll it seemed that the woman we had come to know during our collaboration with her during the early 1990s was rapidly disappearing from view, her personality diminishing with every passing year. Listening to the commentary on her life based on evidence from the trial, it was as though the jigsaw puzzle of her personality had been scattered – so much had been forgotten but also exaggerated or distorted. The letters which Prince Philip sent to the Princess following the publication of my 1992 biography, for instance, were discussed during the trial and given a quite disproportionate significance. In any case, the letters had been comprehensively discussed a decade before by myself and others.

This distortion has gone on apace since her death. Some of those who knew or worked for the Princess have offered their own recollections of her character, often exaggerating their own importance in her life, airing their disappointment with her, or continuing their own vendettas in the pages of their memoirs. Her private secretary Patrick Jephson, for example, probably burst into print too soon with *Shadows of a Princess*, about his years as the late Princess's private secretary, the bitterness of his departure colouring many of his judgements. It is noticeable that in his subsequent newspaper articles he now writes much more warmly and sympathetically about Diana, perhaps realizing, from his own experience, the difficulties she faced in trying to forge her own life outside the royal compound. Similarly, Diana's butler Paul Burrell allowed the anger he feels towards the Spencer family, whom he blames for his trial for theft at the Old Bailey, to infect the narrative of his memoir, *A Royal Duty*.

Stories and opinions abound, the bewildered public treated to a parade of witnesses giving often contradictory impressions and anecdotes from their own necessarily narrow perspective. Harrods owner Mohamed Fayed, father of Diana's last lover Dodi, for example, has consistently argued that his son was going to marry her. This contention, together with his staunch advocacy that there was a conspiracy to murder his son and the Princess, has affected the way the world assesses Diana's last days. Others insist that she herself had told them she had no plans to remarry, while there are those who believe that it was Hasnat Khan she truly wanted to marry.

So even for those who know the characters involved, much has to be decoded. What is said or written is often not what is meant. This is difficult for someone who knows the royal terrain – it is virtually impossible for interested observers. The fact that Diana lived her life in compartments, closing off whole areas of her life to those who now say they knew her well, has made the process of assessing her life in the round even more complicated.

All the while, the continuing description of her life is via the distorting prism of the mass media. This is a trap for the unwary chronicler, for much of what is, and has been, written about the Princess bears scant relation either to events or to her personality. The article in the *Sunday People*, although particularly outrageous, is merely a vivid example. It means that judgements and conclusions based on its evidence are unavoidably distorted. In this book I have tried, as far as possible, to place Diana's decisions in the context of what was actually going on in her life, rather than what the public and media assumed was taking place.

Traditionally when an important public figure dies, the memoirs from friends, staff and others enrich the subject's life. But in Diana's case she seems to have been diminished, the impression that, following her separation and divorce, her life had little meaning, direction or worth, escalating since her untimely death. The Princess had been, to quote one respected biographer, 'spiralling out of control', a woman who was much loved but basically unstable.

Could it be that all the heartache and endeavour she had gone through to present her story to the world through *Diana: Her True Story*, and subsequently to take control of her life, were wasted? If that was indeed the case, though, how then was it possible to explain the spontaneous outpouring of grief at her death, an upsurge of emotion surely linked to the esteem and respect in which she was held?

What seems to have been lost is any sense or acknowledgement that here was a woman, who – still relatively young and often alone – struggled to make sense of an awesome public position and a difficult private life. As Diana's life was cut short, the starting point of her search for a life of her own – her collaboration with her biography – has assumed a greater importance than we realized at the time. That too needed comprehensive re-evaluation, as did her other major mass-media undertaking – her famous 1995 BBC Television *Panorama* interview. The secretive causes and far-reaching consequences of that interview have now assumed historic proportions.

In trying to make sense of a complicated and extraordinary life, all too often little consideration is given as to how far Diana had travelled, and the personal and social obstacles she had striven to overcome. Here was a woman, who in the words of Hillary Clinton, showed 'courage and persistence in getting up and going on whenever life knocked her to the mat'. This book is an attempt to describe and celebrate that journey.

ANDREW MORTON
London, April 2004

PROLOGUE

A Grotesque Tableau

For Ken Lennox, an award-winning photographer and picture editor of the *Sun*, that Saturday night in August was no different from any other. Something of a night owl, the Scotsman was pottering quietly around his apartment in Primrose Hill, North London. As picture editor of Britain's bestselling tabloid, he was idly considering the following day's selection of photographs – images that could make the paper. Naturally, coverage would be dominated by sport, although the ongoing romance between Diana, Princess of Wales and Dodi Fayed, son of the Harrods owner Mohamed Fayed, would feature somewhere. Given the fact that Britain's public had been teased and titillated over the last few weeks with pictures of Diana on holiday with her latest lover, Lennox knew that any snaps had to be exceptional to captivate a public becoming sated with the tale of Diana's romance.

At 12.20 in the morning he was just getting into bed when his mobile phone rang. The voice of his caller was compelling, excited and French. Although Lennox did not know his face, he knew the voice – and the reputation – of the distinguished photographer Romuald Rat, who had exchanged conflict in the Congo and other trouble spots for celebrity chasing. It was 1.20 a.m. in Paris and not the time for small talk – this was strictly business.

'Ken, there's been a crash,' said the urgent voice at the other end of the line. 'Dodi is very badly injured but Diana looks all right. I have pix from the scene showing them still in the car.'

Lennox asked how much. 'You can have first publication, one day's use only. I want three million francs [about £300,000 or US $540,000].'

Lennox agreed without demur and told him to wire the images to the *Sun*'s picture desk in Wapping in East London. As he dragged on a pair of jogging pants and running shoes he told the Frenchman not to speak to anyone else.

Even before Lennox had clambered into the taxi he had hurriedly summoned, the pictures of Diana and Dodi were on his 'electronic picture desk', a sophisticated computer system that allowed him to view pictures from agencies all over the world. Other exclusive deals, with the potential to make many thousands of dollars, were already under way with publications across the globe. At that moment those photographs were among the most valuable goods on the planet.

While these business deals were being made, the dying princess was gently being removed from the wrecked Mercedes and carefully placed inside an ambulance. As she made her painfully slow last journey to the Pitié-Salpétrière hospital, the ambulance stopping twice to give the paramedics a chance to stabilize the grievously injured woman, her last moments alive were being sold to the highest bidder. That she should have become a prisoner of the flashbulbs even as her life ebbed away was a crude, cruel reflection of her life as an iconic commodity.

By the time Lennox had reached his office and opened up his electronic picture desk he had already dispatched the veteran royal photographer Arthur Edwards and a dozen more cameramen to Paris. Ken and Arthur were old sparring partners. They had both been on the banks of the River Dee at Balmoral in the summer of 1980, taking part in the annual stalking of Prince Charles and his latest love. This new girlfriend seemed much smarter than the others. When she had spotted the photographers as they materialized on the opposite bank of the river she had turned smartly and marched up the slope, never once looking back. Then she had used the mirror from her powder compact to get a better view of her media adversaries. As she explained to me some ten years later: 'I saw them appearing from the other side. I said to Charles I must get out of the way. You don't need any aggravation.' Her reaction meant that the only picture Lennox snapped that day was a back view of what looked like an attractive young girl. At the time he was intrigued that this young woman had shown such presence of mind.

Now, some seventeen years later, the man who took the first-ever press photograph of Lady Diana Spencer was looking at the last pictures of a dying Diana, Princess of Wales crumpled in the back of a black Mercedes limousine in the Pont de l'Alma underpass in central Paris. The pictures had been taken perhaps a minute or two after the accident, and certainly before the first fire engine arrived on the scene at 12.32 a.m. Lennox had little time for reflection as he looked at the pictures, but as he gazed at the grotesque tableau of the photo marked 'BIS.JPG@100%' it was clear to him that Dodi, his jeans ripped by shards of glass and metal and one leg twisted at an impossible angle, was seriously injured, probably dead; as was the driver, Henri Paul, who was sprawled motionless over the driving wheel.

At first sight it seemed that Diana had escaped relatively unscathed. She was hunched up on the floor facing away from the front passenger seat. A smear of blood on her right hand and in her blonde hair seemed to indicate that at some point she had been conscious and had tried to brush her hair away from her face. But the blood trickling from her left ear and from her nostrils gave Lennox an uneasy sense of foreboding – she did not look like someone who was going to be 'all right'.

When the managing editor of News International, Les Hinton – a veteran newsman who made his name on the Washington beat – hurried into the newsroom, shouting 'What do you know?' Lennox told him of his concerns. A newly arrived picture, labelled 'DI3.JPG(RGB)', confirmed his growing feeling of apprehension. It showed Frédéric Maillez, a young doctor working with SOS

Médecins, who happened to be driving by and had stopped to help, crouching over the Princess, trying to introduce air from an oxygen bottle into her nose and mouth. With her head lolling downwards and a glassy stare in her eyes, Diana seemed to be slipping away.

As the two men deliberated on whether to use the pictures, their conversation was punctuated by a babble from a bank of TV screens and the racking sobs of a young female freelance reporter sitting on the news desk. 'Les, if she is dead we can't use them,' Lennox told Hinton. 'If she is injured, we can.' There was no debate. The executive simply nodded, then raced across the office to warn the editor of the *News of the World*, Phil Hall, who was still in evening dress, having been summoned from a formal dinner when news of the crash came in.

Even as the front page of the *News of the World* was being changed to make room for the story and photographs from Paris, word was filtering through that photographers at the scene of the crash were being rounded up and arrested. 'That was the first time I felt sick,' recalls Lennox. 'I couldn't believe the names as they came over the wires. These were not paparazzi but brilliant, award-winning photographers who had worked in trouble spots around the world. But in our celebrity-obsessed world they earn more from a pavement shot of Diana than in two months working in central Africa.'

In Paris, as the medical team at the Pitié-Salpêtrière hospital tried in vain to revive the Princess, Father Yves Clochard-Bossuet was summoned and asked to administer the last rites to her. The first indication waiting photographers had of the drama unfolding inside the hospital was when they saw an official from the British Embassy step out of a hospital room, lean back, and then start sliding down the wall, clearly in deep distress.

At four o'clock in Paris (3 a.m. in London), Diana was pronounced dead. At once the photographs of her lying in the back of the wrecked Mercedes were transformed from a valuable commodity into a curse, a veritable plague that infected everyone who touched them. 'Delete, delete, delete,' Lennox shouted to his technician, Mark Hunt. 'Bury them in the machine.' From that moment on the pictures, for all intents and purposes, ceased to exist, and anyone who asked about them was given a curt and abrupt answer regarding their whereabouts. For they were now evidence of a terrible complicity in the shameful ending of the fairy tale; a damsel in distress exploited by commercial greed to feed the public's shameless voyeurism. As for the photographers who had milled around the wrecked car only seconds after the crash, they now began their own journey, a nightmare that started in a police cell and ended in prosecution, financial ruin and, for at least one, suicide.

While the pictures of the dying Princess became a liability rather than an exclusive, Lennox was enough of a seasoned campaigner to realize that one day they might well surface. In his work in the war zones of the world, the award-winning photographer had a rule of thumb for some of the gruesome images he witnessed and captured on film: today, tomorrow, and maybe never. He put the Diana pictures into the 'maybe never' category, believing that one day someone, somewhere might take a chance and publish them. Seven years later, in April 2004, he was proved right when, in America, CBS TV broadcast grainy shots of the Princess trapped in the car as part of a documentary 'investigating' the crash.

On that fateful night, 31 August 1997, Diana had been on a different journey, one that began in hope and ended in tragedy, a life cut short just as it was truly beginning. While it was the journey of only one woman, somehow it came to embrace and involve us all. In a life of many contrasts and contradictions, one of the most savage of ironies is that Diana's life ended in a tunnel just as she was seeing light at the end of her own long march to fulfilment and happiness.

CHAPTER ONE

Hard Road to Freedom

THE PRINCESS OF WALES was deep in dinner-table conversation with the film producer David Puttnam. They had
known each other for years and Diana regarded Puttnam as one of
the uncle figures in her life, a shoulder to lean on and a sympathetic ear always there to listen during times of trouble.

At that time, in March 1992, Puttnam, who was part of a growing group of insiders who had some inkling about her troubled life,
sensed that Diana was under greater stress than usual. As they
chatted at an AIDS symposium at Claridge's Hotel in central
London, the conversation turned to crossing bridges – making
momentous decisions where there is no going back. Conspiratorially, she said to him, 'David, I think I've done the thing in my
life that is going to change it the most. I've been talking to a journalist and there's a book being published. It has reached a point
where there is no way back. And I'm terrified.'

She then stood up and gave a barnstorming speech about her
involvement with and commitment to the fight against AIDS,
before coolly answering questions from her audience of media and
medical experts including Baroness Jay and Professor Michael Adler.

Diana was once asked if she gambled. 'Not with cards but with
life,' was her reply. She was now on the threshold of the first of
several throws of the dice.

The journalist to whom she was referring was me and the book was *Diana: Her True Story*, first published in June 1992, which, with her enthusiastic collaboration, explored her unhappy life inside the royal family and exploded the myth of her fairy-tale marriage.

The book had its origins in the incongruous setting of a hospital canteen in October 1986. Here Dr James Colthurst was relaxing after escorting the Princess of Wales on an official visit to open a new CT scanner in the X-ray department at St Thomas' Hospital in central London where he was at that time working. I was there as the royal correspondent for the *Daily Mail* newspaper, and over tea and biscuits I asked him about the visit. It quickly became clear that Colthurst was rather more than just a hospital medic acting as a guide to the royal personage, but a friend who had known her for years.

Over the years Colthurst and I became friendly, enjoying games of squash in the hospital courts followed by large lunches in a nearby Italian restaurant. In the time-honoured fashion I initially tried to cultivate him as a contact but soon discovered that he was the classic royal insider, happy to talk volubly about anything but the royal family. Our early acquaintance gradually mellowed into friendship as we established a tacit understanding that when we met for lunch the subject of Diana was strictly off the menu.

During the late 1980s Colthurst, the son of a baronet whose family have owned Blarney Castle in Ireland for more than a century, was rekindling his friendship with the Princess, which had been cemented a decade earlier on a skiing holiday in the French Alps in the winter of 1979.

In the course of that holiday Lady Diana Spencer, who had been introduced to Colthurst and his chalet party by a mutual friend, joined them at an expensive disco in the Tignes resort Val Claret one evening. She enthusiastically participated in a ruse devised by Colthurst so as to enjoy the dancing without paying for the overpriced drinks pressed on the clientele by hovering waiters. Colthurst deliberately bumped into a pillar on the dance floor, bit into a blood capsule for dramatic effect, and in the fracas was 'helped' out of the club by Diana and another girl. The stunt, albeit rather juvenile, was very much in keeping with the rest of that skiing week, which Diana later described as one of the best holidays of her life.

While Diana liked innocent and rather silly practical jokes, Colthurst recollected one not-so-innocent prank of which Diana and her friends were the victims, when, during a weekend at a friend's farm cottage in Oxfordshire, they unknowingly consumed large quantities of hashish that had been mixed into the chilli con carne. Diana got unstoppable giggles and had a severe attack of 'the munchies', making night-time raids on the kitchen to devour chocolate bars and sweets. Others, though, were violently ill, and Colthurst, then a medical student, had to keep an all-night vigil by the side of his sky-high friends even though he too was affected.

Most of the time though their encounters were rather more mundane. Colthurst and others of their set became regular visitors to Diana's apartment in Coleherne Court during her short but jolly time as a bachelor girl. From time to time she cooked him dinner, they danced together at the Hurlingham Ball and on occasion she visited his flat in Pimlico, usually accompanied by her friend Philippa Coker. 'She was good fun and good company, it was as simple as that,' Colthurst later recalled. 'There was never any suggestion of a romance; she isn't my type, nor I hers.' Indeed, during her courtship with Prince Charles in the autumn of 1980, James Colthurst got an idea of the way the wind was blowing when he arrived at her apartment one evening for dinner. Diana, who was busy getting ready for her royal date, had forgotten all about her dinner guest. She rushed out to the corner store, bought some food and ordered her flatmates to rustle up a meal for him. When she returned from Buckingham Palace at about midnight she was dewy-eyed and her main topic of conversation was Prince Charles's wellbeing. 'It's appalling the way they push him around,' she said, referring to his commitments and his demanding staff.

With her elevation to the role of Princess of Wales in 1981, the easy familiarity that had characterized Diana's bachelor life was lost, and for several years there was an inevitable distance between herself and her 'Coleherne Court'. She did, however, attend the occasional get-together with James Colthurst, now working in various hospitals in the Home Counties, and a handful of other old friends, including Colthurst's fellow old Etonian Adam Russell and her schoolfriend Carolyn Bartholomew, who became godmother to Prince William. Even so, it was not until after Diana's formal visit to St Thomas' Hospital in 1986 that she and Colthurst began again to see each other more frequently.

They enjoyed a number of jolly lunches at Italian or Chinese restaurants in their old Fulham stamping grounds and it was at these meetings that Colthurst noticed how she would bolt down her food and then go to the ladies' – a classic feature of the binge-and-purge symptom that characterizes the so-called slimmers' disease, bulimia nervosa. At first he didn't think too much of her behaviour as she had always had a hearty appetite as a teenager. But some time later Carolyn Bartholomew expressed to him her concern about Diana's eating habits and they discussed the illness and its dire long-term effects. It was after this conversation that Carolyn Bartholomew decided to make her famous threat – that if Diana did not get help she would go to the media and tell them about the Princess's eating disorder.

By degrees Colthurst began to catch glimpses into the true nature of the life Diana was trying to come to terms with. Her marriage had failed, and her husband was having an affair with Camilla Parker Bowles, the wife of his army officer friend Andrew, but she was expected to keep up the appearances required by the royal family, and live a life of pretence. At Kensington Palace she felt she was controlled by courtiers who preferred her to be seen – looking quiescently attractive – and not heard. It was a claustrophobic life, made worse in that everyone, from the Queen downwards, was in some way, knowingly or unknowingly, colluding in the duplicity. In Dianaland conspiracies were not theories but a daily reality.

Everyone felt the strain of this deception. When Dickie Arbiter first began working for the Waleses as a press officer in July 1988 he found himself in an 'impossible' position, maintaining to the world the illusion of happy royal families while turning a blind eye to the private distance between them. At the end of an engagement in London, for example, the Prince and Princess would leave together – but they would only travel together as far as Friary Court at St James's Palace before one of them would get into a second car. 'She would return to Kensington Palace and he would go off and make, ahem, late-night visits to museums and art galleries,' Arbiter recollected. 'It was best not to ask where he really went.' When Prince Charles broke his arm in a polo accident in June 1990 and was taken to Cirencester Hospital, his staff listened intently to the police radios reporting on the progress of the Princess of Wales on her journey to the hospital, so that they could usher out his first visitor – Camilla – before Diana arrived.

Other royal staff were pulled, often against their will, into the deception: the bodyguard who accompanied the Prince on his nocturnal visits to Middlewick House, Camilla's home, eleven miles from Highgrove, the Waleses' country house; the butler and the chef ordered to prepare and serve a supper they knew the Prince would not be eating as he had gone to see his lover; the valet who had to take a pen and circle programmes in the TV listings guide, *Radio Times*, to give the impression that Charles had spent a quiet evening alone at home in front of the television. 'We've all kept his secrets and the strain made me very ill,' Ken Stronach, a former valet to the Prince, admitted to the *Daily Mail* in January 1995. 'Everything he told us to do was a lie.'

Diana was effectively the focus of a conspiracy, a conspiracy to deceive and hoodwink both herself and the public that would have continued indefinitely, and which involved those she trusted, admired and loved. When she questioned Prince Charles's friends about Camilla, they told her that her suspicions were misplaced, that Mrs Parker Bowles was merely an old friend. As Diana's concerns multiplied they told each other that she was paranoid, fanciful or obsessively jealous. The Queen Mother dismissed her misgivings as the imaginings of a 'silly girl' – a view echoed by other senior royals – while Lord Romsey and his wife Penny, who had spent a wasted hour trying to persuade the Prince not to propose to Lady Diana Spencer when he asked for their counsel during a visit to their home of Broadlands, dubbed her 'that madwoman'. She was all too often so called by the members of Prince Charles's set, who continued to say she was paranoid to the end of her days and beyond.

Making her situation untenable was Diana's belief that by labelling her mad it was only one step away from admitting her to a psychiatric ward. 'It's almost as if they want to put me away,' she told Colthurst. After all, during the desperate days of depression and bulimia she suffered at Balmoral soon after becoming a member of the royal family, the first response had been to summon psychiatrists. The Princess also knew that, under British law, the Queen had legal guardianship of the immediate heirs to the throne, rather than the boys' mother. If she was 'put away' or if she fled, Diana would lose her children.

Far from being the ravings of a madwoman, Diana's suspicions were to prove regrettably correct, and the painful awareness of the way she had been so grievously deceived, not just by Prince Charles but by so many inside the royal system, instilled in her an absolute distrust of the Establishment and all its works that would shape her behaviour for the rest of her life.

In the late 1980s the Princess was coming to realize that unless she took some drastic action she faced a life sentence of unhappiness and dishonesty. Her first thought was simply to pack her bags and flee to Australia with her two young sons. There were echoes here of the behaviour of her own mother, who, following her acrimonious divorce from the late Earl Spencer, and a subsequent remarriage and divorce, now lives as a virtual recluse on a remote cottage on the bleak island of Seil in north-west Scotland, a world away from her earlier life at the heart of Norfolk aristocracy.

While more and more insiders were becoming aware of the circle of deceit, only a handful of her friends were aware of Diana's increasing desperation. Sometime in 1990 James Colthurst was made graphically aware of the gravity of her plight when she spoke seriously of standing in the middle of Kensington High Street and shouting out her tale of woe to an astonished world. 'As your enemies think you are mad,' Colthurst reminded her drily, 'that course of action will hardly strengthen your position.'

While his comment snapped her out of her reckless mood, Colthurst and others now began to appreciate how very critical her situation had become. 'At that stage she wanted to shout her outrage from the rooftops. She wanted to bring the whole house down,' he recalled. 'The consequences didn't bear thinking about.' He continued, 'Her anger about the duplicity practised by her husband and the organization had reached a pitch where at times she was out of control, sometimes in tears, others quite depressed. Indeed, the reason why she went for long car drives on her own or had colonic irrigation was to come to terms with the anger she felt.'

Matters were not helped by the instability in the marriage of the Princess's friend, the Duchess of York, who was in the midst of an affair with a Texan playboy, Steve Wyatt. At the same time, though, Diana was downplaying her own relationship with an army officer, James Hewitt, whom she passed off as a friend who was teaching her boys to ride. Even when she was eventually confronted with her own infidelity she rationalized her behaviour as a reaction to her husband's long-term relationship with Camilla Parker Bowles.

Watching his friend's emotional pendulum swing back and forth, Colthurst considered her plight. He realized that she would gain some moral strength if she could control at least a small fragment of her life inside the royal system – then she would have a fighting chance of making reasoned decisions about her future.

For someone as emotionally fragile as Diana, little things could mean a great deal – a haircut could change her outlook on life, for instance. A new hairstylist, Sam McKnight, a friend of her favourite photographer, the Frenchman Patrick Demarchelier, had impressed her because, in her words, he 'let out something quite different' when he shaped her hair, giving her greater confidence and sense of self-worth. But minor morale-boosters aside, the bigger question lay unresolved: how to give the public a true insight into her side of the story while untangling the emotional and constitutional knots strangling her life and her marriage. It was a genuine predicament. If she had simply packed her bags and left, as she would have liked to do, the public, which still believed in the myth of the fairy-tale marriage, would have considered her behaviour irrational, hysterical and profoundly immature. More than that, she would have been in danger of losing her children, just as her mother had done a quarter of a century before.

'We hacked around a number of options,' Dr Colthurst reminisced. 'It was obvious that it was an issue she had discussed with others and that it preyed constantly on her mind. The first and simplest solution was for Diana to confront her husband. But she had tried that. By then Prince Charles's relationship with Camilla Parker Bowles had become quite blatant and even when she had shouted at him, ranted and raved, she had been ignored. She felt totally disempowered. She had seen the Queen, who sympathized, knew what was going on but had nothing to offer.

'The second scenario was to continue her silence and seek psychiatric help. She had already tried that. The problem was that she knew that she wasn't ill – it was the circumstances affecting her, not her mind. No amount of psychiatric counselling would change the circle of deceit. A constant refrain from her was: "I've had enough, I've really had enough."'

The third scenario was to go public and reveal to the world what her life was truly like. But how could she smuggle her story out? She considered a range of alternatives, from producing a series of newspaper articles, to cooperating with a book about herself, to giving a TV interview. 'She was concerned to express her point of view in a controlled way, which people would understand and in a way which gave her due recognition as a human being rather than an adjunct to the royal system,' explained James Colthurst. 'The difficulty was finding the medium to deliver the message.'

Over the past ten years Diana had seen the way newspapers misrepresented and sensationalized her life, and thought that, while a series of articles would create a huge impact, the effect would be short-lived and out of her control. She was wary too of any involvement with TV or radio because of the close, almost incestuous, relationship most media outlets enjoyed with Buckingham Palace. She was especially anxious to have nothing to do with the BBC, given that the wife of the then Chairman of the Governors, Marmaduke Hussey, was Lady Susan Hussey, senior lady-in-waiting to the Queen. The fear of censorship and exposure was always uppermost in her mind. Diana was not overly enamoured with the world of publishing, either, as that year's crop of royal books, by authors such as Penny Junor and Anne Morrow, painted what she considered to be an entirely misleading picture of her life.

On the other hand, she knew that I was at the time writing a full-scale biography of her, and was reasonably pleased with my earlier book, *Diana's Diary: An Intimate Portrait of the Princess of Wales* (1990) – mainly because it had irritated Prince Charles with its detailed description of the interior of Highgrove, causing his private secretary, then Richard Aylard, to initiate an inquiry to uncover my source. She was also amused, as she told Colthurst, about the day I had annoyed the Queen in a Sandringham farm-yard. During the winter of 1986 I was showing a new royal photographer around the Sovereign's 20,000-acre Norfolk estate. A member of the Queen's staff suggested, rather mischievously, that I should drive down a country track marked 'Private' where we might 'see something that would interest' us. No sooner had we arrived in the farmyard than, like a scene from a Western, the Queen, Prince Edward and the Duchess of York appeared on their horses over the horizon and galloped purposefully towards us. Clearly furious that we had intruded on their morning ride on her property, the Queen leant over her mount and said, 'I hope you are proud of yourself, Mr Morton.' We eventually hightailed it out of town, suitably chastised after our confrontation with the Head of State. It seems the Queen voiced her disapproval at a subsequent family gathering, for the Princess had come to hear about the encounter and had been much amused. She considered me something of a rebel and an outsider, a fact that, though I was unaware of it at the time, counted heavily in my favour when she was considering telling her story.

While I had met Diana at numerous cocktail parties where the royal couple chatted to the media at the start of overseas tours, exchanges had normally been bright, light and trite, usually about my loud ties. As far as I was concerned, there was nothing to suggest a hint of the future working relationship we would later enjoy. However, in March 1991, Diana gave Colthurst advance warning of the sacking of Prince Charles's private secretary Sir Christopher Airy in the knowledge that James would pass the intelligence on to me. She was, I learnt, quietly thrilled that the resulting article, which appeared in the *Sunday Times* under my by-line, accurately reflected the situation inside the royal household as conveyed by the Princess. I now believe she was testing me out. As I was later to realize, it gave her a heady sense of control in a life that was closely monitored. She had been so used to Prince Charles and his team calling the shots that, in the undeclared war of the Waleses, it was satisfying to launch a sally of her own.

It was not a feeling that lasted long. In May 1991 an article by the gossip writer Nigel Dempster was published, portraying Diana as petulant and ungrateful for having turned down her husband's offer of a party at Highgrove to mark her thirtieth birthday. She had her reasons – apart from the fact that she disliked Highgrove, which to her was the province of Charles's mistress, Camilla Parker Bowles, and Charles's set of fawning friends, she felt that a party in her honour would be nothing more than a sham, a cover for the Prince and his mistress to meet and mingle in public – but the public was given a very different impression. When I wrote a feature for the *Sunday Times* on the 'War of the Waleses' a few days after the Dempster piece, again with a briefing from Diana via James Colthurst, it seemed to cement in her mind the notion that she could control her image. 'She had been toying with the idea of going public for some time and the birthday party issue finally made up her mind,' Colthurst later observed. 'She realized that somehow she had to get her message across.'

Diana knew now that unless the full story of her life was told, the public would never understand or appreciate the reasons behind any action she decided upon. It was at that time that she asked James Colthurst if he would sound me out about the possibility of conducting an interview for a book. Before approaching me, Colthurst asked her if she really wanted to try again with Prince Charles. 'She was very clear and said "Yes",' Colthurst remembered. 'That response conditioned my approach to the book.' That is to say, as far as he was concerned, Diana's wellbeing and future took priority over the book.

In keeping with the undercover nature of the whole operation, James and I met to discuss her thoughts in the incongruous surroundings of a working men's café in Ruislip, north-west London, close to the place where he was, at the time, attending a course. What I heard changed my life for ever. Amidst the sizzle of frying eggs and bacon, he unveiled an extraordinary story about Diana's desperation, her unhappiness, her eating disorder – bulimia nervosa – and her husband's relationship with a woman few had ever heard of, Camilla Parker Bowles. He also tentatively alluded to her half-hearted suicide attempts. It was bewildering, alarming and disconcerting. Day after day for the last ten years I and other members of the so-called royal rat pack had followed the couple around the world and never sniffed the story taking place under our noses. For a couple of years or so now there had been signs that all was not well with the Waleses' marriage, but I had not for a moment imagined that it could possibly be this bad. I left the café reeling. I had been given the key that had unlocked the door to a parallel universe, a world where nothing was as it seemed and everything was in disguise.

Deeply affected by the day's revelations, when I got on the Underground for my journey home I felt compelled to cast a furtive glance behind me, to check whether I was being watched or followed, such was the mistrust and unease with which I now felt burdened.

CHAPTER TWO

———

The Year of Living
Dangerously

I T WAS NOT LONG before I was brought down to earth. My
American-born publisher, Michael O'Mara, was deeply sceptical
when I told him about my discussion with James Colthurst. With a
TV drama about the forged Hitler Diaries then in the news, he
unsurprisingly suspected that I was being set up by a con man, but
he agreed that he, James and I should meet in his office in south
London. The meeting was tense; James did not really trust me
completely, and he did not know Mike and felt that he was getting
in over his head. Instinctively he wanted to protect his royal friend,
while O'Mara wanted to test his integrity. 'If she is so unhappy why
is she always smiling in the photographs?' he wanted to know, indicating the small library of royal picture books he had published
over the years.

As the meeting proceeded O'Mara warmed to Colthurst. 'He
was clearly no con man because he didn't ask for money,' he
reasoned. But a test was set – a tape recording of Diana's 'memoirs'
was to be made before the amateur conspirators met for a second
time.

While I was keen to interview the Princess myself, it was out of
the question. At six-foot-four and as a writer known to Palace staff,
I would hardly be inconspicuous. And as soon as it became known

that I was talking to the Princess, the balloon would go up and courtiers would step in to prevent her from speaking her mind. James, as an old friend, was, on the other hand, perfectly placed to undertake this delicate and, as it proved, historic mission.

Armed with a list of questions I had prepared and an old tape recorder, Colthurst set off on his bicycle and pedalled up the drive to Kensington Palace. It was May 1991 and he was about to conduct the first of a series of interviews that continued through the summer and autumn and would ultimately change for ever the way the world saw the British royal family.

'I remember it vividly,' Dr Colthurst recollected. 'We sat in her sitting room at Kensington Palace. Diana was dressed quite casually in jeans and blue shirt. Before we began she took the phone off the hook, as she did each time I asked her questions, and closed the door. Whenever we were interrupted by someone knocking she removed the body microphone and hid it in cushions on her sofa.

'For the first twenty minutes of that first interview she was very happy and laughing, especially when talking about incidents during her schooldays,' Colthurst went on. 'When she got to the heavy issues, the suicide attempts, Camilla and her bulimia, there was an unmistakable sense of release, of unburdening. Yet I felt that she had said these things before to other people as there was an air that her answers, while genuine, were well practised. It was obvious that she had often vented her concerns.'

As Diana spoke, the sense of injustice she felt at the way she had been treated by Camilla, Prince Charles and the royal family grew all the more keen – articulating the sacrifices she had made seemed to define her feelings of grievance and anger. In spite of her raw emotional state, what the Princess had to say was highly believable and many pieces of the jigsaw puzzle of her life began to fall into place. Deep-seated and intense feelings of abandonment and rejection had dogged her for most of her life – ever since, when she was just six years old, her mother, Frances Shand Kydd, had walked out on her father.

It was a bleak emotional landscape that Diana described in recalling an unhappy childhood – her sense of guilt at not being born a boy to continue the family line, her mother's tears, her father's lonely silences and her younger brother Charles sobbing in the night. There were other distressing revelations in store as Colthurst went through the list of questions I had prepared. As it was, many questions were made redundant simply because once she started talking she only needed a brief prompt for her to discuss some aspect of her life, such as her schooldays.

'When I left after that first long interview I realized that I had a large job on my hands,' said Colthurst. 'I felt that she needed to be protected from herself, so in the early months there were several issues, such as the suicide attempts, which I rather soft-pedalled on. At the same time it was obvious that the situation had to be resolved, otherwise it would have meant the end of her. She was certainly not mentally unstable but the circumstances were so crushing that it had the potential to create instability. The potential for her taking her own life was always there.'

Early in their first conversation, Colthurst said to her, 'Give me a shout if there is something you don't want me to touch on.' Her reply was telling: 'No, no, it's OK.' 'Even though I had known her since she was a teenager I was most surprised by the way that she discussed her suicide bids so freely,' Colthurst commented. 'She was very open too in the way she talked about Camilla, her family and the royal family, and one could feel her anger around these issues.'

At the second meeting with Michael O'Mara, James brought along his battered tape recorder. As soon as he played the tape O'Mara's worries about its authenticity evaporated – to be replaced by another worry. 'How the hell are we going to prove this stuff?' he asked.

Clearly, we would have to find evidence to substantiate everything the Princess told us. What was more, since we were not able to quote her directly, we needed to find close friends of hers who could back up Diana's story in their own words.

In the early weeks of this project, it was the Princess who was setting the pace. My notes from the evening of 2 July 1991, the day after her thirtieth birthday (which in the end she had spent alone at Kensington Palace), gives a flavour of her impatient mood. At 5.10 p.m., while Colthurst and I were deep in conversation, his bleeper went off. It was Diana. 'Sees major urgency for the book,' I jotted down in my notebook. 'She thought it could be brought out in weeks. Going to Earl Spencer to pack up a few photo albums and bring them down. If Camilla Parker Bowles leaked the story of the ball to Dempster then the mistress is running the show. Disgusted by the way it has gone.'

If I needed any signal about how tricky this project would be, it came a few days later when I wrote another article for the *Sunday Times* headlined 'Truce', detailing the behind-the-scenes moves by such unlikely characters as the former DJ Sir Jimmy Savile to bring an end to the warfare between Charles and Diana. Even though the story was accurate, my long-term thinking was to put rival journalists off the scent by giving the impression that all had gone quiet inside the Waleses' household, as well as underlining my credibility as a writer with an inside track – thus, I hoped, ensuring that when the book was published it would be taken seriously. I was trying to be too clever by half – the strategy crumbled to dust the moment the book was published. In the *Sunday Times* article I mentioned how, for Diana's birthday, her sitting room was decorated with helium-filled balloons. It was a point the Queen's private secretary, Sir Robert Fellowes, asked Diana about when courtiers carefully scrutinized the article to find clues as to my impeccable source. A few days later, the *Sun*'s veteran royal photographer, Arthur Edwards, phoned me with a warning. 'You've got them rattled,' he said. 'For f—k's sake be careful. They are looking because you are getting it right. They are turning the place over very quietly.' His counsel of caution was echoed by the *Daily Mail*'s royal reporter Richard Kay, who had been told by his newspaper's crime correspondent that the police had been asked to find my mole. A few months later, my tatty office above an Indian restaurant in central London was broken into, a camera stolen and files rifled through.

With the need for caution paramount and Diana eager to press ahead, it was clear that James would have to take on a much bigger role than he had previously envisaged. He had thought he would be able to bow out after making a couple of tapes – instead he found himself visiting Kensington Palace on a regular basis armed with lists of questions that I had carefully compiled, to ask her to fill in the gaps she had left in her early testimony. For the next year he acted as the go-between, as the three of us – Mike O'Mara, James and myself – became her shadow court, not only writing, researching and producing what was to all intents and purposes an 'unofficial official' biography, but advising on her day-to-day life. Everything from handling staff problems, to dealing with media issues to drafting speeches came under our umbrella, as she used us to second-guess her small team of courtiers. It was exciting, exhilarating and amusing as this ill-assorted triumvirate helped shape the life and image of the world's most famous young woman.

At one of our first 'editorial' meetings it occurred to us that Diana would feel much more comfortable if her participation in the project was not acknowledged, thus giving her the opportunity to deny her involvement. The Princess was in fact the last of us to realize the importance of 'deniability', and it was, according to my notes, not until 4 January 1992, when the book was well under way, that she asked James, almost as an afterthought, to make sure she was kept in the background. 'She knew from the start that the enterprise was not without risks,' Colthurst said. 'But with the proviso that she had deniability she became much more excited.'

This strategy did give us an extra problem in that it became absolutely vital that we verified the Princess's every claim independently. The emotional torrent that was her first interview raised many sensitive, not to say libellous, issues, particularly about Camilla Parker Bowles. This was my task for the next year – interviewing Diana's friends, acquaintances and employees in order to acquire corroboration to underpin the original thesis. Some in her circle, like Carolyn Bartholomew and James Gilbey, were aware of her involvement although they did not know the full extent of her cooperation. When, for example, I interviewed Carolyn she told me that Diana had been 'besotted' with Prince Charles before they married. Just to make sure she called Diana to check that the word reflected her feelings. 'I said the right thing, didn't I?' she asked. 'Yes. I was. Totally,' Diana said with emphasis. While Carolyn was almost in with us, most of the others in Diana's circle were out of the loop and she had to choose her words with care when they called her to ask if they should speak to me. With many she was noncommittal, with some downright negative – 'Don't touch it [a proposed interview] with a bargepole,' she counselled her masseur Stephen Twigg. (Thankfully he ignored her advice.) When I eventually interviewed James Gilbey at his Knightsbridge apartment in November 1991, he was explicit about what she wanted to achieve with the book: 'She wants to make her point loud and clear. She doesn't want any beating about the bush. She wants people to know the grief she has had to endure and the way she's been abandoned.'

After her first session with James Colthurst, Diana knew that she had crossed a personal Rubicon. She had thrown away the map and was striking out on a journey with only a hazy idea of the route, let alone the destination. But she was determined to continue, and as the months passed she became increasingly energized by the process, suggesting topics herself, such as her bulimia, which she wanted to put into its proper context. While I busied myself with the Princess's friends, James continued with his interviews: 'Usually we chatted in the morning, then had lunch and sometimes had another session in the afternoon. But by then she had had enough. There were lots of interruptions especially when Paul Burrell [then her under-butler] and other staff were around. She clearly didn't trust them so then we would move on to general conversation when they entered the room.'

(It is worth pointing out that, after he published his memoir in 2003, Burrell told the American talk-show host, Larry King, that in 1991 he and Diana used to discuss the secret interviews that were taking place for *Diana: Her True Story*. Straight-faced, he told millions of American viewers: 'I knew about it. I was there and I knew it was happening. I helped the Princess to have a voice. And that's the only time that she could ever sort of say how she felt and thought. It [the book] didn't shock me because I was aware of the whole situation.' The truth is very different. Far from being an intimate of the Princess, at the time she did not trust him because, as a butler based primarily at Highgrove with Prince Charles, he was in the 'enemy' camp. In fact, when Burrell was in Kensington Palace while Diana was being taped for my book, she insisted that loud music should be played in case Burrell was listening at the keyhole.

At the time what struck Colthurst forcibly was the invasive atmosphere which suffused her home at Kensington Palace. In a world where everyone wanted a piece of her, the Princess had to shield her personal space with the tenacity of a guard dog, hiding anything about her inner life, such as her astrological charts or a book on eating disorders. Her first instinct, demonstrated by the fact that she had a shredder on her desk, was to trust no one – not staff, not courtiers and certainly not the royal family.

While it is easy to scoff, in such an environment, where it seemed that every breath she took, every move she made was watched, monitored and commented upon, it did appear quite possible that Diana's mail was being tampered with and her phones bugged. There was no doubt that she became noticeably more relaxed after the three of us had bought scrambler telephones to deter potential eavesdroppers.

The Princess was also concerned about Colthurst cycling around London, not just for his safety, particularly when he was carrying around with him the interview tapes or the Spencer family photographs, which she passed to us in November 1991. Her anxiety was justified when one day in the summer of 1991 James was knocked off his bicycle by a car after one of his interview sessions with her at Kensington Palace.

In this atmosphere of distrust and suspicion, the very fact that Diana was prepared to give frank and, at the time, deeply shocking interviews to an old friend for a writer she barely knew graphically demonstrates her desperation.

For Colthurst, the role he had taken on, somewhat reluctantly, of conduit between the Princess and her biographer brought responsibilities and concerns far greater than he had expected. 'At the time, as far as I was concerned,' he explained, 'I was helping a chum at a bloody and difficult part of her life. I was quite uncomfortable with the role and never envisaged that helping her would become virtually my full-time job for the next few years. I saw it as a one-off – that once she had said her piece she would then be free to make her own decisions. It didn't happen like that.'

In her emotionally fragile state Diana turned repeatedly to her friend and interviewer for guidance and encouragement, and soon James found himself with the added responsibilities of adviser, counsellor and occasional speechwriter, shadowing and pre-empting decisions made by her paid officials, notably her private secretary, Patrick Jephson, who was appointed in November 1991 after working in a similar capacity while he was her equerry.

In the meantime, I was concentrating on the Princess's biography, which meant that Colthurst and I had different, and at times diverging, agendas. For, naturally enough, in Colthurst's mind where there was conflict between her needs and the book, Diana always took precedence. 'Whereas the book was a means of her gaining recognition as an individual,' he later observed, 'my over-riding concern was what she was going to do with her life and how she was going to run it.' In many respects his most significant contribution to Diana's life was not as a mere go-between for a book, but was in the help he gave her through the slow and painstaking process of shaping a new life and channelling away negative thoughts and emotions, and his encouragement to her to focus on a positive and productive future. It was work Diana was to continue with her therapist Susie Orbach, her astrologer Debbie Frank, and a loose-knit group of surrogate 'father and mother' figures, who included the film-maker David Puttnam and Lady Annabel Goldsmith.

The Princess trusted Colthurst with many of her most intimate secrets, and used him as a sounding board for her problems and concerns. She telephoned him constantly and the calls – usually around eight a day, more if there was a crisis – gathered momentum and took on a rhythm of their own. Morning conversations were short, dealing with contents of the newspapers and how to counter negative publicity. She would outline her engagements for the day, asking advice on how to handle a range of social situations. On one occasion, for example, she asked him what conversational gambits she could use to engage her lunch partner, the French President, François Mitterrand; on another occasion,

Diana, who was, until late in her life, intimidated by intellectuals, called in a fluster and asked how best to interest the formidable former American Secretary of State, Henry Kissinger. Colthurst's advice, just to be herself and ask him what really fascinated him, certainly seemed to strike a chord – over the years Kissinger became a great admirer of the Princess, agreeing to present her with a humanitarian award in New York in 1995.

Afternoon telephone calls usually involved an inquest into the Princess's official duties; then in the early evening she would call to discuss her life and emotional situation. Invariably this involved her husband, her marriage and her future – although, once, while she was staying at Balmoral she asked Colthurst how to resolve a ticklish problem of protocol. It seems that for a time the Queen took to singing hymns unaccompanied after dinner was over. The Princess did not know whether to sing along, start clapping or remain silent. For once Colthurst was at a loss.

He was more helpful when Diana called from Sandringham during Christmas 1991. In the oppressive and accusatory atmosphere of this unhappy family gathering – the last before both the Princess and the Duchess of York separated from their royal husbands – she was desperate to find an excuse to leave, especially after a tart encounter with Princess Anne, who remarked, 'It's difficult for Charles with a wife like you.' When Colthurst suggested to Diana that she visit the homeless in London, she seized on the idea, quickly making arrangements so that she could make her excuses and leave.

The final call, after the day's torrent of requests for advice and support, was what Colthurst labelled the 'bored call', where, before she went to bed, she would chit-chat for up to ninety minutes about nothing in particular. Colthurst, who was then working full-time developing a medical device with British Oxygen and planning his own wedding, found himself juggling his own career with his shadow life as her de facto private secretary. In those days, when mobile phones were the size of house bricks, he regularly received urgent summons on his pager and often had to leave meetings to find a quiet public telephone from which to send his response. In June 1991, for instance, a worried Diana was constantly on the telephone to him seeking reassurance when Prince William suffered a depressed fracture of his skull following a golfing accident at school.

Over time Diana came to rely on James Colthurst for suggestions and solutions to all manner of delicate or thorny problems. When she decided to replace her regular hairdresser, Richard Dalton, but was anxious to do so without hurting his feelings or provoking him to sell his story to the media, she turned to James. He suggested that she write a letter tactfully explaining her decision and give him a present in appreciation of his years of service. His counsel proved effective and while it was little more than sensible man-management, for someone floundering and vulnerable it was a welcome lifeline.

A greater test of his ingenuity came when Diana got herself in a rather sticky situation with Prince Charles's valet Michael Fawcett. She had come to dislike Fawcett heartily and when he married Debbie Burke, a housemaid who was eventually to work for Prince Philip, in September 1991, the Princess rather childishly did not give the couple a wedding present. Fawcett recognized the slight as deliberate and in his anger complained to all and sundry, his gripes so vociferous that at one stage Diana's detective, Ken Wharfe, told him, in no uncertain terms, to 'get a grip'. Too late, the Princess realized that most people would conclude that she, Diana, with her reputation as a generous giver of presents, was being mean-spirited. She talked the issue over with Colthurst, who came up with the diplomatic suggestion that she should give Fawcett and his bride an engraved photograph album and make some excuse for the delay – such as that they had misspelled his wife's name. He then went to a store in Bond Street and bought her an album, which he had appropriately engraved. When she presented it to Charles's valet – at a very public occasion – he was genuinely taken aback and socially wrong-footed, a reaction which ensured that Diana, for once, was able to enjoy a frisson of satisfaction from a small moral victory.

Much as the Princess depended on him, however, she did not tell Colthurst everything. While she was raging against her husband's infidelity, she was hiding the fact that she had enjoyed a long if sporadic love affair with Captain James Hewitt from 1986 to 1990; and a dalliance with James Gilbey, who was later to be exposed as the male voice on the notorious 'Squidgygate' tapes, telephone conversations illicitly recorded over New Year 1989–1990. Throughout her sessions with Colthurst she dismissed Hewitt as a friend and nothing more, always speaking of him in less than flattering tones. Colthurst was not entirely convinced by her assertions, but she was never open about Hewitt, just as she avoided discussing her friendship with James Gilbey. Until, that is, she needed Colthurst's help.

The first indications of her relationship with James Hewitt, which was alluded to in a Sunday newspaper in March 1991, came during the 1991 Gulf War when the dashing but indiscreet tank commander borrowed a news reporter's satellite phone in the Gulf to call the Princess at Kensington Palace. Diana was so alarmed by the prospect of Hewitt being confronted on his return from the war by newsmen who would link her romantically with him that she asked Colthurst to draft a statement for Hewitt to read out to the media. 'She was worried because she couldn't trust him to open his mouth and come out with joined-up sentences,' Colthurst said. 'Understandably she was never explicit about the true nature of her relationship with him.'

Hewitt flatly turned down our request for an interview for the book, and with Diana passing the relationship off as a friendship there was nowhere left to go with the story. We did not have the faintest inkling either about her infatuation with the art dealer Oliver Hoare, who was the object of her love and devotion by early 1992. It was one of Diana's enduring, and, for many, intriguing, qualities that no matter how close individuals thought they were to her – family, old friends like Colthurst, fortune tellers – she never revealed absolutely everything.

Rather less dramatic than his function as repository for the Princess's confidences (some of them), but in the long term more effective, was Colthurst's capacity as her unofficial speechwriter. She complained that the texts prepared for her by charity officials or the Palace were 'heavy, formal and dull' and wanted James to inject a 'Diana element' into the address. They would discuss what Diana wanted to say, James would prepare a draft and she would contribute further thoughts and refinements. I too would find myself involved, and quite often even the Princess's bodyguard, Ken Wharfe, would be found sitting in the royal limousine polishing her speeches minutes before an engagement.

'The speeches meant a lot to her,' said Colthurst. 'It was an area where she gradually realized that she could put across her own message. It gave her a real sense of empowerment and achievement that an audience actually listened to what she had to say rather than just gazed at her clothes, hairstyle and general appearance. She used to ring up very excited if there had been coverage on TV or radio, delighted that she had received praise for her thoughts.'

The procedure, while amateurish, was highly effective – even though it was usually undertaken in an atmosphere of barely suppressed frenzy and panic. Once, in August 1991, Diana rang in agitation from a Mediterranean cruise on board a yacht owned by the tycoon John Latsis because a speech she was due to give to the Red Cross had not arrived. In fact, Colthurst had faxed it to the boat two days earlier but a crew member had forgotten to give it to her. On another, later, occasion the Princess rang him in a panic as he was eating his breakfast at his farmhouse near Pangbourne in Berkshire. She was due to attend a retirement lunch for her friend Lord King, the former British Airways chairman, and had decided at the last minute to say a few words. In between munching his morning toast, James, pacing around his kitchen in his dressing gown, dictated his hasty thoughts to the Princess who painstakingly wrote them down in long hand.

One lunchtime meeting in September 1991 summed up the frantic mood of her life at that time. James and I were enjoying a liquid lunch in the Stag's Head public house in London's West End, editing and rewriting a speech she was due to give to a child-psychiatry symposium. This was the famous 'hugging speech' – which won her an award – in which the Princess informed her highly qualified audience of some 800 doctors of the enormous value of a hug, saying that a cuddle was 'cheap, environmentally friendly and needs minimal instruction'.

As we tinkered with the phrasing, Colthurst's bleeper went off. We initially thought it was an amateur photographer we had asked, with Diana's knowledge, to take informal snaps of the Princess and her boys as they entered San Lorenzo's restaurant where they were having lunch. In fact it was Diana herself. When James found a public telephone and called her, she informed him that his carefully crafted address had quickly to be cut from 2,100 to 1,600 words. The tone also had to be softened, she said, because the reference to hugging might be seen as a criticism of the Queen and the distant way that she had brought up her own family. During the conversation she made a wry comment about a fellow lunchtime diner, the Marchioness of Douro, a one-time friend who had fallen out with Diana when the Princess discovered that she was reportedly allowing her Scottish estate to be used by Prince Charles and Camilla for a romantic tryst. In delighted tones, Diana related how her former friend had been suitably embarrassed during their chance meeting.

This was by no means the first conversation of the day, nor would it be the last. Earlier, Diana had dismissed as 'nonsense' a Nigel Dempster story about the Queen ordering Diana to be with Charles – a point she was happy to have publicized if a journalist should call to ask me about it. On the same day, in between rewriting Diana's speech, I briefed Stuart Higgins, then deputy editor of the *Sun*, about a secret trip Prince Charles was taking to a friend's château in southern France. At the time Diana thought that Camilla was going too and we were very anxious to obtain independent confirmation of that, preferably photographic, to support her allegations of Charles's infidelity. At the last minute, however, Camilla decided against joining the Prince.

Indeed, throughout the summer of 1991, the Camilla question was the most difficult. As the Parker Bowleses had successfully sued an author who had inadvertently linked Camilla to Charles, the prospect of fighting a court case was very real. We needed independent proof of Diana's assertions that her husband was engaged in a long-term affair with Mrs Parker Bowles.

In late August 1991, irked because I seemed to be doubting her word, the Princess, who was staying at Balmoral, rummaged through her husband's briefcase and came across a cache of letters. In doing this she exposed herself to the cold and conclusive realization – rather than the abstract suspicion – that another woman was in love with her husband, and that that love was clearly returned. The letters – and a couple of saucy postcards – which I was shown in August 1991 were from Camilla Parker Bowles. As Diana read the passionate letters it was quite evident to her that Camilla, who called Charles 'My most precious darling', was a woman whose love remained undimmed in spite of the passage of time and the difficulties of pursuing the object of her affection.

The tone of the letters was adoring. I recall the lengths to which Camilla went to contact Charles, on one occasion writing to him while secreted away in a lavatory on the Queen Mother's ninety-first birthday, 4 August 1991. 'I just hate not being able to tell you how much I love you,' she wrote. The note, on her headed writing paper, continued in a similar vein, saying how much she longed to be with him and that she was his for ever. I particularly remember one vivid passage that read, 'My heart and body both ache for you.'

She apologized for breaking into gibberish during a secret phone call with Prince Charles, blaming her husband in a memorable turn of phrase: 'The erstwhile silver stick appeared through the door looking like a furious stoat – pity they did not stuff him.' It was a sentence that stuck in my mind because Brigadier Parker Bowles had held the largely ceremonial post of 'Silver Stick in Waiting' to the Queen. I recall that she went on to proclaim her undying affection for Prince Charles with phrases like, 'I yearn to be with you day and night, to hug, comfort and love you.' She reminisced about a 'magical night' with her prince at a friend's country house, lamenting the difficulties of their illicit relationship. 'I dread the acting part,' she wrote, referring to a forthcoming lunch where she, with her husband in tow, was to join Prince Charles.

As Diana absorbed the depth of her rival's love she was also able to see the extent of the duplicity that her husband and his lover connived in to pursue their affair. In one of the letters, Camilla carefully outlined the dates and places when she was available to see him while her husband and children were away. It must have been horrible for Diana to realize that the venues where her love rival was waiting for Charles included the homes of people she called her friends. Camilla mused that the long periods of separation were a test of her love and affection for him.

Just as shocking to Diana must have been the letter which referred personally to her in very unflattering terms. Camilla advised Charles to erase any thoughts of guilt about their relationship from his mind and rise above what she termed 'the onslaughts of that ridiculous creature' – clearly a reference to Diana.

Camilla, calling herself, 'your devoted old bag', reminded the Prince that she loved him above all others, and signed off, 'Your hopelessly besotted old friend'. Having read this sheaf of passionate love letters Diana told Colthurst that any hopes she might have harboured of saving her ten-year-old marriage were doomed.

While the letters, which we were given sight of, removed any doubts we might have had about Diana's tale of woe, they cut little ice with the libel lawyer we saw in February 1992. We were, of course, unable to tell the lawyer of Diana's involvement in the book and he did not ask how we had had sight of the letters. In the circumstances it is hardly surprising that he appeared to view the enterprise (and Colthurst, O'Mara and Morton) with some distaste. He informed us that the letters could not be used in court in any circumstances, and that we did not have sufficient evidence, under English libel law, to prove that Charles and Camilla were lovers. He put me well in my place when he said, 'Who do you suppose the judge would believe, Mr Morton – you or Prince Charles?' When Diana was told that all her undercover efforts had come to nothing, she was understandably furious, seeing it as another example of the whole world standing against her.

Our distinguished legal adviser did, however, come up with a method of conveying to the reader that Prince Charles and Mrs Parker Bowles were lovers without actually saying so. 'If you refer to their "close friendship" often enough, and in the correct context, your reader will assume they are lovers,' he advised. And he was absolutely right. Although I never said outright that the pair were lovers in the first edition of *Diana: Her True Story*, the whole world assumed I had.

*

The Princess was now thinking soberly about life after the contents of the book had been revealed. During the late summer of 1991 she went to Colthurst's home in west London to see his astrologer friend, Felix Lyle, for a reading that might yield clues to her future. During their conversation, which she had tape-recorded, she forecast that her marriage break-up would come about in around eighteen months – she was just a few months adrift. She realized there would be turmoil for two or three years before she could remarry, and in any case she wanted space between relationships. But, she wondered, what should her next suitor's star sign be? Taurus and Capricorn were deemed too slow for her, but a man born under Aquarius, an air sign, would be best suited to the new Diana who was gradually emerging, Lyle told her.

Gravely, the Princess recognized his prediction that she must endure many trials and tribulations before she could find the new life that she craved. The doubts and concerns were evident as they discussed her future. 'Will I be allowed to break away?' she asked, then added significantly, 'And will the public let me?'

These were difficult and trying days as the pressures began to mount. The Princess's private secretary, Patrick Jephson, lost no time in warning her, before Christmas 1991, that the 'men in grey suits' knew about the book and her involvement in it. Nevertheless, Diana forged ahead. She knew there was a cataclysm in the offing, but had no doubts that she would survive it. In a letter to James Colthurst some six months before the book's publication, she wrote:

> Obviously we are preparing for the volcano to erupt and I do feel better equipped to cope with whatever comes our way! Thank you for your belief in me and for taking the trouble to understand this mind – it's such a relief not to be on my own any more and that it's *okay* to listen to my instinct.

Diana was not the only one considering a future life free of royal constraints. During the summer and autumn of 1991, the Duchess of York was continually beseeching her sister-in-law to jump ship with her. Not only did her unhappiness encourage further instability in Diana's marriage, editorially it pushed us to produce the book as quickly as possible. So nervous were we of Fergie's unbridled influence that publication was brought forward from September, the traditional date for potential bestsellers, to June 1992. The warning signals were coming thick and fast. Just before Christmas 1991 we heard that a very well informed individual had placed a £500,000 bet on the Waleses' marriage not lasting a year; and in the same month Fergie, who was secretly seeing her lover Steve Wyatt in Texas, asked Diana if she could look after her children, Princesses Eugenie and Beatrice when she left the royal family.

Diana was becoming increasingly anxious as she waited for her book to be completed, worried that in the PR war with her husband and the Palace, the enemy were gaining advantage. In late February 1992 she was appalled when a book entitled *Diana in Private: The Princess Nobody Knows* by Lady Colin Campbell was serialized in Britain's bestselling tabloid, the *Sun*. The book took the view that if there was a problem with the Waleses' marriage, it was Diana. Worse, it hinted that Diana had romantic attachments to men other than her husband.

The Princess immediately passed on her fury to James Colthurst, who phoned me on the 'scrambler'. I too was deeply concerned but, as I told James, there was little I could do – the only thing that could remove Lady Colin's version of events from the front pages of the tabloids would be an even bigger royal story and there were none available (that is, not until my book arrived in June). Colthurst relayed this information to Diana, who to his astonishment instantly provided the blockbuster story we required. She had recently learned that Fergie had visited the Queen to talk about a separation from Prince Andrew; after much discussion the Queen had agreed that a separation was the best option in the circumstances.

When Colthurst passed the story on to me I was dumbfounded. I had not dreamed for a minute that a royal scoop to blow away Lady Colin's account could ever be revealed – but here it was in spades. I duly wrote the front-page story for the *Daily Mail*, which the

Queen's press secretary, Charles Anson, later described as 'inch-perfect'. As we had nail-bitingly hoped, Lady Colin Campbell's anti-Diana stories were submerged by the new feeding frenzy in the tabloids.

Our main objective, however, was to ensure that the book measured up to Anson's assessment of the article – that it reflected Diana's life, both in words and in pictures, as accurately as possible.

As she had promised, in November 1991 the Princess supplied us with several large, red family albums together with a selection of photographs taken by Patrick Demarchelier, which she pulled from a desk drawer in her sitting room. From time to time, however, Diana would get cold feet about the project. For a long while there was a debate between Kensington Palace and the publisher about the proposed title. We thought '*Diana: Her True Story*' the only possible choice, as the book told the story very much from her point of view; Diana, though, nervous that the choice of title would hint at her involvement, wanted it to be called '*The True Story*'. Eventually, she was persuaded that her choice, in the circumstances, would have been misleading – but only after she had been secretly shown mock-up covers of the book featuring both versions of the title. She even changed the jacket blurb saying that her wedding day was not, as she had alleged previously, the 'worst day' of her life but the most 'emotionally confusing'.

As each chapter was written, Colthurst would deliver it to the Princess to read, although when he was on holiday I cycled one Saturday morning to the Brazilian Embassy, where Diana was seeing her friend, the Ambassador's wife Lucia Flecha de Lima, to drop off a chapter. She admitted to finding herself by turns moved by her own story and anxious about its content, occasionally deleting material that she thought would implicate her. In fact, many of Diana's deletions concerned other people or material already in the public domain – a comment to Sarah Ferguson during her first engagement on board HMS *Brazen* to see Prince Andrew; her sister Sarah's anorexia nervosa, and stories about Camilla Parker Bowles (the deletion of which would have undercut Diana's case against Camilla) – and once James had pointed this out she agreed to reinstate the material. Time and again, the Princess returned to the driving imperative behind the book – to allow her voice to be heard clearly.

It was a theme she articulated in a letter she drafted to her father, Earl Spencer, a few days before his final fatal illness in March 1992. In the short note she talked about her involvement with the book and tried to explain her reasons for cooperating so fully. She wrote:

> It is a chance for my own self to surface a little rather than be lost in the system. I rather see it as a lifebelt against being drowned and it is terribly important to me . . .

For a few weeks in February 1992, as the final manuscript was being prepared, it looked as though the book would surface with a whimper rather than a bang. Serialization was crucial and both the newspapers we approached, the *Daily Mail* and the *Sunday Times*, turned it down. When Michael O'Mara approached the editor of the *Sunday Times*, Andrew Neil, and briefed him on the book's contents, Neil's response was: 'I think it would be better off in a tabloid.' In spite of all O'Mara's arguments, Neil turned the book down out of hand, making it clear that he was simply not interested in serializing royal books. While he ran royal stories, at that time usually written by me, he was still sore about having serialized a previous royal book of mine, a frothy lifestyle tome about the Princess of Wales called *Diana's Diary*. He had been criticized by both senior editorial executives and some readers for serializing a lightweight book in a heavyweight newspaper and he was not prepared to go down that road again. At the time his judgement was backed by his paper's proprietor Rupert Murdoch. The outlook was bleak; we needed a reputable newspaper backing the book otherwise it could easily be dismissed as tittle-tattle and hearsay. In the last throw of the dice, I had a word with Diana's friend Angela Serota and asked her if she would speak to her friend, and Andrew Neil's boss, Andrew Knight, chief executive of News International, which owns the *Sunday Times*, and assure him that the book was authentic and came with Diana's approval.

The last-ditch appeal worked. Just a few hours later, O'Mara received a phone call from Sue Douglas, executive editor of the

Sunday Times, saying that they were now very interested in looking at the book. She arrived soon after at O'Mara's office and, after reading the manuscript, made it clear that the paper would like to serialize the book. Within a matter of days a deal was done. Andrew Neil, the man who initially rejected the book, became its staunchest defender, effectively laying his job on the line to support it. However, as the weeks ticked by and speculation about the book's contents reached fever pitch, even the notoriously pugnacious Andrew Neil began to appreciate the enormity of what he was about to do, realizing that if the individuals who had spoken to me during the course of my research for the book did not stand by their statements he would have to resign. In late May, a few days before serialization was due to begin, he called O'Mara and me into his office at Wapping, in London's East End, and asked us to provide signed statements from the book's main witnesses. This we duly did. We had a reciprocal request to make of him: Diana had complained that she had heard that Murdoch himself was gossiping about the contents of the book, which were then secret, at New York dinner parties. This was a cause for considerable concern and we now formally asked Neil if he could prevail upon his boss to keep quiet.

The prospect of Rupert Murdoch himself blowing the gaffe did little to calm Diana's nerves and she had to have her hand held by the sisterhood, notably Carolyn Bartholomew, Angela Serota and healer Oonagh Shanley-Toffolo, who independently reassured her that the book would, despite the coming upheaval, ultimately be a positive force in her life.

As well as talking to her friends, the Princess was making her own internal preparations for the coming storm. Towards the end, a week before serialization began, she arranged a meeting with the Queen to discuss the possibility of having her own home, staff and money, made independent from the Prince of Wales. In conversations with James Colthurst, the Princess made it clear that the Queen was aware of the problems in her marriage, and had indicated that, if the couple were so unhappy, she felt that there was no reason why the Prince and Princess should be artificially pushed together.

For his part, Prince Charles had already discussed the prospect of a royal separation with the august lawyer, Lord Goodman. While these behind-the-scene manoeuvres were taking place, on the surface, in the face of the mounting flurry of media speculation, the Prince of Wales's supporters were trying to downplay the book's potentially explosive contents. When Prince Charles's private secretary Richard Aylard briefed journalists, he told them dismissively: 'You know Morton – a bit of insight, a bit of invention and the colour of the tablecloth.'

An unguarded comment by Andrew Neil on *Sky News* gave an indication that domestic furnishings did not form a part of *this* royal narrative. A couple of days before the book was serialized for the first time, Neil mentioned that Diana thought that she would never be Queen. Next day it was splashed across two pages of the *Sun* newspaper.

This, however, was nothing compared to when the first extract appeared in the *Sunday Times* on 7 June 1992. The front-page story carried the headline: 'Diana driven to five suicide bids by "uncaring" Charles'. Underneath was the sub-heading: 'Marriage collapse led to illness; Princess says she will not be Queen'. It is hard now, some twelve years later, when the narrative of her unhappy life has been accepted as conventional wisdom, to convey the shock, disgust and astonishment that greeted that first instalment. The criticism came from all sectors of society and was severe and unrelenting. I, as the author, suddenly became an object of hatred – to the extent that when I appeared on *This Morning*, hosted by Richard Madeley and Judy Finnegan in Liverpool one morning in June 1992, security guards patrolled the roof of the building, the car park next door was evacuated, and a helicopter flew me away from the studio because they feared some crazed attempt to attack, even kill, me. A tad extreme but indicative of the public mood.

Hours before the first serialization appeared in the *Sunday Times*, Rupert Murdoch phoned Andrew Neil from New York to warn him of the coming onslaught from the Establishment. 'They will try to destroy you,' he said. 'Be careful; they are not nice people and you are about to become their number-one enemy.' He was proved to be absolutely right – the snobbery, class divisions and instinctive deference to Britain's ruling elite all came to the fore in the days and weeks following the book's publication.

The Archbishop of Canterbury warned about the damage to the boys; the Labour politician Peter Mandelson complained that the book was 'scurrilous' and that there were 'no longer any boundaries between fact and fiction'. The former Arts Minister Richard Luce said that the book went beyond the pale of decency and could only serve to undermine the monarchy, while his Tory colleague Sir Nicholas Fairburn was rather pithier, saying that I should be put in the Tower of London. Sir Peregrine Worsthorne, who was editor of the *Sunday Telegraph* from 1986 to 1989, declared that Andrew Neil ought to be horsewhipped for serializing the book. Indeed, the media – which in a free society should by its very nature believe in disclosure rather than censorship – were the most damning in their criticism. The *Sunday Telegraph*'s editor Charles Moore said on BBC's *Newsnight* that journalists should use 'hypocrisy and concealment' when writing about the royal family, while Max Hastings, then editor of the *Daily Telegraph* and since knighted, told listeners to *Today*, BBC Radio Four's flagship morning current-affairs programme, that I was not fit to play a piano in a brothel, dismissing the story as 'a deluge of rubbish and a farrago of invention' that lacked a 'single reliable fact'.

In the rush to condemn, supercilious book reviewers exposed their own class prejudices: Hugh Montgomery Massingberd dismissed me as a 'tabloid vulgarian from Leeds', old Etonian Philip Ziegler called me a 'little hack' and Lady Elizabeth Longford described the book as 'Crawfie [the Queen's former nanny who wrote an anodyne account of their nursery life] with strychnine'. Even the *Sunday Times*'s sister paper, *The Times*, was unconvinced about the veracity of the book. Its headline 'Royal book serial provokes distaste' made clear its disapproval.

During the days that followed, the chairman of the Press Complaints Commission, Lord McGregor, accused the media of an 'odious exhibition' and of 'dabbling their fingers in the stuff of other people's souls', although his complaint was not directed at the book. If anything, the reaction to the book's serialization was proof positive of what Diana had been up against all her adult life.

In the ensuing furore the book was banned by Harrods, major bookshops such as Hatchards in London and James Thin in Edinburgh, supermarkets such as Tesco, and various independent bookshops throughout Britain. 'We are not stocking that book and we never will,' declared Philip Foster, owner of a bookstore in Tetbury, near the Waleses' country home. It is one of the ironies of this whole affair that a biography written and produced with the enthusiastic cooperation of its subject should be piously boycotted on the grounds that it was believed to give an entirely false account of its subject's life. It became the most banned book in Britain of the 1990s. Even to produce it and bring it into Britain had involved something of an undercover operation. As British printers were nervous about printing the book, it was in the end produced in the far north of Finland and the first consignment was brought into Britain inside a truck also carrying confectionery.

While *Diana: Her True Story* was dismissed as a confection by the media and the political establishment, in the days after the first extract was published it became clear that we had to show that the book was not disapproved of by the Princess, or at least had the support of her friends; somehow we had to try to halt the accelerating juggernaut of disbelief and censure. After twenty-four hours in the hot seat, even a seasoned campaigner like Andrew Neil was rattled, concerned that the book's most contentious story, that of Diana's suicide bids, was going too far. On Monday 8 June, after a bruising encounter with Max Hastings on the *Today* show, Neil called me to say that before he appeared on the ITV lunchtime news, this time in battle with Tory peer and royal confidant, Lord St John of Fawsley, he needed more ammunition to back these claims. Diana's friend James Gilbey, who proved a steady and stalwart friend in these difficult days, agreed to issue a statement confirming that the Princess had told him and other friends about her suicide attempts. We cobbled together a form of words on the phone, which I then read to Neil, who took them down in longhand just minutes before his TV appearance. He then proceeded to read Gilbey's statement out on air: 'I can confirm that I was interviewed by Andrew Morton when he was researching his book *Diana: Her True Story*. My interviews are represented fairly and accurately in the book. I did not receive nor ask for any payment. I can confirm that the Princess discussed with me, on numerous occasions, her attempted suicides, as she has done with other close friends. Her friends have given interviews freely in the knowledge that the information would be treated in a responsible manner. I have no further comment to make.'

While St John lamely tried to dismiss Gilbey's statement with the cliché, 'With friends like that you don't need enemies', at least the dam was holding against the torrent of foaming ire. Of most concern to all of us was the Princess of Wales. She had had a very wobbly weekend when the book was first serialized. Hours before the *Sunday Times* was made available to the public she called the Buckingham Palace duty press officer Dickie Arbiter – who, like everyone else, knew of the book's existence but not its contents – and asked plaintively: 'What shall I do, what shall I do?' His advice was simple – 'Pour yourself a stiff whisky.'

Events were moving quickly. On Monday 8 June, the same day that St John, Moore and Hastings were on TV and radio shows denigrating the serialization, the Prince and Princess of Wales met at Kensington Palace and for the first time seriously discussed their broken marriage. The first person she contacted after that momentous meeting with her husband was Colthurst: 'The phone rang and she said, "He's agreed, he's agreed [to a separation]." I've never heard her so ebullient, she was out of control with excitement. So when she subsequently said on television that she didn't want a divorce, what she was really saying was that she didn't want to be *blamed* for the divorce. That was always very important to her.'

In the years since the publication of *Diana: Her True Story*, I have often wondered whether this issue of blame was not one of the chief reasons that Diana pursued the publication of 'her true story'. As I have mentioned, both James Colthurst and I were unaware of the exact nature of her relationships with James Hewitt and James Gilbey; we did not even know of the existence of Oliver Hoare. Could it be that Diana, knowing that her husband had been unfaithful to her for many years, was worried that one of her dalliances might be made public and that she would be blamed for the failure of her marriage? How bitter this would have been for a wife who felt that her husband had loved another throughout their marriage.

Neither did the Princess want to be blamed for the book, for that matter. Irrespective of her conversation with her husband, the pressure on her from senior courtiers to renounce and denounce the book was intense. She, however, refused to yield to their demands that she make a statement of criticism. At the same time she was acutely aware that her friends, themselves under attack from their family and friends for their perceived betrayal of the Princess, were desperate for her to give them some public indication of support. There were numerous tearful phone conversations with friends worried that she was going to let them hang out to dry. 'When Andrew goes on the road it will be fine,' Diana argued, when referring to my publicity tour for the book, and being rather over-optimistic in her efforts to wriggle out of the entreaties of her friends. She faced a tricky dilemma: how could she tread the narrow path between endorsing their statements and distancing herself from complicity?

We came to the conclusion that, although it was a risk, the only way would be for Diana to be seen publicly with one of the friends who was known to have cooperated with the book. The choice was obvious, for she was in any case due to visit William and Carolyn Bartholomew at their Fulham home that week. Diana viewed this with dread, but Colthurst and Carolyn Bartholomew between them convinced her that it was imperative that she kept that appointment. A picture of Carolyn and Diana together would do more than any argument advanced either by myself or Andrew Neil that the book was authentic. She agreed to take the chance. So on the morning of Wednesday 10 June I called Stuart Higgins, then deputy editor of the *Sun*, who was due to serialize the book after the *Sunday Times*, and told him to send a couple of discreet photographers to Carolyn's home where they might see something of interest. None of us, not even Diana herself, knew exactly when she would arrive so I didn't want to take any chances. At seven in the evening, while the Princess was on her way, I got a frantic phone call from William Bartholomew. He had walked up and down his road and could not see any photographers. With Higgins unavailable, I took a chance and called my former colleague, Ken Lennox, the photographer who had been my partner in the days when we had worked together as the royal duo on the *Daily Star* and who was now employed by the *Sun*'s rival, the *Daily Mirror*. It was a high-risk phone call. While Ken is totally trustworthy and would never reveal his source, I thought it would not take anyone long to link us and come to the conclusion that Diana was part of a surreptitious photo opportunity and therefore behind the book. It was a gamble we had to take. As Ken lived nearby, in Chelsea, he was quickly outside Carolyn's house, though not in time to capture Diana's arrival. An hour or so later she emerged from the Bartholomew's home, and while Ken clicked away she embraced Carolyn and William on the doorstep before leaving. The *Daily Mirror*'s headline accompanying the photographs said it all: 'Seal of approval.' True to form, Lennox resisted pressure from his editor Richard Stott to tell him who had given him the tip-off. The following day when Stott was discussing the implications of the story with his royal correspondent James Whitaker, the veteran reporter stated that he had no clue as to the identity of Lennox's informer. 'He hasn't got any royal contacts,' said James confidently. 'Well, he seems to have one more than you,' his editor replied acidly.

For years, everyone has believed the story that it was a 'well-spoken woman', possibly Diana herself, who had called the news desks of several national newspapers and tipped them off about her private visit to a friend. Like so much concerning this aspect of her life, the *Daily Mirror* piece was unplanned, an improvised but remarkably effective operation, which staunched the flow of unrestrained criticism. Certainly Richard Stott, the *Daily Mirror* editor, who, in a typical knee-jerk fashion, had tried to rubbish the book because his rivals the *Sun* were serializing it, was given cause to look with fresh eyes at the evidence before him.

Privately Diana paid a high price for supporting a friend. The following day she was hauled over the coals by the Queen's private secretary, Sir Robert Fellowes, for having visited Carolyn Bartholomew, someone so closely associated with the book. Just minutes after her confrontation with Fellowes, she called James Colthurst and told him that she felt like having a good weep. 'If you want to cry, just do it, don't hold back,' he said. But public duties denied her the luxury of throwing herself down on her bed – she was about to leave for a scheduled visit to Liverpool. There, a woman in the crowd stroked her face and, as if on cue, the tears coursed down her cheeks. While her obvious distress gained her immediate public sympathy, it sent out mixed messages about her feelings towards her biography. Andrew Neil, who heard the news on his car radio, recalled saying to his driver, 'Oh, no, I'm going to go down in history as the editor who made the Princess cry.' As ever, Diana had been much cleverer than anyone truly suspected, her tears to some degree premeditated. While she had given her friends support, through her show of tears in Liverpool she had also distanced herself from the book while winning over public sympathy.

In fact, all Diana's theatricals would have counted for nothing if one of her other friends had had his way. On 8 June, the day after the first extract was serialized, Michael O'Mara received a phone call that made his blood run cold. It was from a man acting for the photographer Terence Donovan, who was a friend of the Princess. He pointed out that a picture of Diana used by the *Sunday Times* and attributed to Patrick Demarchelier had in fact been taken by his client, Mr Donovan. The picture had been used without Donovan's permission and he wanted £70,000 in payment. O'Mara's explanation, that we had used the photograph under the innocent impression that it had been taken by Demarchelier, cut no ice with either Donovan or his negotiator. They informed us that they knew exactly how we had obtained the picture, since Donovan had given it only to Diana, and that if we did not pay this inflated price – the usual fee at the time for a picture used in a book was £500 – they would reveal to the world who had supplied the picture. It meant that Diana's complicity with the book would be exposed in spite of all our attempts to camouflage her involvement. Both sides dug their heels in; at one point O'Mara had a group of employees on standby, ready to cut the offending picture out of the book with razor blades. In the end O'Mara paid Donovan a five-figure sum for the use of his picture, a price which also guaranteed his silence.

Had that story come out at the time it could well have tipped Diana over the edge. For, as Colthurst, Carolyn Bartholomew, James Gilbey, and others, witnessed, the first few days after the book's appearance in the *Sunday Times* tested the Princess's resolve to the limit. But very soon she began to receive the kind of support that always meant so much to her, from her public. 'The flak was intense and for a time she did get cold feet,' said Colthurst. 'Then the letters of support came pouring in. There were thousands of them, many from women who had suffered from eating disorders and accepted their lot in silence. Many told her that they were inspired by her example. She knew that somehow she had touched the heart of humanity and had been able to make a difference. That meant so much to her.' Just as encouraging was a report from the Eating Disorders Association, shortly after the book was published on 16 June, saying that they had had an enormous increase in first-time callers asking for help. The response was entirely due to the Princess's courage in making public her private difficulties.

Even as these supportive letters were landing on her desk, an article appeared in the *Sunday Express* headlined 'My Regrets by Diana', which implied that the Princess wished she had never become involved. She was quick to telephone James to repudiate the article and to apologize for any implication that she was in any way responsible for it. Over the years there have been endless suggestions that she regretted her part in the book, that her involvement was an example of aberrant behaviour which she entered into at a low point in her life. The truth of the matter is that she had put what she called 'the dark ages' of her royal life behind her and was keen to move on to a more fulfilling future. Certainly she was nervous but she was also resolved to break out of the prison her life had become. David Puttnam was certain she never regretted her involvement in the book, saying, 'She owned what she had done. She knew what she was doing and took a calculated risk even though she was scared shitless. But I never heard one word of regret, I promise you. With all her faults she was a good woman.'

*

The original idea behind the book was for the Princess to tell her side of the story, and to dispel the myths that had been woven around her marriage, but it soon became clear that collaborating with the book had psychological benefits for Diana. For those intense twelve months, she went through a process of purging the past, a kind of confessional-through-reminiscence in which she was able to give voice to her anger and her regrets, as well as her dreams and ambitions. The book was a biography – but given the extent of its subject's participation, it was also the nearest the Princess could come to an autobiography and self-expression – and so had the additional benefit of boosting her self-confidence.

In mid-June, a matter of days after the book's publication, James Colthurst was driving to Solihull in the Midlands for a board meeting at his medical company when he received an urgent page from Diana. He pulled off the M6 motorway and found a phone box in the nearest service station. Diana was waiting frantically for his call. She told him that she and her husband had had a meeting with the Queen and Prince Philip at Windsor Castle to discuss their marriage and the wider impact on the monarchy of any suggestion of a separation. She had expected her husband to stand by the decision they had made and argue for a formal separation, but to her disgust he had remained silent during a tirade from his father.

While her husband's failure of nerve in the face of parental disapproval was no more than she had come to expect, what had frightened her was the moment when her father-in-law confronted her about her involvement with the book. When she denied any knowledge of it, he retorted that they had a tape of a telephone discussion in which she was talking to an unidentified person about which newspaper should be given serialization of the book: the *Sunday Times* or the *Daily Mail*. Once more she stonewalled, denying his accusation, but when the meeting ended she left Windsor Castle alarmed and confused. Unless this was an elaborate bluff, which seemed extremely unlikely, what she had suspected for years had now been confirmed – that her telephone conversations were routinely tapped by an official government agency, whether it be the police or security services.

Yet, as she told Colthurst and, later, others in her intimate circle, she could not clearly remember if she had had any such conversation.

When she returned to Kensington Palace she contacted Sir Robert Fellowes and asked him what the Queen and Prince Philip were playing at. While he was sympathetic and told her that he had never realized how 'awful' her life was inside the royal family, he again confirmed that there was an incriminating tape of her conversation. More than that, he told her that the Prime Minister, John Major, had been informed and that she would be given a copy of the tape the following day. The next day Diana was understandably on tenterhooks as she waited for the axe to fall. But the Palace blade remained sheathed and the alleged tape was never made available to her. Instead, she was told later that, as the tape could not be used as evidence of her involvement with the book – the implication being that the recording had been made illicitly or its veracity was in doubt – the episode should be forgotten.

Shaken and disturbed, Diana now began to see the full extent of the opposition lined against her. If she wanted her freedom, she would have to fight, and fight skilfully. 'I'm a threat, you see,' she told her astrologer, Felix Lyle, 'I've got to be very sprightly.'

She had succeeded in making herself heard. Now she faced a more difficult challenge, the search to find herself.

CHAPTER THREE

The Comfort of Strangers

WHEN STEPHEN TWIGG held Diana's face in his hands for the first time, the feelings and emotions that emanated from his royal client alarmed him. He sensed, according to his notes, 'a deep and abiding fear, flashes of intense anger, bordering on rage, crippling self-judgement, an extreme sadness, but most of all a profound sense of loneliness and overwhelming despair'.

Stephen Twigg, therapist, counsellor and masseur, first met the Princess in December 1988, when he went to see her in Kensington Palace. During the hour-long massage he gave her he saw the scars where she had disfigured herself and recognized, from his encounters with clients who were on the brink of taking their own lives, that here was a young woman in utter despair. 'It was quite frightening as I have had experience in the past working with suicidal people,' he said. 'I could feel a woman who was definitely considering that life wasn't worth carrying on with.'

He was so concerned that at their next session, when they felt more comfortable with each other, he invited her to make an affirmation, a powerful vocalization of faith in front of a witness. At his behest she repeated: 'From this moment on I choose to be alive,' a statement indicating a conscious choice about her life rather than a passive acceptance that life goes on. For the next seven years Twigg was on hand to observe those words become reality. His intervention had been successful. 'He used to teach me affirmations about myself [at a time] when I could never believe [in myself],' Diana later acknowledged. 'He said that if I wanted to get better I could. I never gave anyone else [that] credit.'

Twigg, who now lives in the south of France, was one of a disparate band of outsiders who, in the late 1980s, were admitted into her real life, charged with carrying the heavy burden of her unhappiness in secrecy. The astrologer Penny Thornton, introduced to Diana by Sarah Ferguson, was one of the first to see the flip side of the fairy tale, discovering a young woman who was 'clearly angry, desperate, disappointed', a far cry from the saccharine image of the popular photographic poses for the public. 'She felt abused, rejected, betrayed, alone,' said Penny remembering the first time she saw the Princess in her sitting room at Kensington Palace in 1984. 'Prince Charles was the focus for much of that anger because she told me that the day before they married he told her that he didn't love her. He told her that categorically.'

Another outsider to meet the Princess during her dark days was an acupuncturist, Oonagh Shanley-Toffolo, a former nun, who when she first met Diana in September 1989 saw a woman who 'presented a very tormented landscape. Diana was very fragile, very low in energy and in extreme need of affection,' she recollected. 'Diana was constantly searching for love, for appreciation.'

Yet, bleak as Diana's world presented itself, she had by the end of the 1980s, come a long way from what she called the 'dark ages' of her life inside the royal family: the time when she cut her body out of frustration; when she famously hurled herself down the stairs at Sandringham while pregnant with Prince William, because her husband had ignored her concerns about his relationship with Camilla Parker Bowles; and when her eating disorder was at its most pernicious.

A skiing tragedy at Klosters in Switzerland in the spring of 1988, in which a member of the royal party was killed in an avalanche, was a watershed for the Princess. Though suffering from flu, and shocked by the news of the death of a good friend, she was jolted into calm, sensible, decisive action. She packed their dead friend's possessions and firmly discouraged her husband from staying on to continue his skiing, insisting that they must accompany their friend's body home.

Possibly emboldened by her own firmness – 'I took charge there,' she was to comment later – she sought to take charge of herself too, and, with a push from Carolyn Bartholomew, received medical help for her eating disorder. Not long after that, she was able to force a confrontation with her husband's mistress at a party, remaining calm and self-controlled throughout. These achievements had combined to give her a greater sense of self-worth, a belief in herself that was bolstered and sustained by other affirmative actions, such as helping to nurse her friend Adrian Ward-Jackson, who eventually died of AIDS in 1991. Such shoots of personal recovery were nurtured by the reception she received from the public – she was particularly touched by the growing crowds of well-wishers who greeted her on public occasions – and by the stalwart support of a growing group of friends and advisers.

The publication of *Diana: Her True Story* in June 1992 blew open the secret little world of deception and illusion in the Palace and revealed to the public the millstone that had been carried for so long by those inside the freemasonry of the royal inner circle. As recounted in the previous chapter there was considerable anger and resentment within the royal circle at Diana's 'betrayal', and among many people at the puncturing of the collective dream of monarchy; but there was also a deep sense of relief, amongst friends, courtiers and royal staff that the charade was over. In this epic drama of kings and queens, princes and princesses, the book was the literary equivalent of Gollum, the unlovely and unloved creature from Tolkien's *Lord of the Rings*, who none the less plays a critical part in resolving the titanic conflict between the forces of light and darkness. As crude and jolting as it was, *Diana: Her True Story* went some way to resolving a phoney royal peace that was causing crippling casualties all round.

Even before the book was published, lawyers from both sides of the marriage had been secretly negotiating a separation. The strain of maintaining the illusion of happy families had left everyone drained and exhausted, not least because the Princess, acutely aware of the forces now ranged against her, had refused to go along with the pretence. 'It's so bloody dishonest, a damned farce,' she declared repeatedly. That said, Prince Charles himself seemed to be dropping the charade, his behaviour becoming more blatant. In May 1992 the Princess went on an official visit to Egypt at the invitation of the President's wife, Mrs Mubarak. The aircraft on which she was travelling had to make a detour to Turkey in order to drop off the Prince and his entourage, so that he could go on a cruise with some friends – one of them being Camilla Parker Bowles – while Diana went on to Egypt to carry out the tour solo. As the aircraft approached Cairo, she broke down in tears of self-pity, rage and sadness.

A Mediterranean cruise on board a yacht owned by the Greek billionaire John Latsis, which was unwisely billed as a 'second honeymoon' by Prince Charles's private secretary Richard Aylard, was an unmitigated disaster. Diana, who had only agreed to the holiday for the sake of her boys, was miserable and hated the pretence. She was, with reason, convinced that her husband was spending a great deal of time on the telephone to Camilla Parker Bowles, and she demanded to fly home early; this would have been very difficult to manage and she was eventually dissuaded by her bodyguard Ken Wharfe.

A few months later, in November 1992, it once again took the combined efforts of various courtiers – as well as considerable cajoling from James Colthurst – to convince her that she should go with the Prince on a joint tour of South Korea. As soon as the warring couple landed, their press secretary, Dickie Arbiter, waiting for them at Seoul airport, took one look at their body language and commented to a royal aide: 'Oh, f—k, we've lost this one.' Headlines referring to the sullen couple as 'The Glums' later endorsed his view. So when, on 9 December 1992, the then Prime Minister, John Major, announced the couple's 'amicable' separation there was an audible sigh of relief inside the Palace.

The woman at the centre of the storm was calm, controlled and determined, brimming with humour and sunny spirits, a world away from the brooding malcontent of the autumn. In the days following the announcement it was as if a huge weight had been lifted from her shoulders. 'I see you have bought yourself another German car,' someone remarked on seeing her new Audi outside Kensington Palace. 'Well, it's more reliable than a German husband,' Diana replied.

The impact went way beyond surface banter. Her bulimia, which tormented her in times of stress, was subdued; a sign of her inner strength and serenity. A triumphant three-day tour of Paris on her own, just before the announcement, had given everyone a tantalizing glimpse of how the Princess, unfettered and unencumbered, could perform on the world stage. 'She glowed under the rapturous attention, responding as usual to the stimulus of public expectation by producing a flawless display of how to be a royal celebrity,' her private secretary Patrick Jephson wrote in *Shadows of a Princess*. 'Every gesture, every glance, every stop of every walkabout revealed a professional at the peak of her form.' Exhilarated by her solo success and exulting in the heady sense of impending freedom, she enjoyed a late-night drive through the empty Paris streets with only her bodyguard Ken Wharfe for company. As they drove along the Champs-Élysées, she suddenly remarked, 'By God, Ken, *this* is living.'

If the book had given Diana the chance to be heard, then the announcement, six months later, of the separation of the Prince and Princess of Wales had presented her with the opportunity to be herself. Once the initial euphoria had subsided, Diana gradually came to realize that she faced a journey of self-discovery more challenging than anything she had hitherto encountered. 'I am going to own myself now and be true to myself,' she declared bravely. 'I no longer want to live someone else's idea of what I should be.' Who was the person she saw when she looked in the mirror of her dressing room at Kensington Palace? Perhaps more importantly, who was the woman she would like to become? These were questions easier to ask than to answer. She had been barely out of her teens when she had married the Prince, inexperienced and impressionable (although perhaps not quite as malleable as Charles and his clique had hoped). As her friend and astrologer, Debbie Frank, pointed out, the days following her separation were a time of re-evaluation and reassessment. 'She had to really look at herself and where she was going. She only knew herself through her iconography, so she had to find out who the real Diana was.'

Diana was well aware that, because of her title and status, she had become a living icon, a real-life fairy-tale princess on whom the public could focus their hopes, and feed their starry-eyed dreams of princes and princesses. The famous photograph from the Spencer family albums showing the teenage Diana sitting engrossed in one of Barbara Cartland's romantic novels demonstrated how far the young Diana was herself initially captivated by the idealized image of courtly love and romantic marriage. By the time of her separation, the spell had been savagely broken. 'They [the public] are told there is this fairy princess with a bleeding tiara on her head and it is fairy-story stuff for them,' she said bitterly during our interviews.

She had spent all her adult years in an institution where her life had been controlled – either by courtiers who managed her timetable and massaged her ego; by her bodyguard, who monitored her movements; or by the media, who defined her personality through bewildering distortion, unthinking contradiction and facile cliché. By and large, however, the media was the only day-to-day yardstick Diana had ever had to judge herself by.

'The process of finding herself was very hard,' James Colthurst observed. 'For most of her adult life, decisions had been made for her – she was, to a degree, institutionalized. After the separation it became very much a question of her regaining control of herself and building momentum. The focus was always on trying to move *towards* something, rather than simply *away* from the royal family.'

The weeks following the official announcement of the royal couple's separation were, to put it mildly, stressful, as members of the royal family closed ranks and a perceived whispering campaign started up against the Princess of Wales – and against the Duchess of York – while the Queen lamented her *annus horribilis*. Diana had to get away.

The much-needed tonic was provided by a sun-drenched holiday with her sons on the Caribbean island of Nevis in January

1993 – 'You saved my life,' she told Ken Wharfe, who had organized the break. Back at Kensington Palace, it was now time for her to take control of her life.

Like any injured animal, the Princess needed a safe refuge where she could lick her wounds in peace. She had resisted urgings from Prince Philip and others to move out of the former marital apartment at Kensington Palace and into the much smaller and semi-derelict apartment no. 7. As far as she was concerned she wanted to be surrounded by the familiar, even though many of the memories were painful. Also painful was the division of the spoils, including in some cases the disposal of the staff, a number of whom were made redundant while others were moved. Prince Charles's under-butler at Highgrove, Paul Burrell, and his wife Maria, a housemaid at Highgrove, for instance, moved to Kensington Palace, and very reluctantly too. The feeling was mutual – the Princess instinctively distrusted the loyalties of anyone who had ever worked for the other side.

As her slimmed-down staff settled down, every scrap of her marital past was being scrubbed, brushed and painted over. Charles was history. Everything of his, from the Prince of Wales carpet to his antique lavatory, was removed and the Princess asked her interior designer friend Dudley Poplak – who had helped her decorate the Kensington Palace apartments twelve years before, in the weeks ahead of her marriage – to freshen up a number of rooms; she even talked about asking another of her friends, Gianni Versace, to design distinctive uniforms for her staff.

Diana also brought in a New Age healer, Simone Simmons, to exorcize and cleanse the negative energy from her former marital home, as well as an expert in feng shui to reinvigorate some of the rooms. 'I feel as though I have died here many times,' she explained sadly. While it would take much more than new wallpaper and a coat of paint for Diana to forget her unhappy past, it was a start. From the purchase of a new double bed to the slightly risqué cartoons in the downstairs loo, there were signs of new beginnings.

It was a similar, if less exhaustive, story at Highgrove House, where another interior designer, Robert Kime, was giving the

Prince's country seat a makeover, to remove traces of the Princess's original decoration.

Diana's London home, while still a place of much sadness and anger, was – even though she called it a prison – at least a safe refuge. This secure base helped her body to heal, which was important as for most of her life her body had been her master. In the first months of her newly single life she demonstrated consistent control over herself, in particular over her eating disorder, bulimia nervosa, which had plagued her ever since she joined the royal family. As this illness involves feelings of control, now that she had more control over her life the bulimia had less control over her – as opposed to the early days of her royal career, particularly when she stayed at Balmoral and Sandringham with the rest of the family, when her bulimia was at its most intense. As the prospect of a life of her own grew, the Princess was able to speak lightly of the disorder. When she refused to attend a shooting party on the Sandringham estate with her husband in November 1992 – a decision that precipitated the separation – she remarked to Patrick Jephson, her private secretary, 'Nicholas Soames [the Conservative politician and rotund grandson of Winston Churchill] can eat all the food they have brought for me. I'd probably only have sicked it up anyway.' That she could now joke about her illness with staff showed how far she had come. Her appetite now was for life rather than binge eating. Even on the occasions her bulimia returned it was more as a sporadic coping strategy than an endemic problem.

In other areas, the Princess gradually and consistently moved away from the days where her body controlled her life, slowly weaning herself off her dependencies. Thus she replaced the sleeping pills in her medicine cabinet for sessions with a sleep therapist who monitored her oxygen levels; and she went for colonic irrigation to deal with her inner rage rather than, as she had done in the past, cut and mark her body. In time, colonics would be replaced by kick-boxing sessions with Keith Rodriques, the husband of her therapist Chryssie Fitzgerald, although Diana's bodyguard did not share her enthusiasm for visiting Rodriques' seedy basement gym in the rundown East End of London. While her endless experimentation with New Age therapies – from casting runes and sitting under copper pyramids to sitting in a stone circle and absorbing energy from the sun – became widely derided, they were part of a long, haphazard process of healing, not to say self-absorption. The absurdity of some of her experiments was not lost on Diana. When her detective Ken Wharfe encountered her 'wired up as if for a NASA launch' in a treatment room in Beauchamp Place he asked her quizzically, 'Are you enjoying that, ma'am?' From the tangle of tubes and wires she retorted with cheerful irony: 'It's very therapeutic.'

A more conventional form of therapy was Diana's daily exercise routine; apart from her regular workouts being physically invigorating, they gave her a powerful feeling of being in charge of herself. When her fitness coach Carolan Brown was first introduced to her in 1990, Diana exhibited all the classic signs of insecurity and low self-esteem. Her shoulders sloped, making her chest look droopy, her chin jutted out, and rather than looking up at her coach she peered at her through her blonde fringe. More surprisingly for a young woman celebrated for her fashion sense, Diana wore shapeless T-shirts and baggy shorts as if she were ashamed of her body. Over the next few years, particularly after the separation, she worked on her body, gaining self-confidence as she developed a toned torso that she allowed herself to be proud of. Indeed, she reached the point where she was actually prepared to reveal it to strangers. Wearing nothing more than a flesh-coloured Lycra thong leotard, she offered to see Carolan out after a workout session at Kensington Palace. As Carolan and the Princess made their way into the courtyard, Diana's next-door neighbour Princess Michael of Kent, and the art historian Sir Roy Strong came out on their way to the Chelsea Flower Show. As they prepared to drive off Diana made idle chit-chat, all the while slyly amused at the impact her display had had. 'It was showing off in a way,' Carolan commented, 'but it was much more than that. When I first met Diana she could never have done it. It was a sign that at last Diana felt comfortable in her own skin and wanted to enjoy her new-found confidence in her body.'

*

While she worked to control her petulant body, Diana also sought to expand her mind, displaying the same kind of voracious appetite for knowledge that she had once shown for food. She was a curious, and for many, an unsettling combination – a sophisticated woman of the world able to discuss death and dying with the Archbishop of Canterbury one minute, yet innocent of the ways of the world. A socially accomplished woman who could face a sophisticated cocktail party and say to her companions: 'Hold your nose and dive in', she had never been to a pub or a bar on her own, and neither could she boil a pan of pasta. 'She had a sheltered upbringing and was very immature when she married,' Dickie Arbiter, the press secretary she shared with Charles, pointed out. 'She went from one fantasy world to another.' Yet as the dust settled surrounding her separation, the upper-class girl who left school without a significant academic qualification demonstrated a wide, if untutored and unselective, breadth of reading. This student princess was as experimental as any undergraduate, cherry picking from an eclectic range of texts. She herself remarked, 'I'm going to be amused by people's reactions to the titles of the books.' From pious texts by the philosopher Omraam Mikhael Aivanhov, New Age books on tarot cards and the I Ching, medical books such as *Gray's Anatomy* and the seminal *Fat is a Feminist Issue* by the psychotherapist Susie Orbach, Diana displayed her growing and continuing interest in the spiritual, medical and psychological. According to Debbie Frank, 'She read anything she could get her hands on. Some things she found hard to digest, but she wanted to find out why she was in this position, how she could help herself and others in times of difficulty and stress. She didn't want to be a victim who was out of control any more.'

While Diana was the first to admit that she was no academic, she was using her growing knowledge to change and control the vision she had of herself, to see herself less as a helpless victim and more as a woman empowered and energized. 'Diana is on a voyage of discovery at the moment – she is discovering who the real Diana is,' observed Stephen Twigg.

As part of that journey, she acted on the advice of her osteopath Michael Skipwith and made an appointment to see Susie Orbach, whose work on the female psyche, particularly in relation to eating disorders, has gained international repute. It was a brave step, especially as a central feature in the pathology of bulimia is to deny that one has a problem. As Susie Orbach is the first to say, therapy is no easy option. She did not present a professional shoulder to cry on during the hour-long sessions at her clinic in Belsize Park, North London, in the spring of 1993. 'Therapy makes you look at who you are,' she says. 'It's not about saying, "You are fine" or about reassurance and consolation. It's about asking who you are and why you act the way you do.' These are demanding questions, but Diana now felt that she could ask them of herself.

Indeed, the Princess even felt able to articulate and explore these questions on a more public stage when, in April 1993, she agreed to make the opening address at the first London conference on eating disorders. She had done her homework for the speech and had written sections of it herself. As a result, while she was intensely nervous beforehand – 'I could do with a gin and tonic,' she told the psychiatrist, Dr Bryan Lask, who had organized the conference – she was for once truly speaking from the heart. 'I have it on very good authority that the quest for perfection in society can leave the individual gasping for breath at every turn,' she said, not afraid to own to her problem. She went on to call bulimia a 'shameful friend' and described childhood feelings of 'guilt, self-revulsion and low personal esteem creating . . . a compulsion to dissolve like a Disprin and disappear.' Her speech, personal, perceptive and revealing, was a startling departure for a member of the royal family. Most important for Diana, she was the one who was in charge of her thoughts, her words and her voice.

'Not bad for a whore!' yelled a voice as she left the conference, still flushed with adrenalin and nerves.

For a moment the Palace officials accompanying the Princess were aghast, but Diana explained through ecstatic giggles that it was her speech trainer, the actor Peter Settelen, who in his work with her, had used role play, which included impersonating people from all walks of life. Indeed, his influence was typical of the informal, rather haphazard way people came into the Princess's life. Just before Christmas 1992 Diana had asked her fitness trainer for her verdict on how she had delivered a recent speech that had been broadcast on BBC Radio Four. 'Rubbish,' came Carolan's unvarnished reply. 'You sounded like a ten-year-old with a little-girl feel-sorry-for-me voice. If you want to make a powerful speech it has to sound like you mean it.' Carolan lost no time in recommending her friend Peter Settelen as coach, and while he was taken on to train the Princess in the art of speech delivery it was not long before – much to Patrick Jephson's irritation – he added speech writing to his royal duties. By mid-1993 he, Stephen Twigg and James Colthurst were involved in her speeches, sometimes in competition.

There were other ways in which the Princess sought to present her new self to the world – a new hairstyle and a new wardrobe of sophisticated business suits made their appearance, while she chose to release portraits of herself by her favourite photographer, Patrick Demarchelier, that would display the fresh face of a determined, self-confident young woman who was eager to address serious issues and move on with her life.

But these were only images; the real-life Princess was still prone to doubt, depression and anxiety as she faced an uncertain future. She was, as one friend noted, 'very tidal'. For every business suit she wore, she also appeared in public in severe black outfits, as if in mourning. In a woman who was acutely aware of her public image – 'They [the public] don't want to see me looking dowdy; they want to see me out there doing my thing,' she told Ken Wharfe – the plain and sombre garments gave an indication of the continuing struggle in her heart and mind. It was not long before the tabloids were criticizing her dress sense, censure that hit a raw nerve. 'Dowdy, am I?' she snapped at one hapless tabloid royal correspondent after a spate of stories were published, caustically commenting on her gloomy wardrobe.

It was left to James Colthurst to broach this thorny subject over lunch at Kensington Palace. Diplomatically, Diana's old friend told her what, deep in her heart, she already knew – that the public wanted to see a bright and colourful princess. Surprisingly, she accepted his comments, and for a period there was the amusing situation of the world's most famous fashion plate asking a man who thought that 'haute couture' was a brand of up-market porridge for suggestions on her wardrobe. In reality what really changed her mind was the argument that a new, brighter look would also confuse 'the enemy' – Prince Charles's camp – who were silently cheering her public difficulties at that time. Indeed, the Prince would throw a fit of petulant anger every time he saw a prominently displayed newspaper photograph of Diana. 'He's simply got to learn to grow up some time,' commented one courtier.

In the intense atmosphere before the separation Diana was fully aware of the hostility she faced not just from her husband and his supporters but from Buckingham Palace itself. Much as the Queen and Prince Philip tried to remain above the fray, it was clear that ultimately they would side with their son and heir. Blood ties mattered most. She had seen the way the wind was blowing at the royal showdown at Windsor Castle in June 1992 when Prince Philip stated that they had a tape recording of her telephone conversation with an unnamed man about the newspaper serialization of *Diana: Her True Story*.

While that came to nothing, it was extremely unnerving; then, in late June, Diana received a letter, the first of a series, from her father-in-law about the marital breakdown and her perceived involvement with the book. She was outraged and upset. Much has been written about these letters, most recently by her former butler Paul Burrell, who was working for Prince Charles at Highgrove at the time. His benign interpretation of Prince Philip's letters – citing the fact that they were signed 'With fondest love – Pa' – as proof of Philip's concern about her well-being, does not sit easily with Diana's initial reaction. She was so alarmed when the first letter was delivered that she telephoned a friend and asked him to recommend a solicitor to help draft a suitable reply. He in turn contacted me, but in the time that it took me to produce a couple of names, the Princess had already found her own lawyer. Such an agitated response was hardly the behaviour of someone who considered Prince Philip's intervention as friendly. Lucia Flecha de Lima on the other hand – who, with Rosa Monckton, the wife of Dominic Lawson, editor of the *Sunday Telegraph*, helped the Princess draft several replies – found his notes 'warm and helpful', 'Like a father writing to a daughter'. But Diana had never been enamoured of her father-in-law. When, later, she was chatting to Sir Max Hastings, the former editor of the *Daily Telegraph*, she spoke in gleeful tones about the forthcoming publication of a biography by Kitty Kelley, the American gossip writer, of the Duke of Edinburgh (which never came about; instead she published *The Royals* in September 1997). 'He's got away with murder for years,' she told Hastings, a frequent refrain in her litany of complaints about the royal family. Whatever her personal feelings towards him, Prince Philip did, in subsequent letters to Diana, express the universally held belief about his son's liaison with Camilla. 'I cannot imagine anyone in their right mind leaving you for Camilla. Such a prospect never entered our heads,' he wrote.

While these letters have now assumed dramatic importance in the cataclysm of the Queen's *annus horribilis*, then they were just one cloudburst in a season of storms. Diana was at the time the object of a great deal of criticism, disapproval, rumours and allegations. She was criticized for making a speech on drug abuse on a 'Balmoral Day' in August, when the royal family should be on holiday. Not long after, she heard that the Queen had said during her summer cruise on board the royal yacht *Britannia* that the book had confirmed her view that Diana was 'unstable'; and that, according to the royal writer Brian Hoey, no one in the Queen's household had a 'good word to say about her'. Thus the myth of the 'loose cannon' was born, and the whispering campaign, with its claims that she needed psychiatric help and suffered from Borderline Personality Syndrome, gathered pace.

In August 1992, not long after the 'second honeymoon' fiasco on board Latsis's yacht, and while the press had been revelling in disclosures about the Duchess of York and her so-called financial adviser, John Bryan, came another bombshell – the publication in the *Sun* newspaper of illicitly taped telephone conversations between the Princess and a man identified as James Gilbey.

Just days before the extracts of the now notorious Squidgygate tapes were published we heard that one of Prince Charles's closest supporters had been encouraging nervous newspaper executives at the *Sun*, who had had the tapes in a safe for many months, to publish the damning late-night chat of three years before. Ironically, the editors at the normally brash tabloid were so fearful of publishing the contents of the tapes, which graphically revealed Diana's sense of isolation and unhappiness inside her marriage and within the royal family, that they would have held fire if they had been contacted by the Queen's private secretary, Sir Robert Fellowes. He never called. The *Sun*'s executives, having overcome their scruples, even set up a phone line for people to listen to excerpts from the tapes.

Diana, who was staying at Balmoral, was so distressed that she was on the point of packing her bags and leaving even before her lawyers and those representing the Prince had started work on a suitable separation settlement. While she put on a brave face in front of the royal family, The Princess was, according to Colthurst, 'at the lowest ebb for years'. But he and other friends managed to convince her that it was best to stay and fight it out rather than leave.

In spite of the pleasant smiles and polite tone, the negotiations were, as far as Diana's private secretary Patrick Jephson was concerned, motivated by 'spite, hypocrisy and injustice'. 'I wondered if her opponents really understood the bloody-minded determination of the woman they were seeking to banish to the backwaters of royal life,' he wrote in his memoirs. There were many who wished to see her pay a high price for her independence.

Perversely, those attempts to downgrade her status by limiting her use of the Queen's flight and royal train, and access to the Palace machine merely served to shine a light more clearly on the true direction Diana wanted to take. For years she had railed against the flummery and protocol surrounding royal life; now she had a chance to demonstrate an approach to duty that differed in style and substance from the prevailing Windsor orthodoxy. So when in March she flew to Nepal in the company of Lynda

Chalker, the then Minister of Overseas Development, on her first solo trip as a 'semi-detached member of the royal family', the media sharks were circling in the water, sensing blood. A secret media briefing by Prince Charles's aides, which pointed out Diana's reduced status, served to define the news agenda for the visit. 'We may be witnessing early signs that Diana is no longer a royal of the first order,' announced a headline. That she had travelled by scheduled airline with her sister Sarah McCorquodale as her lady-in-waiting for the five-day visit was seen as merely underlining her inferior status.

In fact, Diana was only too glad to have the chance to shape an important overseas visit to fit in with her vision of how it should be, shorn of protocol and formality, with an emphasis on meeting ordinary people. It was a style she had been working towards for some time; at the height of the furore over the royal separation, for example, Diana was making secret visits to see London's homeless at the Passage Day Centre in Victoria, run by the Catholic Church, to which she had been first taken by the late Cardinal Basil Hume in September 1989, and to hospices in London's East End, Blackpool and Hull.

These visits were part of her healing process. In the world she lived in, everyone's motives were suspect, everyone had an agenda, either to influence her judgements or further their own careers and lives. On the other hand, the people she was visiting lived in a different world – one which had no hold over her. As her friend Debbie Frank observed, 'She was used to never having a relationship that was pure and clean. They all wanted something. It's one reason why she got on so well with children and the dying. They didn't want anything from her. Sad, really.'

The Princess's day-to-day life was filled with rumour and hearsay of plots and counterplots. Rarely a day went by at Kensington Palace without there being some excursion and alarm.

In this uneasy atmosphere loyalty and trust were highly valued, and any perceived transgression assumed an importance out of all proportion to the event. Family, friends, staff, courtiers and police: they all came under her gimlet eye.

*

An incident involving a new full-time member of staff, Paul Burrell, her junior butler, represented everything about life at Kensington Palace which the Princess found constraining, invasive and alienating. When the royal couple parted, in December 1992, Diana had only agreed to take on Burrell and his wife Maria after representations from her private secretary and her butler, Harold Brown. Her first thought was that Burrell, like anyone who had worked for her husband, might turn out to be an enemy spy. While he was personable and flattering, her initial doubts seemed to bear fruit when one day in 1993 the Princess arrived back from the gym to find him rifling through her private letters on the desk in her sitting room. She was furious and sent him from the room, but minutes later, fearing the humiliation of dismissal, he returned to her, threw himself on the floor in tears and started kissing her feet. The astonished Ken Wharfe came by just in time to witness this bizarre spectacle and in an appropriately policemanly manner rebuked the butler for his 'unforgivably disloyal' and 'deeply unprofessional' behaviour. Unable to explain himself, Burrell scuttled from the room.

Shortly after, as Diana was leaving the apartment for a public engagement, Princess Margaret's chauffeur Dave Griffin, who usually engaged her in cheery banter, commented to her that she did not look too happy. 'He [Burrell] will have to go,' she said firmly as she outlined the story. 'She had caught him spinning the bins, going through her letters,' recalled Griffin. While the Princess did see the funny side of the unseemly performance (in fact at the time had difficulty stifling her giggles), Burrell was for several weeks out in the cold and was fortunate to retain his position.

If this had been an isolated incident, the Princess would have probably been happy to laugh it off, but she was uncomfortably aware that nothing of hers was truly private.

Again, when Ken Wharfe made a few unguarded, and rather chauvinist, remarks about Diana to the *Sun*'s royal photographer, Arthur Edwards, the rumour mill quickly went into high gear. Edwards passed the comments on to his boss, the paper's deputy editor, Stuart Higgins, who in turn told a royal contact he was cultivating, the Duchess of York. She wasted no time in relaying the news to her royal friend in order to ingratiate herself. Everyone had their own agenda but the end result was that Diana, already feeling restricted by the police presence, was angry and annoyed that Wharfe had, to her mind, been disloyal. That initial spat sowed the seeds for a summer of growing distance between the Princess and her minder. He was angry when she had her rooms swept for listening devices by a private firm without telling him – 'It's my home and I'll do what I want', she told him defiantly – and also briefed journalists about her plans without informing him. Eventually, with a degree of acrimony on both sides, the Inspector and Diana parted company in November 1993. For some time Diana went without official police protection – although she later employed Princess Anne's former bodyguard, Colin Tebbutt, as her security driver. It was an arrangement that worked well – she had protection yet was in complete command, a situation she had craved for years.

Indeed, it was a deep-seated feeling of being out of control that lay at the heart of the Princess's continuing dissatisfaction with Kensington Palace. While Prince Charles had now left, she still did not feel truly comfortable in her apartment. It was not just the obvious signs of being in a prison – the patrolling police and CCTV cameras – that contributed to her perpetual sense of anxiety and unease. Even after the formal separation she felt that she was still being watched and manipulated, albeit remotely. While she might have been mistress of her household, she neither employed nor held the purse strings for her courtiers, police and staff. Ken Wharfe, for example, was employed by the Metropolitan Police and reported directly to Colin Trimming, Prince Charles's protection officer. Whether or not it was the case, to her mind this meant that her estranged husband knew her plans and movements. Every time she wanted to go on holiday, especially with her boys, others seemed to stand in financial and strategic judgement.

Even if Diana's staff were on her side – which most were – she suspected that ultimately their loyalties, in terms of their pay packets and prospects, lay elsewhere. It was only following her divorce in 1996 that she became her own boss and could be sure of her employees. Until then she ran a shadow secretariat she had built up, a motley group of men to advise, guide and protect. It was haphazard and uncoordinated as well as irritating and deeply frustrating for those already in place. As far as Diana was concerned, though, she had a team (even that word may be too defining) who owed their loyalty and allegiance to her alone. 'I trust my own instincts,' she declared. It was a valiant but fatally flawed assertion.

So while she listened courteously to her private secretary, Patrick Jephson, she felt that, like most of the courtiers, he would have been happiest had she remained within the orbit of the Queen and Buckingham Palace, where she could be more easily managed. So she continually pre-empted him, roping in others to do what he felt were his duties. Thus, for instance, she might invite all and sundry – her masseur Stephen Twigg, her voice coach Peter Settelen, the *Daily Mail*'s royal correspondent Richard Kay (who became friendly with her on the return flight from Nepal) and, later, the TV reporter Martin Bashir, among others – to help write her speeches; or she would discuss her future strategy (in everything from her possible involvement with the Red Cross to the style of her Christmas cards) with the likes of the banker Jacob Rothschild, the television presenter Clive James, the film producer David Puttnam, and her old friend Dr James Colthurst.

For example, a couple of days before Colthurst and the Princess had lunch at Kensington Palace in September 1993, I wrote a five-page discussion paper, headed 'Short to Medium Term Strategic Planning', outlining the issues and difficulties Diana faced at the time. The paper mainly dealt with her media image, speeches, public engagements and her search for a country home; one suggestion, as a long-term strategy, was for her to head a Princess of Wales Trust, which would act as an umbrella organization for all her charity interests. Unknown to me, Stephen Twigg, David Puttnam, and doubtless others, had made similar suggestions. Each time the Princess answered in the negative, saying that she did not want to compete with her husband's charitable trust. The intervention of well-meaning outsiders like myself and others must have been deeply frustrating for her private secretary.

In his memoir Patrick Jephson unintentionally exposed the fault line in their working relationship when commenting about the way

Diana embraced fresh thinking: 'I saw it as a kind of laboratory of ideas in which the Princess could enjoy the freedom to take opinions from anyone she chose. I did not have to intervene . . . but I still retained a degree of control.' He was missing the point – the Princess was seeking to control the situation.

Again, she consistently undermined her press secretary, the former Australian diplomat Geoff Crawford, whom she felt was an emissary from Buckingham Palace and therefore ultimately owed his loyalty the Queen. She regularly circumvented him by filtering stories to Richard Kay at the *Daily Mail*, and to several others, including myself. Eventually, Crawford did indeed become the Queen's press secretary, leaving Diana's employment after her interview on *Panorama* in November 1995.

Given the sometimes malign atmosphere at Kensington Palace, it is easy to understand why the Princess was so thrilled when, just a few days after her return from her visit to Nepal in April 1993, she received a letter from her brother, now Earl Spencer, offering her the use of a four-bedroomed house on the Althorp estate as a private country retreat. It would be a safe haven away from prying eyes, unhappy memories and court gossip – for her a godsend. While she could have afforded to buy her own country home, she was concerned that the extra security costs, indeed any suggestion of lavish expenditure, would have invited criticism both inside and outside the Palace. Until there was a financial settlement, any report about Princess's spending struck a raw nerve. At a rental of £12,000 a year, with a cleaner and gardener thrown in, using the Garden House at Althorp would neatly circumvent those concerns. More importantly, it would have given Diana, still only thirty, the chance to make her own 'cosy nest', the first home of her own. She was so excited that she asked Dudley Poplak to join her and the boys on a visit to her prospective country retreat, where they had a picnic lunch and spent a day full of happy anticipation, choosing rooms for the boys, and furnishings and a colour scheme (she had had in mind pale blues and yellows, colours suggesting peace and contentment).

Within days, however, her dreams were dashed. Her brother contacted her again, this time saying that, on reflection, given the inevitable press and police interference, it would be better if his senior land agent took over the property. 'If you are interested in renting a farmhouse [outside the park] then that would be wonderful,' he wrote in a letter first quoted in Paul Burrell's memoir. Diana, though, was heartbroken, more hurt than Earl Spencer could ever have known. She immediately wrote him a letter venting her fury, which he, perhaps sensibly, returned unopened. There then followed, as he described it, a 'brief and bitter silence', not helped when in September he asked her to return the Spencer family tiara which she had worn on her wedding day in July 1981.

Emotionally, Diana had invested very heavily, probably too much so, in the country house. It represented so much more than a weekend retreat – independence, safety and security as well as an opportunity just to be herself. Her anger with her brother masked the anger she felt towards herself. As with other significant events in her life – her mother's departure, her own failed marriage – she blamed herself, distorting a perfectly natural impulse, to have a home to call her own, into a complex psychological drama of guilt and self-loathing. 'She was desperately upset,' recalled Stephen Twigg. 'Once again she felt that she was thrown back on her own resources. In the end she had to sort out her problems on her own.'

'Why would anyone want all the fuss that goes with me?' Diana commented sorrowfully, an instinct that informed and affected so many of her dealings with the outside world, particularly her relations with men. She was to repeat this lament more than once.

It was the first of a series of incidents that tested her resolve to the limit. Every time she seemed to be making progress in living her life on her own terms, the Princess was pushed back; it was a cycle of aspiration and frustration that marked the rest of her life.

While she was licking her wounds following the altercation with her brother, she began to see the therapist Susie Orbach at her basement rooms in Belsize Park, North London. But as the Princess strove to resolve her inner conflicts, especially her feelings of guilt and low self-worth, she discovered that the world was not willing to give her the opportunity to do so in peace. More than that, they – or rather their self-appointed representatives, the mass media – wanted her to feel guilty for even trying. It was not long before paparazzi were lurking outside the clinic, harassing Orbach's neighbours and distressing her other clients. When the Princess emerged from her hour-long sessions they would shout at her to lift her head up so they could get their shots. If she did not, they muttered, 'Bitch,' and photographed her anyway. One, who photographed Diana crying as she left Orbach's home, commented blithely, 'She is used to a number of photographers shadowing her, so seeing just the four of us was no big deal.' When she was inside the royal family, the hunting season was reasonably limited. Now that she had left their smothering embrace, she was the daily prey of the paparazzi, a hunt that lasted until her death. 'She began to see the dark side of human nature,' said Debbie Frank. 'She realized that some people were so primitive that she could never have any connection with them.' The continual pestering Diana faced culminated in her taking out an injunction for harassment against one particular paparazzo, Martin Stenning, who stalked her persistently.

The dirty work undertaken by the photographers was followed up by a steady stream of judgemental features and stories that placed both Diana and her therapist in the media cross hairs, reinforcing the media's presumption of quasi ownership of the Princess by virtue of her position as a public figure. A disdainful headline in the tabloid *Daily Mail* was typical: 'She's left-wing and hates the traditional family. She hasn't even bothered to visit her own sick uncle. Is Susie Orbach really the best person to advise the Princess?' The subtext seemed clear – conform to our agenda or face the consequences.

Indeed, the observations made by the feminist author Bea Campbell regarding the photographers who hounded Diana could also serve as a comment on the mass media's relationship with the Princess: 'They loved looking at her, they loved chasing her, frightening her and simply staring at her. Their work also revealed a determination to dominate her, by never taking no for answer.' As far as the media were concerned, any compromise on her part was a variation on the age-old excuse of 'She asked for it'. That Diana continued to attend her meetings with Susie Orbach, one moment unburdening her innermost secrets, the next braving the shouting paparazzi, was a testament to her strength of purpose and fierce desire to explore the nature of herself and her psyche.

Diana's new life was proving much more difficult than she had expected – pursuing a 'normal' life had a high price tag. While she actually did manage a secret weekend away in Paris with two friends, harassment-free morning workouts at the gym proved too much to expect. After two years using the facilities at Kensington Palace, her trainer, Carolan Brown, suggested in 1992 that they visit her gym, LA Fitness, in Isleworth, West London, for a change of scene. She knew that Diana was sufficiently comfortable with her body shape that she would not be overly concerned about being seen by fellow gym-users. 'I knew how much she wanted to be a normal person and do normal things,' said Carolan. 'It meant so much to her as her life was so controlled and organized.'

The simple suggestion had deplorable consequences. After Diana had made the occasional visit, unknown to both women, the gym owner, a New Zealand businessman called Bryce Taylor, had, with the help of a photographer friend, secretly rigged up a camera in the ceiling of the gym. When the Princess visited he waited until she was using the leg press, which was directly below the camera, and surreptitiously took sneak photographs as she worked out in her leotard.

In May 1993, already distressed by the badgering of the photographers outside Susie Orbach's home, Diana was alarmed to discover the possibility of this latest intrusion into her life. The story the Princess told Ken Wharfe was sketchy and inconclusive. She had been contacted by an elderly lady-in-waiting, Lady Elizabeth Johnston, whose hairdresser, Shane Glavey, happened to be a friend of Bryce Taylor's girlfriend, Lesley Scott. He had seen the pictures briefly and was so concerned that he had spoken to Lady Elizabeth who, in turn, contacted Diana. When, in mid-May, Wharfe looked into the matter he was met with a comprehensive denial from the gym manager. It took a further six months for the photographs to surface, published in November in the *Sunday Mirror*. Amidst the inevitable furore, the most telling result was Diana's reaction. She was shocked and horrified but also very angry, for a time retreating to her bedroom, which was her sanctuary in times of distress. Even the Queen saw the intrusive photographs of her daughter-in-law. 'Oh, my God, no,' was her first reaction as she reviewed the Sunday newspapers over breakfast at Windsor Castle (where the *News of the World* is always at the top of the pile).

In the days that followed the publication of the photographs, Stephen Twigg said, he found the Princess so tense that her whole body, particularly her neck, was rigid and tight. 'I feel like I've been raped,' she repeatedly told Carolan Brown, who had already resigned from the gym in protest. This time the tears of self-pity were shortly replaced by a cold fury and a desire to resolve the matter in a mature manner. Diana instructed her lawyer, Lord Mishcon, to take out an injunction against Bryce Taylor and Mirror Group Newspapers and sue them for damages. In the end, however, the Princess settled out of court, receiving an apology, and, by way of damages, a sum paid to a charity of her choice – as well as the negatives and prints of the photographs. The most satisfying outcome was not lost on those who understood her – for one of the first times in her life she had not blamed herself for the unacceptable behaviour of others. Instead, her feelings of violation and outrage, so long denied or denigrated, were given legal legitimacy and weight.

This was a watershed moment for Diana, a sign of how far she had travelled on the road to recovery. As Stephen Twigg observed, 'If this had happened to her five years before, it could have driven her to suicide or at the very least plunged her into an immensely deep depression. At that time her self-esteem was so low that she would have blamed herself for the pictures being taken just as she blamed herself for problems in her marriage. By now she had the strength and [sense of] self-worth to say that this behaviour was no longer acceptable.'

It was, though, a pyrrhic victory. A year that had started with resolution ended with a necessary retreat, Diana having decided that she needed more time and space to explore and examine her life. The harassment, as she saw it, from the media, coming on top of the ongoing war with her husband, had worn her down. Each time she tried to come to terms with her past and plan her future, there were many people, friends as well as foes, eager to stifle her. There was a constant whispering campaign against her issuing from St James's Palace, while the counsel of friends often left the Princess more confused and unsettled than ever. On one occasion, for example, the Duchess of York rang to tell her that her psychics had forecast that Diana would be in tears for at least two weeks. It was time to leave the stage, at least for a while; a decision that caused consternation among her charities, her staff and her public.

She refused to be swayed, deciding to make her dramatic withdrawal in a speech at a charity lunch on 3 December 1993 in aid of Headway National Head Injuries Association (now known as Headway – the Brain Injury Association), of which she was patron. The first drafts of what came to be called her 'Time and Space' speech, written by her voice coach, Peter Settelen, reflected her sense of resentment and anger towards those who had made her life a misery, notably the media and her husband. She planned to say, 'It would not be unreasonable to assume that the recent plague of photographs has propelled me more rapidly into my decision . . . but the continuing invasion by some members of the media into every aspect of my life has become unbearable.'

'This,' Patrick Jephson was later to write of the speech, 'rather than a statesmanlike offer of reconciliation, irresistibly appealed to the martyr, the emotionally deprived child and the showgirl within her.' His patrician cynicism served to underscore what she instinctively felt – that the true sympathies of her supposed allies often lay elsewhere.

Even so, when she showed a draft to Stephen Twigg, following a massage at Kensington Palace, he was concerned, as indeed was Jephson, that it would not give her any room for manoeuvre. He sat on the edge of her double bed and pencilled in changes, some of which were incorporated into the final, more conciliatory, version, which none the less laid the blame for her departure at the door of the media. While she publicly thanked the Queen and the Duke of Edinburgh for their kindness and support, her husband's name was conspicuously omitted.

Chapter Four

Unfinished Business

THE HANDWRITTEN NOTE slipped under the door of a suite at the Ritz Hotel in Paris was friendly, warm and totally unexpected. As Countess Spencer looked at the distinctive, rounded hand, she could barely contain her astonishment. The letter was from her stepdaughter, the Princess of Wales, whom she had not seen or heard from since the funeral of Diana's father, her beloved husband Johnnie, Earl Spencer, in March 1992. Now, in May 1993, more than a year later, came an invitation to renew their relationship. 'Sorry we couldn't meet up in Paris. Perhaps we could have lunch when you return to London,' wrote Diana, still exultant after managing to achieve one of her long-cherished ambitions – to spend a weekend in Paris as a 'normal' person. It had been a huge success – shopping, eating and sightseeing along the boulevards of France's capital city with her friends Lucia Flecha de Lima and Hayat Palumbo, wife of the billionaire property tycoon Lord Palumbo. A chance meeting in a restaurant with the film star Gérard Depardieu was the icing on the cake. For a few fleeting hours all seemed right with the world at a time when Diana was determined to put her own world to rights.

As Raine Spencer read the letter, she had no clue what lay behind Diana's decision to resume contact with her. While it was clear that Diana wanted a rapprochement, her stepmother was not at all certain she wanted to reawaken painful memories. 'I was frankly uneasy to go back to the past,' she admitted. 'I can't say why she suddenly wrote. I don't know.'

One of life's great survivors, Countess Spencer, now seventy-four, is from a generation and class where personal traumas and tragedies are not for public consumption, preferring always to look forward rather than harking back. She is fond of quoting the words of the nineteenth-century American writer Ella Wheeler Wilcox: 'Laugh and the world laughs with you, weep and you weep alone.'

Not long after she received Diana's note, Raine Spencer was to get engaged to the French aristocrat who would become her third husband, Jean-François, Comte de Chambrun. 'After John died I got on with my life,' she said. 'I don't think about the past; it's horrid enough being a widow. I live totally in the present and the future. I don't need people from a past life – what's finished is finished.'

So while it was unthinkable to decline an invitation from the Princess, she was, to say the least, apprehensive. For the bad blood that existed between the Spencer family and the woman they called 'Acid Raine' had continued even after Earl Spencer's death. Diana's brother Charles, who took over the title and the running of the family estate of Althorp in Northamptonshire, publicly accused his stepmother of the indiscriminate sale of family heirlooms as well as tasteless redecoration of the main house. Indeed, such was the rancour that existed between Raine Spencer and her stepchildren that, following their father's death, Diana and her brother had unceremoniously bundled up her belongings in bin liners and thrown them down the stairs at Althorp. A weaker woman would have been mortally offended. But Raine was made of sterner stuff, resolutely closing that chapter in her life and moving on. While she maintained a dignified silence, her brother, the publisher Ian McCorquodale, sprang to her defence. 'She is unfairly typecast as the wicked stepmother,' he had said to the *Evening Standard* in July 1992. 'The stepmother always gets the stick.'

Inevitably, therefore, there was an initial wariness when Countess Spencer, accompanied by de Chambrun, eventually met the Princess for lunch at Kensington Palace. It was towards the end of a 'very jolly' lunch that Diana expressed what had been on her mind. 'Raine,' she said, 'thank you for looking after my father. I know you loved him.' The two women got up and hugged, a touching scene that left the trio gulping back tears. It was Diana's way of saying sorry for the hurt, distress and misunderstandings of the past. That meeting began an unlikely friendship that lasted until her death.

'I've always thought,' the Countess later said, 'that one of the reasons she wanted to be friends was because she and I were the only people who could talk about Johnnie together. She very generously and endlessly thanked me for what I had done for John when he was so terribly ill. It was very sweet but basically we had fun, and she wanted and needed that as well.'

Behind the jovial banter and the generosity she saw a deeply troubled young woman, a woman striving to come to terms with who she was and where she was going. 'She was incredibly lonely and depressed, and obviously I tried to help as much as I could. I wish I had been able to do more.'

After that first meeting, Diana and her stepmother regularly met for lunch at Kensington Palace or the Connaught Hotel, or Diana would visit Lady Spencer's apartment in Grosvenor Square, near the American Embassy, for afternoon tea. She would sit happily on the sofa, feet curled under her, chatting about everything from the trivial to the confidential. She always brought the 'most marvellous' presents, which reminded the Countess that when Diana was at school she was always being praised for her thoughtful behaviour, particularly towards younger children. One 'present' Lady Spencer will always treasure was bestowed at a particularly difficult time in her life. When her marriage to Comte de Chambrun collapsed in 1996, she was left adrift and feeling sorry for herself. Recognizing that the Countess needed some sort of work to occupy her time, Diana asked Mohamed Fayed, who had come to one of her lunches with the Countess, if he would be able to give her stepmother a job. Not long after, he offered the Countess a directorship of Harrods International. 'It changed my life, and Diana really had a great part in it,' the Countess said.

For a young woman who lived by the unforgiving creed, 'once gone, always gone', Diana's friendship with her stepmother was a genuine sea change. As she reminded her mother, Frances Shand Kydd, who had commented with some annoyance on her daughter's meetings with the Countess, she, Diana, had been the one who had disliked Raine the most; if *she* could forgive and forget, so should the rest of the family. At her brother's wedding in 1989 Diana had taken a perverse delight in confronting her stepmother and telling her how much pain she had caused her and her family. 'I've never known such anger in me,' the Princess admitted later, telling friends that she herself had been shocked by the intensity of her feelings especially as, at the time, Lady Spencer had done nothing to provoke her. But at the time Diana was going through her 'dark days' and her stepmother seemed to present a valid target for her fury.

The subsequent death of Lord Spencer and the tumult in Diana's own life as well as a considered reassessment of her stepmother's role in her father's life – perhaps the understanding gained from her own work with the sick and dying had made her realize that her stepmother's iron resolve in nursing her father when he had his first major stroke in September 1978 had saved and prolonged his life – all combined to bring about this volte-face.

Admittedly, the timing (the spring of 1993) coincided with Charles Spencer being much out of favour with his sister for having taken back his offer of the Garden House – but there was certainly much more to the reunion between the two women than simply family point-scoring. At the time, Diana, who was beginning regular visits to the psychotherapist Susie Orbach, and to the astrologer Debbie Frank, frequently discussed the connection between her childhood experiences and her adult personality. As a therapist, Orbach would have encouraged her to confront and explore the demons from her past, revisiting the country of her childhood to make sense of her present world. And in that country lived 'Acid Raine' – 'We hated her so much,' as Diana once said.

'After that first lunch with Raine she came bounding into the room high as a kite because she was aware that she had done something valuable,' recollected Stephen Twigg. 'She realized that she now had sufficient self-confidence and self-esteem to go and say "I'm sorry for what I did because I didn't understand you sufficiently then."'

The reunion with Raine Spencer was part of the process of clearing the emotional decks as the Princess began the serious task of understanding who she really was. Far from being a woman who was, as one feminist commentator claimed in a *Sunday Times* article of 31 August 1997, 'locked into her old life as morbidly as Miss Havisham', she was struggling to come to terms with her past in order to build a more satisfying and complete future. It was an exploration yielding imperfect results that lasted the rest of her life.

The Spencer family, already surprised and not a little alarmed by the renewal of Diana's relationship with Raine, were further taken aback when she made an appointment to see her maternal grandmother, Ruth, Lady Fermoy at her home in Eaton Square in central London. The meeting, in June 1993, was as awkward as it was symbolic. For it is no exaggeration to say that, but for Lady Fermoy, Diana's early life would have been quite different. When Diana's mother, Frances, then Viscountess Althorp, and Johnnie Spencer, Viscount Althorp, separated, it was Lady Fermoy's decision to testify against her daughter at the custody hearing that proved critical. It altered for ever the way Diana viewed her mother. A constant and compelling refrain in the narrative of Diana's life was her feelings of abandonment and loss brought about by her mother's departure from the family home when Diana was just six years old. 'The biggest disruption was when Mummy decided to leg it. That's the vivid memory we have – the four of us,' she remembered.

Debbie Frank was also to observe that 'The enduring trauma of her life was her sense of abandonment.'

Far from 'bolting' from her children, however, Frances Shand Kydd in fact fought two unsuccessful and bitter battles with her estranged husband to gain custody of her children. Lady Fermoy's intervention in the court hearing bore considerable weight, especially as she was siding against her own daughter. Diana's mother had fully anticipated bringing up her children and she never truly recovered her equilibrium after the case went against her. 'You can imagine how much it hurt,' she said years later.

Diana must certainly have seen her mother's grief in the bitter tears she shed each time she had to say goodbye to her children after their all too brief reunions, but the picture held in young Diana's mind's eye was of her mother leaving Park House, the family home, in 1967. For Diana that incident served as a convenient image to distil the years of insecurity, pain, anxiety and anger surrounding her unhappy home life. With her elder sisters, Jane and Sarah, away at boarding school and her brother Charles only a three-year-old toddler, it was Diana, then a highly intuitive and sensitive six-year-old, who felt most deeply the tensions, tears and tantrums. A former member of the Spencer staff later talked about violent rows between Johnnie and Frances, fights that clearly horrified their watching daughter. 'I remember seeing my father slap my mother across the face, and I was hiding behind the door and she was crying,' Diana told James Colthurst.

Such was the distress she experienced, not only from witnessing that painful incident but also the emotional turmoil surrounding her parents' break-up that Diana later admitted that for a time she was literally struck dumb. At a critical time in a child's development, when she was learning to read and write, Diana became an elective mute. According to her own account she could not remember exactly how long or with whom she deliberately decided to remain silent. Her own memory placed the period as lasting between three and eighteen months – a remarkably long time by any standards, all the more so for a child at an age when an hour can feel like an eternity.

It is a curious story, especially as it is uncommon for a child as old as six to withdraw from speech; at this age they generally find it difficult to refrain from talking. Children who suffer from this behavioural difficulty, which is commonly linked to a traumatic shock at school or in the home, are very strong-willed and determined characters – usually of the type that will also be prone to eating disorders, like Diana was in later life. According to child psychologist Lyn Fry, an expert on elective mutes, there are no long-term effects on either speech or mental health, and in fact more often than not such children choose to remain silent only in certain situations. 'Even elective mutes usually talk to someone. At home they may ignore their parents and speak to their siblings, at school they will chat to their classmates whilst remaining silent with the teacher.' It was likely that Diana followed this pattern, for example refusing to speak when she was around her family but not at school. A classmate from Diana's first school of Silfield in Norfolk, now a television producer, Delissa Needham, remembered a little girl who was painfully shy and quiet, but very watchful: 'Certainly she was insecure, but she was always quite sparky.'

That a young child should withdraw into silence, even if only for a few months and not all of the time, was testimony to her deep unhappiness. 'She never felt good enough as a child, blaming herself for her mother's leaving and subsequently living with a stark sense that those she loved would abandon her,' declared Debbie Frank.

'I hated myself so much I didn't think I was good enough . . . I mean, doubts as long as your leg,' the Princess said. As mentioned earlier, in her speech of spring 1993 at a conference on eating disorders, she told her audience how from childhood she had suffered from feelings of 'guilt, self-revulsion and low personal esteem'. She saw her natural needs, for love, attention and comfort, as greedy, creating the complex dynamic that is at the heart of bulimia nervosa.

With such turbulence in her life, Diana sought to make order out of chaos; as a child it was expressed in the tidy zoo of stuffed animals lined up on her bed, as an adult it was in the systematic way she arranged her wardrobe and her shoes. 'If Diana was in a safe and secure environment, she was fine,' as her former head-mistress, Ruth Rudge, observed.

Remembering, and now beginning to understand, how decisive was her grandmother's intervention on her father's behalf – and its consequence on her own childhood – Diana was very concerned to voice her disappointment at the way Lady Fermoy had behaved during her separation from Prince Charles. Just as the old lady had taken the part of the Norfolk aristocracy rather than her own flesh and blood during her daughter's separation, so she had shown the same loyalty to the Crown, siding with Prince Charles rather than with her granddaughter. Diana could not, perhaps, have expected anything else. Ruth, Lady Fermoy – a close friend of and lady-in-waiting to Queen Elizabeth, the Queen Mother – was a courtier down to the very ends of her elegant fingertips, personifying, in the words of Diana's private secretary, 'an attitude which was anathema to the Princess'. As Diana recalled, 'My mother and grandmother never got on. They clashed violently. My grandmother tries to lacerate me in any way she can. She feeds the royal family with hideous comment about my mother running and leaving the children. Whenever I mention Mother's name in the royal family, which I rarely do, they come down on me like a ton of bricks.' Indeed, Prince Charles refused even to speak to Diana's mother. 'They are convinced she behaved badly and poor Johnnie had a very rough time,' the Princess told James Colthurst. 'I now know it takes two to get into that situation. Mummy's come across very badly because Grandmother has done a real hatchet job.'

During her marriage Diana had come to see Clarence House, then the home of the Queen Mother, as the source of all negative comment about herself, much of it emanating from her grandmother. Before the marriage Lady Fermoy had warned Diana about the dangers of marrying into the royal family – although Diana now realized that the real reason was because her grandmother did not feel that she was the appropriate match for Prince Charles. When the marriage turned sour it was her implacable opinion that her granddaughter should stay with Prince Charles in order to spare the royal family the embarrassment of a marital scandal. As the former Archbishop of Canterbury, Robert Runcie commented, 'Ruth was very distressed with Diana's behaviour. She was totally and wholly a Charles person, because she'd seen him grow up, loved him like all the women at court do and regarded Diana as an actress, a schemer.'

A fairly recent encounter, the year before, between the Princess and her grandmother showed Lady Fermoy in typical light. As the Princess of Wales was leaving Buckingham Palace after a tricky meeting with the Queen concerning her charity work, she met her grandmother, who upbraided her for daring to wear trousers to an interview with the Sovereign. Even though her trousers were well cut and very expensive, in the eyes of Ruth, Lady Fermoy she was little more than a 'strumpet'.

So when Diana finally plucked up the courage to confront her

Royal funny girl Diana meets her Dr Blarney

By ANDREW MORTON, Royal Correspondent

PRINCESS DIANA met an old boyfriend, the Blarney Stone doctor, when she toured a hospital yesterday. And afterwards Old Etonian Dr James Colthurst recalled Diana the joker he first met on an Alpine skiing holiday when she was 17.

'She is one of the nicest, most compassionate girls I have ever met but she is a wicked practical joker,' said 29-year-old Dr Colthurst, whose family own Blarney Castle in Ireland, home of the famous stone.

'On the holiday around 20 of us shared a chalet. It was great fun. I and a friend usually started any practical jokes. But Diana had the last word. Apple pie beds were just the start. She had a very neat sense of humour, very wicked.'

After the holiday Dr Colthurst became a regular visitor to the flat Diana shared with three girls before her marriage and he took her to dinner a couple of times.

At St Thomas' hospital in London yesterday Dr Colthurst, a radiology registrar, showed Diana round a new £750,000 scanner which she opened. He was at her side throughout her 90-minute visit. 'She came as a personal favour but also because she is very interested in this work,' he said.

Greeting for Diana as Dr Colthurst (centre) looks on   Picture by MIKE FORSTER

ABOVE: Where it all began. Diana renews her friendship with Dr James Colthurst at the opening of a new radiology scanner in 1986, as Andrew Morton reports on the event. It was the start of an extraordinary alliance which resulted in the explosive book *Diana: Her True Story*.

BELOW: An informal snap of Diana taken by James Colthurst. She relaxes in her Kensington Palace drawing room, after one of the many interviews Colthurst recorded with her for the 1992 book.

questions..2
School
While you thought you were useless at school, do you remember any
achievement at the time, however seemingly insignificant but
important at the time, such as when you learned to read, memories
of your first Janet and John books (your dates me), making a
model, painting a picture - what are your favourite colours, the
way - the sounds of Riddlesworth and West Heath school, the
smell, polish, boiled cabbage, and making a
subjects, music for example, can you play any instruments besides
the piano, music for example, can you play any instruments besides
the piano teacher. Who was your grad... learn to play. Were you
enthusiastic pupil and what... learn to play. Who was your
piano teacher. Who was your grad... learn to play. Were you
essay you were proud of when did you... your favourite...
being baffled by biology, looking... your favourite...
of your teacher's do you love... (N...
Verdis Requiems, in a dab hand... your favourite...
- Fergie was you got up to - how... your favourite
devilment, in what way was... your favourite
The pranks you got up to - how... your favourite
pellets, shouting out was... your favourite
assembly or church. Were you noisy/quiet/a s...
at were you noisy/quiet/a school prefect...
hool, the head girl/prefect, what...
aly? Can you remember...
career of any old...
ring in public, even...
first sporting event...
on. The best kept...
care for him/her...
did you keep in...
hat treats did...
you are a not...
ou picked...
ay pen friends...
call, how...

you
c
s

[redacted]

Lots of love to you both.
from.
Diana x

Facsimile Cover Sheet

To: Diana
The Mum Who Should Be P...

Fax: 071-937-0239

From: James

Date: 12/12/83

Pages including this
cover page: 3

Dear Diana,

Here is a slightly amended version which improves the end. The
line about providing an alternative is the essential nub of the whole
piece.

...g well at the carols!

Love
James

KENSINGTON
PALACE

February 13th

Dearest Cuthbert
It was lovely
to have a let...
I did appreci...
understand...

J. Cuthbert
c/o J.

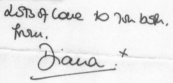

champagne it meant that were ... Dia
...r friends, missed the next race. As guests
... are expected to see the race from the royal
...ered a discourtesy not to return. Fergie's
...ded Carolyn Cotterell, now the Duchess' lady in
... with the awkward dilemma of leaving Diana or
...en's displeasure ... they stayed.

...s far as they ... ned they had earned a bl...
... the Queen. D... smooth things over b...
A trivial i... one which illustrate...
jealousy a... royal sisters in la...
observed... feels that Fer...
her thu... so she does si...
becau... ... her friend...
blam... ... ... worries

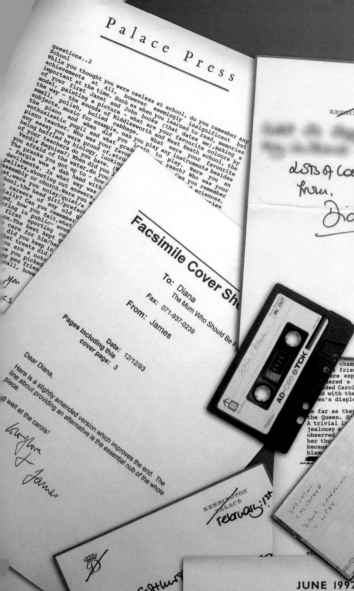

...ter that w...
...net of Charle...
...aying polo. The...
...ssed this pecul...
...make sure that th...
...s of their newspaper...
to this Courtly minu...
much frivolity,' sniff...
...tators accused the girl...
...pera. The focus for this g...
...royal behaviour was the Re...
...ard used a television idea...
...combined royals with showbiz...
...s ... of rather juvenile games based

SPEEDERGE...
CHIC 2469 D
DIANA CUTHBERTSON
IN 6/90

JUNE 1992

1992	MORNING	LUNCH	AFTERNOON	EVENING
TUES 16	Ascot*		Maple Leafs v Tramontana Coworth	
WED 17			Royal Windsor Cup & Mountbatten Cup q/f GPC	
THURS 18				
FRI 19	IWM (S) Torquay	Renfrewshire	Royal Windsor Cup & Mountbatten Cup s/f GPC	
SAT 20			Chester Cathedral?	
SUN 21	Ludgrove Day Out		Royal Windsor Cup of Mountbatten Cup Finals GPC (or Match C. Pk)	
MON 22	HMQ Holyrood	ISDD Press Awards & Lunch, London		PT Concert, King's College Cambridge RT
TUES 23	Holyrood			Royal Marsden Hospital Lise Minnelli Concert RT

...ly a whirlwind of change ripped through Althorp as t...
...ress endeavoured to turn the family home into a payi...
...ion so that the awesome debts the new Earl had taken...
...paid off. The staff were pared to the bone and in ord...
...he house to paying visitors the stable block was turn...
... a room and gift shop. Over the years numerous painting...
... and other objets have been sold, often, claim
... at rock bottom prices while they describe in disdain...
...e way the house has been 'restored.' Earl Spencer h...
...toutly defended his wife's robust management of t...
...aying:"The cost of restoration has been immense."

FACING PAGE: An original tape cassette on which, in conversation with Colthurst, the Princess secretly recorded details of her life for Andrew Morton. Also shown are: correspondence from Diana to Colthurst from that time, in which she expressed her appreciation of his help and support; a list of questions that Morton had asked Colthurst to put to Diana; more pages from the first draft of *Diana: Her True Story*, on which Diana marked her amendments; pages from the official diary of the Prince and Princess of Wales for the period around publication; a fax from Colthurst to 'The Mum Who Should Be Proud', sent more than a year after the publication of Morton's book and accompanying corrections the two men had made to one of Diana's speeches to the Centrepoint charity.

BELOW: A letter from Diana to James Colthurst in which she speaks of 'preparing for the volcano to erupt' – a reference to the coming publication of *Diana: Her True Story*. With it are some pages from Morton's book showing some of her amendments.

KENSINGTON PALACE

December: 1st 1991.

Dear James.

Your support & [assistance] this year, in [particular,] has meant a [great] deal to me & I

Obviously we are preparing for the volcano to erupt & I *do* feel better equipped to cope with whatever comes our way!

observed at the time: "The princess feels that Fergie has stolen her thunder and taken the limelight. So she does silly things and because Fergie feels she has to support her friend she gets the blame. The princess is very insecure and worries ⬛⬛⬛ people ⬛⬛⬛ her."

It was an observation shared by others later that week when they saw Diana deliberately perch on the bonnet of Charles's treasured Aston Martin sports car as he was playing polo. The cynics among veteran royal observers who witnessed this peculiar behaviour believed that this was a ploy to make sure that the Princess of Wales appeared on the front pages of their newspapers.

The watching world, not privy to this Courtly minuet, chorussed its disapproval. 'Far too much frivolity,' sniffed the Daily Express while other commentators accused the girls of behaving like actresses in a soap opera. The focus for this growing public disatisfaction with the royal behaviour was the Royal Knockout Tournament. Prince Edward used a television idea way past its `sell by' date which combined royals with showbiz and sporting stars in a a series of rather juvenile games based on a medieval theme.

... part but resolutely refused. ... her chagrin.

14

Three years later they bought a 1,000 acre farm on the isle of Siel, south of Oban in Argyllshire where Mrs Shand Kydd lives today. When the children came for summer holidays they enjoyed a `Swallows and Amazon' idyll, spending their days mackerel fishing, lobster potting and sailing and, on fine days, barbeques on the beach. Diana had her own Shetland pony and it was on horseback that she suffered a nasty broken arm which has made her anxious about riding ever since. She was galloping on her horse, Romilly, in the grounds of Sandringham Park when the horse stumbled and she fell off. Diana ran into Park House, clutching her arm and screaming in agony.

Here versions vary. The accepted story is that Diana's arm was put in plaster and took three months to heal. However Diana recalls that nobody believed the arm was broken and two days later she went skiing in Switzerland. During the holiday her arm was so lifeless that she went to a local hospital for an x-ray. She was diagnosed as suffering from `greenstick', a childhood condition where children's bones are so flexible that they bend, not break. A doctor strapped the arm but the following day when she tried to go riding again she lost her nerve and dismounted. She still rides but prefers to exercise by swimming or dancing [tennis]

They are also activities where she excels. They stood her in good stead when her father enrolled her at her next school, Riddlesworth Hall, two hours drive from Park House. She learned to love the school which tried to be a home away from home to its 120 girls. However her first instincts were of betrayal and resentment. Diana was nine and felt the wrench from her father keenly. In her motherly concerned way, she was cossetting him as he tried to pick up the pieces of his life. His decision to send her away from her home and brother into an alien world ... interpreted as rejection. She made threats ...
you won't leave me t...

writing was clear and she read fluently, Diana [particular]ly side rather confusing. Miss Lowe remembers [clearly?] the smaller children, her love of animals and [thought]fulness but not her academic potential. She was good [at?] ... her friends couldn't explain why she burst into ... during a painting class one granny ... apparent that she dedicated all her pict...

They do remember that ... and 'Janet and John' and Daddy.'

[mud]dled through her tables of her younger brother, [invaded?] increasingly jealous but well behaved little boy. [s]he says, b... same increasing 'solemn' him in the schoolroom, being b... [need]ed as a as him in the schoolroom, with Diana, charles c... [as?] good as he could wound with words, ... [there?] were fights ... And she pinched, words ... [it?], invaded that he could wound and rather [she?] realised that ... ordered him to stop [he?] mercilessly. Both parents from a slow and rather ['] a nickname derived in a popular children's TV sho... [who?] featured [round]about.'

had sweet revenge with the unexpected hel... [Char]les says, with relish: "I do... [is?]car's wife. Charles would say it was the trauma of [psy]chologist would say the school run one da... [and?] real difficulty telling On the Spencer if ... [em]bellish things. On the Diana walk ho... [s]topped the car and said: to make you rumbled." [l]ike that I am going home she had been ... triumphant because

While the sibling competition was an i... less capable was the growing parental... as Frances and Johnnie vied with each ... their children. Yet while they sho... expensive presents this wasn't acc... cuddles and kisses that the local... already had a reputation... fireworks displays on Guy Fawke... now for Diana's seventh birthday... ... from Dudley zoo fo... ... as the surprise

ABOVE: Diana with Prince William outside the San Lorenzo restaurant in London, an exclusive photo opportunity secretly arranged by the Princess for *Diana: Her True Story*.

BELOW AND LEFT: Diana with her close friend Carolyn Bartholomew who had spoken 'on the record' about Diana's problems in *Her True Story*. Their continued friendship after the publication of the book convinced many people of the veracity of its revelations.

E: In Sydney, Diana openly sobs during
Vales' tour of Australia and New
nd in 1983. Charles smiles at the crowd,
ng no comfort to his young wife, to
distress he appears oblivious.

: Diana pictured alone aboard King
Carlos of Spain's yacht while holidaying
Charles and the boys in 1988. Displaying
otogenic curves that made her front-
ews nearly every day of her adult life,
is conspicuously downcast; feelings that
ould find increasingly difficult to hide in
ming years.

ABOVE: Diana shoots a furious glance at Prince Charles at a public event in 1984. In private, and occasionally even in public, the Waleses' relationship was becoming ever more acrimonious.

RIGHT: The other woman. A married Camilla Parker Bowles prepares to weather the storm over the publication of *Diana: Her True Story*, with its allegations about her relationship with Prince Charles, as she attends the Windsor Horse Show Ball with her husband Andrew in 1992. They were to divorce three years later.

ABOVE: Diana formed a close personal friendship with her police protection officer Sergeant Barry Mannakee, shown here (*second from left, alongside her driver, Simon Solari*) with the Princess on their way to a function in 1985. In July the following year Mannakee's superiors removed him from his post after rumours surfaced in the Palace about the nature of his relationship with Diana. She was devastated when he was killed in a motorcycle accident in the spring of 1987.

LEFT: Diana's friend Oliver Hoare in 1994. Their alleged affair in the early nineties was exposed when Hoare's wife famously complained of nuisance calls from Kensington Palace, as it turned out, to the family home, which led to a police investigation.

ABOVE: Diana's lover James Hewitt, pictured here while on active service with his regiment dur[ing] the Gulf War of 1991. She was incensed when he thoughtlessly borrowed a journalist's satellite phone to call her from Iraq, thus risking the exposure of their affair.

BELOW: Diana at a polo match with Hewitt in 1992. She admitted her adultery with him on national television, declaring in her 1995 *Panorama* interview that she had 'adored' him.

ABOVE LEFT: Diana's friend James Gilbey, who was linked with the Princess after the notorious 'Squidgygate' tapes were published in 1992, suggesting an intimate relationship between the pair.

ABOVE RIGHT: Diana with former England rugby captain Will Carling. Carling's wife sold her story to the tabloids, accusing Diana of 'killing their marriage'. However, a former employee of the rugby star asserts that it was Carling who ran after Diana, like 'a puppy dog'.

BELOW: Diana in 1994 with the American businessman Teddy Forstmann, with whom she was rumoured to have had an affair. This is the only known photo of them together.

T: In June 1994, on the night
Prince Charles admitted his
ery in a TV documentary, Diana
ed the world in this stunning
dress. As well as ensuring that
rabbed all the headlines, the dress
attention to the very flattering
rences between herself and
illa Parker Bowles, triumphantly
oring as it did one of the latter's
ts from a previous occasion
hoto earlier).

W RIGHT: Diana on a private
ly holiday in the Caribbean
93. Now separated from Charles,
beginning to delight in her
pendence, she appears composed
confident at this informal
o shoot, arranged by her police
ection officer Ken Wharfe so
the press would allow her to
lay in peace.

NG PAGE: (*Main photo*) Diana
the Queen Mother and Prince
ry on the occasion of the Queen
her's ninety-fourth birthday.
ously, Diana and the Queen
her had never got on well, but
the Waleses' separation Diana
d that relations became even more
y. Increasingly, her passport into
amily became her sons, and they
e ever more precious to her as her
pendence from the Windsors grew.

t) Diana at an event in 1993,
the Waleses' separation had
formally announced. Becoming
pendent was a hard-fought battle
ch at times became too much for
evidenced here by very public tears.

Being hounded by the paparazzi was a daily occurrence in the Princess's life. The photographers became increasingly aggressive after the separation and more determined than ever to take their pictures. Their constant presence was both a worry and an irritant to Diana.

ABOVE: Diana being interviewed for the BBC's *Panorama* by journalist Martin Bashir. She saw the programme as an opportunity to put her side of the story, but questions have since been raised about the methods Bashir used in persuading the Princess to appear.

RIGHT: The picture that made all the front pages. As it turned out, the *Panorama* programme was to be the final nail in the coffin of Diana's marriage.

LEFT: Diana's therapist Susie Orbach, a specialist in eating disorders. Learning to fight her personal demons was something that Diana was incredibly proud of, and Orbach helped her every step of the way.

RIGHT: Diana with her good friend Lucia Flecha De Lima, wife of the Brazilian Ambassador to Britain. Diana relied on the older woman's support throughout her life and saw her as a mother figure.

LEFT: Diana with her friend Rosa Monckton at Rosa's daughter's christening. Following her separation, Diana relied ever more heavily on her friends for support and affection.

IGHT: The Princess and her ecretary, Victoria Mendham, rriving back in Britain after a oliday to Antigua in the winter f 1995. Diana had agreed to a ivorce following her *Panorama* nterview and wanted to get away absorb her impending freedom.

eighty-five-year-old grandmother, whose physical frailty did nothing to blunt her sharp tongue, it was a defining moment – the errant granddaughter taking on the powerful matriarch. While Diana had much to be angry about, given that her grandmother had refused to stand either by her own child or, later, her grandchild, she spoke more in sorrow than anger, telling her how disappointed she was that her own kith and kin had failed to support her during the marriage breakdown. It was a mature and considered approach and her formidable grandmother was embarrassed and shaken, not just by Diana's courageous decision to raise such personal issues in the first place, but also because her behaviour was both even-handed and politely conciliatory.

At least, when, in July 1993, just a few weeks after their meeting, Ruth, Lady Fermoy died, Diana could feel some satisfaction in having reached an understanding, if not made peace, with a woman who had so affected her life.

It is significant that the Princess's meetings with Raine Spencer and Ruth, Lady Fermoy both took place during 1993, the first year of her life on her own. It was a time when she was inevitably undertaking considerable spring cleaning, not just in her relations with her own family, the royal family and her circle of friends, but also in her endeavours, through intensive counselling, to reconcile and reinterpret her past through the eyes of an adult rather than the impulses of a child. Even so, while she gradually came to appreciate her mother's sorrowful life – particularly the unresolved grief Frances felt following the death of her baby son John, an event which precipitated the breakdown of her marriage – Diana's relationship with her mother remained uneven, complex and ultimately unresolved.

Both sharp-witted, strikingly attractive and capricious; both displaying a superficial sociable cheeriness beneath which lay a deep-seated sadness, usually well-hidden – as Diana told us in one of the interviews, 'However bloody you are feeling you can put on the most amazing show of happiness. My mother is an expert at that and I've picked it up. It kept the wolves from the door.' Both taking solace in eating when troubled, the Princess and her mother were more similar than Diana would ever have cared to admit. So too was the trajectory of their lives. 'Two peas in a pod,' declared her friend Vivienne Parry, who knows all the Spencer family. For all their disagreements, there was no denying the bond between them – 'loving and trusting' as Frances described it, even though it was not always visible – or the daughter's admiration – sometimes grudging though it was – for her mother. When Diana reflected on how the Duchess of York's father, Major Ronald Ferguson, had, according to Frances, asked her to marry him, it reminded her that her mother was one of the celebrated beauties of her era. 'Mummy was quite special to look at when she was young,' she commented. 'She's dynamite, not unlike Princess Grace in a funny kind of way.' (It is worth noting that Diana formed an instant rapport with the former American actress when she met her, soon after her engagement to Prince Charles; and insisted that she should represent the royal family at Princess Grace's funeral in Monaco in 1982.)

Times of closeness – such as when Diana, her mother, her sister Sarah and their children went to Necker Island in the Caribbean in 1989; when her mother visited her at Kensington Palace; or when she, William and Harry spent week-long holidays with 'Granny Frances' at her cottage home on the remote island of Seil off the north-west coast of Scotland – were, however, matched by long periods of distance and silence, a pattern that continued until Diana's death. As her New Age healer friend, Simone Simmons, remarked of the mother-and-daughter sporadic get-togethers, 'Diana wanted to be pleased to see her, not least because she was keen to talk through the unfinished business of her childhood. But these were troubled and uneasy encounters.'

An emotional ebb-and-flow is part of the Spencer family's character: sharp, witty, and intuitive but with a reckless willingness to say or do the unsayable, a quality that is as careless of the consequences as it is of the feelings of those involved, whether family, friends or complete strangers. 'They were a very volatile family,' Vivienne Parry observed, 'in that you could never be sure which one had fallen out with which other one. Yet they were close despite the fact that they constantly had rows and if an outsider criticized one of them it would be seen as an attack on them all.'

What regularly strained their relationship to breaking point was Diana's feeling that ultimately she could never truly rely on her mother, whose interventions in her life, while ostensibly supportive, were unpredictable and often tactless. It was a pattern first established in the build-up to her wedding, when the princess-to-be complained that her mother was 'driving her mad' with her tears and moans about the strain she was under. ('I tended to think *I* was the one under pressure because I was the bride,' she later remarked.) That led to a period of some months during which Diana refused to speak to her mother – although Frances was on hand to offer advice and consolation during her difficult first pregnancy with Prince William. And while Diana appreciated the way her mother fiercely supported her at Prince Harry's christening, when Prince Charles grumbled that he had wanted a girl and had carped about the baby's red hair, she was less happy when Frances wrote to her husband criticizing him for going to the opera in 1991 while Prince William was undergoing surgery for a head injury following an accident at school, leaving Diana to cope on her own. The Princess, fortunately, intercepted the letter, which presumably her mother had told her about, and disposed of it before Charles had a chance to read it.

Again, during the fateful summer of 1992, when Diana's own life was in turmoil, her mother's erratic and impulsive behaviour gave her real cause for alarm. When Frances called in a state of deep distress, accusing her youngest daughter of abandoning her and threatening to harm herself, Diana was so concerned that she sent a panic-stricken message to James Colthurst, who had to leave a board meeting abruptly to help her deal with the family crisis. His advice to Diana to keep her mother talking for as long as possible until she had calmed down eventually worked.

By another unhappy coincidence, in April 1996, just as the Prince and Princess of Wales were finalizing their divorce, Frances Shand Kydd was arrested for drink-driving and subsequently banned from driving for a year. Diana, who had Old Testament views on crime and punishment and believed that drink-drivers should be disqualified for life, felt that her mother had once again let her down, and, particularly at a time when she herself was under critical stress. Tragically, their tidal relationship ended at the low-water mark after Frances was interviewed for *Hello!* magazine in May 1997. In the course of the conversation, she remarked that it was 'wonderful' that her daughter had relinquished the title of Her Royal Highness: 'At last she is able to be herself, use her own name and find her own identity.' Diana considered her remarks, which of themselves seemed blandly supportive of her daughter, hurtful and unnecessary, especially as the Princess had made a vain last-ditch appeal to her brother-in-law, the Queen's private secretary, Sir Robert Fellowes, to keep the honorary title. The initial altercation between the two women widened into an unbridgeable rift after, according to Paul Burrell, her mother phoned her at Kensington Palace and launched into a tirade of slurred abuse about the men her daughter was seeing. While Mrs Shand Kydd has disputed Burrell's account, she acknowledges that the Princess refused to accept her subsequent phone calls and returned, unopened, her mother's letters. Even the butler's attempts to act as an unbidden go-between came to naught. They never spoke again.

While the Princess acknowledged her mother's virtues as well as her faults, and came to realize that she had not willingly left her children when her marriage broke down, in her heart Diana could never escape the childhood trauma of abandonment and loss. 'Everything in her tormented psyche turned on what had happened to her at the age of six, when her parents separated and left her to a loneliness that nothing could cure,' wrote her friend, the Australian-born author and television presenter Clive James.

During the Princess's last meeting with Debbie Frank in July 1997, shortly before her death, she went over the story once again, underlining her almost visceral need for solace, succour and safety, a desire that was manifest in the numerous substitute mothers and surrogate families that she collected during her life.

Distant from her own family and increasingly alienated from the royal family, during the 1990s especially, the Princess increasingly turned to a collection of older women who, while strong independent characters, came from different societies or were only on the fringe of the British Establishment. In the mid-1980s Mara Berni, who, with her husband Lorenzo, was the owner of the famous San Lorenzo restaurant, was the most significant maternal figure in her life; the expansive Italian mother something of a spiritual guide, reading her tarot cards, recommending clairvoyants and interpreting her stars. They fell out for a time when la Signora Berni invited Diana to the opening of a new dress shop and failed to tell her that there would be photographers present. While that friendship waned, as so many did, the Princess formed bonds with others, notably Lucia Flecha de Lima, Annabel Goldsmith, Hayat Palumbo and Elsa Bowker, all of whom nurtured, supported and comforted the Princess during the years following her separation. Sophisticated, worldly-wise and outside conventional circles, they provided a cosmopolitan counterpoint to the life she had hitherto been leading. At the same time, these mature women were conservative, cautious and constraining in their advice – both Lucia Flecha de Lima and Lady Palumbo, for example, were opposed to her collaboration with my 1992 biography.

The oldest of Diana's substitute mothers was Elsa Bowker. They had first met in 1993 when Lady Bowker was already well into her eighties. She had been a close friend of Diana's Spencer grandmother, and also of Raine Spencer, and the Princess was immediately attracted by her exotic background. Born in Egypt to a French mother and Lebanese father, Elsa married a British diplomat, James Bowker, and spent much of her life travelling the globe. 'She liked my way of living, my experience and she could tell me everything,' Lady Bowker recalled before her own death.

It was in 1990, as her marriage was collapsing, that the Princess met Lucia Flecha de Lima, the wife of the Brazilian ambassador to London. They did not fully cement their relationship until Diana made an official visit to Brazil with them the following year. 'I loved it,' declared Diana. 'I was on a high from the day I arrived to the day I left.' For a woman driven by her emotions, a country of such sensuous sensibilities immediately appealed. The Brazilian Ambassador and his wife represented those values of warm, sensibility family togetherness, an exuberant Latin-American susceptibility as well as a solid Roman Catholic faith, conservative, certain and secure, to which the Princess, in her search for stability and security, was naturally drawn. A mother of five and grandmother, Lucia, who was twenty years Diana's senior, not only opened up her home to the Princess but on occasion her bedroom. After her husband Paulo Tarso had left the marital bed Diana would jump in and join her just like a little girl. 'She was one of the family and we came to treat her like our own children,' Lucia told the *Daily Mail* in November 2003. 'I think it gave her a sense of belonging that she did not have elsewhere. I know I was a mother figure to her and she was like a daughter to me. Diana just became another one of the family.' The Princess even had her own room at their London residence in Mayfair's Mount Street where she would join them for weekends. 'At my house Diana was a girl in trouble and I would listen to her and give her advice if she wanted it. Mostly I listened.'

When Paulo was posted to Washington in November 1993 and her surrogate family left her, Diana was bereft. It did not help that their move coincided with the resignations of her detective Ken Wharfe and chauffeur Simon Solari as well as with her decision to withdraw for a time from public life. None the less, the friendship continued to flourish, and the Princess visited them regularly, on one occasion meeting Hillary Clinton with Lucia, another time flying to Washington especially to visit Paulo when he was recuperating from a heart operation. While she enjoyed her holidays with them, it was the fact that Lucia was always there at the end of the telephone to offer support and counsel that Diana most valued.

If the Princess was emotionally simpatico with her Brazilian family, then she adored the bohemian if very well-bred chaos of life with the Goldsmiths. Even though Lady Annabel Goldsmith, a daughter of the eighth Marquess of Londonderry, is from Diana's social milieu, the fact that her flamboyant husband James, the late food billionaire, lived in England with her and openly in France with his mistress, put the family on the wilder shores of social convention – this spoke to the rebel in Diana, who perhaps felt more at ease with those who lived beyond standard social norms. That their daughter Jemima married Imran Khan, the former

Pakistani cricket captain and erstwhile politician, added to the family's glamour. At least twice a month the Princess joined this larger-than-life family for a chaotic and very rapid Sunday lunch, often bringing Harry and William along to play with the Goldsmith children. On these occasions she was at her most relaxed and giggly, bantering with James, when he let her get a word in edgeways, chatting with staff, helping with the dishes and swimming in the pool. 'My home was simply the rock or the haven that she could turn to for escape, where she knew she would never be betrayed,' Lady Annabel wrote after Diana's death.

While the Goldsmiths offered lunch and safety, Lord Palumbo and his wife Hayat shared the trappings of their fortune, giving her the use of their private jet, entertaining her at their homes in England and France, and inviting her on board their yacht, *Drumbeat*. They used their considerable connections to assist the Princess; Peter recommending media-relations expert Sir Gordon Reece, a close friend of Margaret Thatcher, to help burnish her image, as well as the venerable lawyer, Lord Mishcon, to advise on her divorce negotiations. It was Hayat, the daughter of a Lebanese newspaper editor, a moderate Shi'ite Muslim, who was assassinated by terrorists, who organized Diana's first, much treasured trip to Paris, where, with Lucia Flecha de Lima, they spent the weekend shopping and sightseeing. The fact that Lady Palumbo had converted to Roman Catholicism from her Muslim faith gave their friendship an absorbing dimension, given Diana's own spiritual journey (see Chapter Six). At the same time, the Palumbos' friendship with Princess Margaret's former husband, the photographer Lord Snowdon, as well as with the Duke and Duchess of York – Peter Palumbo is godfather to their elder daughter, Princess Beatrice – gave Hayat a telling insight and rounded appreciation of the endless intrigues and personalities at court, which someone like Lucia Flecha de Lima could only glimpse from afar. While she disagreed profoundly with Diana's collaboration with my book – as too did Lucia – she would have understood more clearly than most the demands, constraints and tensions that came with life inside the royal family.

*

Where the Princess did not find a mother figure was within the royal family itself. Those dreams that she may have cherished, conscious or unconscious, of the Queen Mother or the Queen being some kind of maternal guardian, guiding, nurturing and nourishing her, were quickly dashed. When she raised her concerns about Camilla Parker Bowles before the wedding, the elderly Windsor matriarch suggested that she should not be such a 'silly girl', effectively telling her to do her duty. Far from feeling that she could confide in the Queen Mother, Diana was always wary. 'I don't really trust her. She comes to ask me about various people's marriages in this family,' she said. 'Can I help and what do I think.' Years later she ruefully explained to Max Hastings, the historian, author and at the time editor of the *Daily Telegraph* that the Queen Mother was a much tougher proposition than the public understood.

For an emotional, needy young woman, life in a family whose instinctive response to personal matters is silence or an averted gaze – 'ostriching' as they themselves call it – was barely tolerable. She saw herself as an outsider; they saw her as a problem, viewing her eating disorder, manifest by her frequent absences from family dinners, as the cause of her marital problems rather than a symptom. They came to see her as 'a cracked vessel' who probably needed professional psychiatric care.

David Puttnam was indignant. While conceding that she was a 'very, very, very hurt girl', a 'nutcase' she was not, he told me: 'If my daughter, who is the same age as Diana, had got involved with that dysfunctional family and had the same pressures and lack of support it wouldn't surprise me if she had cracked. One of the things that drove me to real anger was that if I had been her father I would have gone ballistic at her treatment. They had a duty of care to her that was never fulfilled. If you bring somebody into the family they have enormous responsibility.'

While her separation from Prince Charles in 1992 severed many of the bonds between Diana and the rest of the royal family, she was politically astute enough to maintain close links with the Queen. Invariably it was the boys who were her admission ticket into the corridors of power. When they were young she took them to swim at Buckingham Palace and afterwards for tea with the 'chief lady'. 'The Princess also used these opportunities to express loyalty and give assurances about her wish to do no harm either to the institution or to her husband who would inherit it,' Patrick Jephson wrote. 'These assurances,' he added, 'were not always entirely sincere. To judge from the lack of effective rejoinder, they had also probably been heard too often in the past.'

As far as possible the Princess followed a similar pattern from 1992 onwards, aware of the need to maintain close links with the fountainhead of authority and power, not just for her own sake but for her boys'. Early on she had realized that it would be a one-sided relationship – the Queen very rarely visited her and her children either at Kensington Palace or Highgrove. 'She never wants to see them [the boys] but they are always there,' the Princess said in response to a newspaper story claiming that the Queen had complained that Diana had prevented her from seeing her grandchildren. 'William and Harry go to people who warm to them,' the Princess said pointedly in one of her interviews with Colthurst. Her overriding aim, as she said frequently, was to do what was best for her boys. 'The royal family would just like me to disappear into some desert somewhere and leave the children to them. I just won't do it,' she told Max Hastings.

Unlike Diana's chosen mother figures, the Queen exercised genuine control over Diana's life, from the shape and style of her public duties and decisions about her foreign visits to her relations with the government; and, ultimately, Diana's eventual title and divorce settlement. While not naturally confrontational, the Queen has long experience in clipping the wings of over-influential subjects, whether politicians or princesses. After the separation, Diana fell to earth on numerous occasions, often after an intervention from Buckingham Palace at the Queen's behest. According to Vivienne Parry, however, 'Even though the Queen must have been consulted on many of the things concerning Diana, she [Diana] preferred to believe that it was the Palace grey men who were at fault rather than the Queen herself.'

When two young boys were killed by an IRA bomb planted in Warrington town centre in 1993, for example, the Princess telephoned Wendy Parry, the mother of one of the victims, Tim, and said that she would dearly love to hug and comfort her at the service. Even though she had left her diary clear to attend the memorial service, she explained that the Duke of Edinburgh was representing the family. When news broke of Diana's call to Mrs Parry, the Palace made it plain that the Duke was the 'appropriate choice'. 'I really had my wrists slapped, it was a monumental cock-up,' she admitted afterwards, accepting that she had a 'lot of growing up to do'. The withdrawal of an invitation to give the prestigious Dimbleby Lecture and the decision to veto a proposed visit to Dublin to see the Irish President, Mary Robinson, in September 1993 for 'security reasons' impressed on the Princess that her life was not in her own hands. It never changed. In March 1997, on the first anniversary of the Dunblane massacre where a crazed gunman had killed sixteen children and a schoolteacher, she complained that the Palace had prevented her from visiting the Scottish town. 'I just wanted comfort those families. I still think of them all the time,' she said.

While the awestruck reverence which characterized Diana's early, tense dealings with the Queen modified over time to a duti-ful if nervous respect, there was, following the separation, an inevitable wariness on both sides. The confrontation at Windsor Castle over the taped telephone conversation and Prince Philip's letter-writing campaign following the publication of *Diana: Her True Story* meant that their relations were never trusting or easy. Diana felt a kind of baffled admiration for the Queen, in awe of her quiet stoicism in the face of the mundane treadmill of monarchy, but she was fearful, if not a little frustrated, at the extensive influence the Monarch wielded over her life. She was quietly infu-riated that the Queen, whom she continued rather naively to see as an omnipotent family referee, had not intervened to end her eldest son's relationship with Camilla Parker Bowles, and always seemed to take his side. Her complaints were endorsed by courtiers from that period. 'She was wholly sympathetic towards Charles – in fact rather one-eyed in her approach,' commented one. Diana, how-ever, also frequently grumbled that all too often the Sovereign sat on the fence, never putting a foot wrong because essentially she never moved her feet. 'My mother-in-law has been totally support-ive but it's so difficult to get a decision out of her,' she observed diplomatically. While she could mimic the Queen well, Diana was on less certain ground when it came to assessing her personality. During our interviews the one question Diana stumbled over was about the Queen's character. 'Very difficult to answer.' Over time Diana began to feel 'pity and sadness' as she learned to appreciate that the Queen was as much a woman trapped in a gilded cage as she was herself. She articulated that view more clearly in a letter, said to date from October 1996, that she wrote to herself, outlining some of her thoughts about the Queen and the institution she had served for most of her adult life: 'I just long to hug my mother-in-law, and tell her how deeply I understand what goes on inside her. I understand the isolation, misconception and lies that surround her and feel very strongly *her* disappointment and confusion.' While these words revealed part of her thinking, it would perhaps be more accurate to say that this rather patronizing attitude masked her confused feelings of powerlessness and inarticulate affection in the presence of an iconic figure whose influence over her life was continuing and considerable.

The sense of perplexity was felt on both sides. The Queen never really tuned into Diana's complex personality, which was a fact acknowledged by her elderly cousin Lady Kennard, godmother to Prince Andrew, who gave a rare insight into the Monarch's think-ing. 'The Queen or anybody else would never quite understand what Princess Diana was about,' she said in a BBC documentary that was officially sanctioned by the Queen. 'She [Diana] was very damaged – her background and her childhood – and it is very difficult to know.' The fact that the only letter Diana ever received from the Queen was a formal note in late 1995, requesting that she and Prince Charles should divorce, symbolized the distance and dissonance in their relationship.

While the Princess always tried to build bridges, however unsuc-cessfully, with her mother-in-law, she made little attempt to accommodate herself with the rest of the family. An icy formality existed between herself and the Queen Mother, whose circle – including her lady-in-waiting, Diana's grandmother, Ruth, Lady

Fermoy – unreservedly took the side of the Prince of Wales in their marital dispute. Other members of the royal family, whatever their personal misgivings about Prince Charles and his tendency to self-indulgent introspection, were distant or overtly hostile to his estranged wife. Family gatherings – which had always been an ordeal for Diana, bringing on outbreaks of her eating disorder – now had an embarrassing *froideur*. When the Queen invited her to attend the D-Day celebrations with the rest of the royal family in June 1994, for example, her private secretary saw how the Princess was anxious beforehand, nervously adjusting her hat and fretting about what she would say to their hostile ranks. Far from the veteran of countless public engagements, Diana appeared more like a freshman attending her first college dance.

Even when Diana was not present, members of the royal family were very cautious in articulating their opinions when her name came up in conversation. And her name came up with alarming frequency. They did not understand her, found her eccentric and could not handle her temper, her bulimia or her mood swings. 'The family worry desperately about the damage she is doing,' one of their number said to a mutual friend.

Shortly after Diana made her famous Time and Space speech, in December 1993, Prince Edward's then new girlfriend, Sophie Rhys-Jones, now the Countess of Wessex, was caught in the middle of this unspoken conflict between Windsor and Spencer. From the royal family's perspective, Sophie, the daughter of a retired salesman for a tyre company, was a living rebuke to the Princess of Wales, proof positive that a low-born commoner could rub shoulders quite happily with them. For her part, Sophie had heard many of the horror stories concerning the Princess from Prince Edward, who never disguised his loathing of the media or for those who breach the royal code of silence. So when Sophie, then a public relations executive, met Diana with other members of the royal family for afternoon tea with the Queen at Windsor Castle she was very much on her guard. As the Queen and the rest of the family sat round drinking tea and making polite conversation over sandwiches and small cakes, Diana cupped her face in her hands and silently stared at Edward's girlfriend. Sophie felt so intimidated that she walked out of the room – after first asking the Queen's permission according to royal protocol. Away from the Sovereign's presence, Sophie, unnerved and upset, broke down in tears and was later consoled by Prince Edward.

At subsequent meetings Sophie was always wary. While they chatted briefly on the steps of the church after the marriage of Princess Margaret's daughter Lady Sarah Armstrong-Jones and Daniel Chatto in July 1994, Edward's girlfriend suspected that Diana had an ulterior motive – that she was subtly trying to engineer a joint picture for the watching photographers. While Sophie's blonde hair and demure manner regularly earned her comparison with the young Diana, in truth the only similarity was that she could mimic Diana's voice perfectly. That day the Princess looked sleek, elegant and tanned and, as she was standing a couple of steps above Sophie, she literally towered over her. Edward's girlfriend, who later admitted that her own choice of outfit was 'ghastly'. Sophie was sufficiently media-savvy to be aware that any pictorial comparison between the two women would do her few favours so she kept out of the way of the cameras. Whatever Diana's motives – and at the time she told friends that she liked the new arrival – Sophie's view was shaped by the royal one, that the Princess was 'manipulative, cunning and conniving'. 'She has been brainwashed by the royal family,' noted a friend. 'She feels sorry for the way Diana has treated them.'

The family that Diana once held in such esteem, and had so longed to become a part of, saw her as tainted and troublesome. 'In their view she had put herself outside their charmed circle and was now relegated to the role of outsider,' observed Patrick Jephson. Their feelings, however, went well beyond indifference or dislike. The Princess of Wales was, in a phrase used by several members of the royal family on numerous occasions, simply 'evil in their midst'.

CHAPTER FIVE

In Search of Love

W HEN DIANA MADE her emotional Time and Space speech
in December 1993, she argued that she was bowing out of
public life for a time because of the media attention that had made
life in the first year after her separation such a misery. There was,
though, another reason for her dramatic decision. She was head-
over-heels in love and saw the opportunity to indulge her passion
away from the demands of her public or the attentions of the
police.

Her secret four-year relationship with art dealer Oliver Hoare
was to leave her with a bruised ego, a damaged reputation and a
broken heart. 'It was a very, very painful relationship for her,'
recalled Debbie Frank. 'We often talked about it. But through the
pain she learned something about herself.' As for escaping the
attentions of the press, that was plainly unrealistic.

With hindsight, the Ascot-week house party at Windsor Castle in
June 1985 might be seen as a momentous occasion. One of Diana's
guests was her friend Sarah Ferguson, the rumbustious daughter of
Prince Charles's polo manager Major Ronald Ferguson. Sarah was
to find herself seated next to Prince Andrew at dinner: they got on
like a house on fire, and the rest, as they say, is history.

Another guest was Oliver Hoare, who was there with his wife,
Diane, the daughter of a very wealthy French heiress, Baroness

Louise de Waldner, a friend of the Queen Mother. On meeting this man, sixteen years her senior, with saturnine good looks and an urbane and courteous manner, the Princess – as she afterwards admitted to Ken Wharfe – felt shy as she flirted mildly with him. In some ways he must have seemed to her to represent what her husband might have been. There are some similarities between the two men, both having a sophisticated appreciation of the finer things in life as well as an interest in the holistic and esoteric. An Old Etonian and art connoisseur, Hoare moved in cosmopolitan and cultured circles that fascinated the Princess, his friends including the late Russian ballet dancer Rudolph Nureyev and David Sulzberger of the American publishing family that owned *The New York Times*. 'He is a bit of a sybarite, not in the bad sense, but he likes to live well and not make a huge effort,' a friend of Hoare's said of him. He had lived for a time in Tehran, and he and the Prince of Wales struck up a friendship based on a common interest in Islamic art – a subject in which Hoare is an expert. Indeed, in 1985, the Prince attended an exhibition of Islamic art at Hoare's gallery in Belgravia and, while the business came under judicial scrutiny during a theft trial that same year, the friendship between the Waleses and the Hoares flourished.

Ironically, as the marriage of the Prince and Princess of Wales collapsed into mutual animosity and bitterness in the early 1990s, it was Diana's jealousy of Camilla Parker Bowles that drew her closer to Oliver Hoare. Not only were he and Diane friendly with Charles and Diana – they were also part of the royal inner circle who were aware of Prince Charles's relationship with Camilla Parker Bowles. Charles and Camilla attended dinner parties at the Hoares' Chelsea home, and Diane's mother, Louise de Waldner regularly invited the Prince to her château near Carpentras in the south of France to paint and relax, which was also where he went to recuperate after breaking his arm in 1990. In 1991, Diane and Oliver Hoare, together with improbable characters like the TV personality Jimmy Savile, were drafted in as intermediaries to try to resolve the differences between the Prince and Princess of Wales.

To begin with, Diana (by now cooperating enthusiastically with me for *Diana: Her True Story*) turned to Hoare for advice and comfort – and in order to tease information out of him about the movements of Camilla and Charles – as much as to develop their relationship. Under normal circumstances, Hoare's friendship with Camilla would have put him beyond the pale, a figure to be treated with suspicion and circumspection. At that critical time in their marriage, as far as both the Prince and Princess were concerned, friends, courtiers and staff had to choose whose side they were on. There was no middle way. So the fact that Diana was prepared to pursue her friendship with Oliver Hoare was a sign of her interest. As for Hoare – 'He was flattered that Diana had a crush on him,' a friend told the American writer Sally Bedell Smith. 'He encouraged her without knowing it.' That remark is rather disingenuous given that some eighteen months before, Hoare, then forty-six and most certainly a man of the world, had ended a four-year friendship with Ayesha Nadir, a former Turkish beauty queen and the estranged wife of Asil Nadir, the disgraced business tycoon.

While Diana was pursuing this new secret relationship – having given James Hewitt his marching orders over lunch at Kensington Palace in December 1991 – her obsession with Charles and Camilla remained. Questions about when they met, who they saw, what they did, constantly gnawed at her, undermining her self-esteem as they stoked her jealousy. The specific information she got from Oliver Hoare helped to relieve her lurid imaginings – and, more practically, it meant that she had details about the times that Charles and Camilla were together, and if applicable, who they were with, that she could pass on to me. I would then have some concrete information for which to seek independent corroboration. On one occasion, for instance, she sent me the dates when Prince Charles was due to visit the château owned by Oliver Hoare's mother-in-law, even including the château's telephone number. The source was presumably Oliver Hoare – although neither I nor James Colthurst had any idea at the time of how she was receiving her intelligence.

It was during the feverish summer of intrigue and plotting in 1991 that Diana became a regular visitor to Hoare's art gallery in Pimlico, calling in a couple of times a week. Indeed, to celebrate her thirtieth birthday in July, Hoare bought her a birthday cake, and he and his staff sang 'Happy Birthday' as she sat on his desk, smiling at the discordant throng assembled before her. While she saw him at his gallery, Diana was also spending much time at Lucia Flecha de Lima's home in Mount Street, where she had been given the use of a bedroom. It was just a few hundred yards from the apartment of Adrian Ward-Jackson, a prominent figure in the arts world and also a friend of Oliver Hoare, who was in the terminal stages of AIDS. She helped her friend Angela Serota, now Lady Bernstein of Craigwell, nurse him, on one occasion driving from Balmoral to be at his bedside in August 1991.

For a time Mount Street became her second home, the Princess staying there at weekends when the Brazilian Ambassador and his sons were away. Indeed when I dropped off a chapter of the book for her there on one occasion, Diana said afterwards she had read it in the company of her Brazilian friend. By now the Princess was besotted with Hoare, and despite the knowledge that when my book was published it would focus intense attention on her romantic life, it did nothing to curb her infatuation. To Ken Wharfe, who in his position as bodyguard knew more than most about what was going on, Diana confided that she 'absolutely adored' Oliver Hoare (though she insisted that 'We just talk'). During a trip to Egypt in May 1992, as speculation about the contents of the forthcoming *Diana: Her True Story* intensified, the Princess apparently told her butler Paul Burrell about her secret liaisons in Mayfair. As he noted in his memoir: 'The Princess regularly used their [the Brazilians'] embassy in Mount Street, London to meet someone. Not James Hewitt.' It was a risky confession – at the time Burrell was nominally in the 'enemy camp', as he and his wife Maria were still living at Highgrove in the employment of the Prince of Wales.

While the Brazilian Embassy in Mount Street was a favourite meeting place, according to Hoare's former chauffeur, Barry Hodge, who was interviewed by the *News of the World* in February 1995, the Princess and the art dealer also saw each other at a number of other locations, including the home of the restaurateur Mara Berni in Walton Street, as well as cafés and restaurants in Kensington and Knightsbridge. Shortly after her separation in December 1992, the Princess and Hoare frequently had breakfast

together at the Chelsea Harbour Club, which she started frequent-
ing in the spring of 1993, after she and her trainer Carolan Brown
were alerted to the possibility that sneak pictures might have been
taken of her at Bryce Taylor's gym, LA Fitness. 'He would come
over and try and kiss or touch her,' said Carolan, who now runs her
own health club. 'He was openly flirtatious towards her and she
would push him away with her hand. She made it clear to me that
she was having an affair with him.'

As was her habit, Diana courted Hoare by taking an intense
interest in his life. She visited his mother Irina, and after Hoare
had talked to her about Sufism, a mystical branch of Islam that he
had embraced, it was not long before she was spotted reading
Discovering Islam by Professor Akbar Ahmed, and was asking
friends to explain the finer points of the abstruse subject of Sufism.

In the view of her protection team, Diana took things a little too
far on one occasion in March 1993, when she was on a skiing holiday in Lech with her boys. It seems that late one evening, when
everybody assumed she was safely in her room for the night, she
threw herself from the first floor of the hotel, a fall of twenty feet
but cushioned by a huge snowdrift. Then she walked off into the
night. While her detective never did find out exactly what had happened, he knew that at five-thirty in the morning she had walked
back into the hotel, which she had not been seen to leave. He saw
for himself clear evidence of her escape in the snow – and he knew
that her friend Oliver Hoare was skiing at a nearby resort, so it was
not hard to get a rough idea of what she had been up to.

It was not only snow into which the Princess made daring leaps:
Elsa Bowker was to relate how Diana once jumped out of Hoare's
car into Sloane Square in the middle of a traffic jam because she
suspected that he was going to see his wife rather than, as he told
her, his sick daughter. Hoare later found her sitting sobbing on a
park bench outside Kensington Palace. The Princess in tears was
not an unfamiliar sight. On several occasions around this time,
Princess Margaret's chauffeur, Dave Griffin, found her in her car
outside her royal apartment, crying her eyes out. In his unofficial
role as an uncle figure, Griffin also gave her friendly advice about
the clumsy manner in which, for a time, she smuggled her friend

into her apartment. She would drive in with him hidden in the boot of her car, which she would park in the courtyard of her next-door neighbour, Princess Margaret. Hoare would then slip out and sneak through the rear entrance into Diana's apartment. The Princess of Wales's behaviour both irritated and intrigued her royal neighbour. When Diana drove into her courtyard, Princess Margaret was annoyed that her private space was being invaded – but her displeasure did not stop her peering round one of the double doors she kept open to try to spot Diana's secret visitor. After a while, Dave Griffin respectfully advised the Princess that she was drawing more attention to herself by this cloak-and-dagger behaviour than if her visitor came in through the front door.

On another occasion the art dealer drew attention to himself because of his nocturnal activities. At about 3.30 in the morning the smoke alarms in Diana's apartment went off. The Princess's detective hurried there to find an unkempt and embarrassed-looking Oliver Hoare, who had been standing in the hallway smoking a cigar.

In her relationship with Hoare, the Princess seemed for the first time to be presented with both an emotional dilemma and a possible resolution. While she saw my book as her escape from the constricted life inside the royal prison and a stifling marriage, it is now clear that she probably imagined life with Oliver Hoare as the Promised Land once she had made her getaway. She told Lady Bowker, to whom she had been introduced by Oliver Hoare, that she fantasized about leaving England and buying a house in Italy with the art dealer. She talked gaily of having two daughters to match William and Harry. Idle daydreaming was one thing, though – she had talked of buying a house in the country with her former lover James Hewitt – the reality was quite another.

With the Waleses' separation in December 1992, there was now before Diana the possibility of one day genuinely pursuing this romantic vision. Within a year she had dispensed with her Scotland Yard protection officers, which meant that there were now no watchful bodyguards spying on her movements. At the same time, her decision to take a breather from public life in

December 1993 gave her an opportunity to explore life with the man she loved. This was, as she told Stephen Twigg, the real reason for bowing out of public life. 'Her heart truly ruled her head,' he observed. 'She was always driven by her emotions.'

It was not a one-way street. Hoare, too, according to his driver, Barry Hodge, seemed to be building his future around their liaison. A matter of weeks before Diana made her Time and Space speech, in October 1993, Hoare left his wife and moved into a friend's apartment in Pimlico. The die was cast, the Princess was in touching distance of making a long-cherished dream come true. She was passionately in love with Hoare, or so she thought, and he had demonstrated his commitment to the relationship by leaving the marital home. As she engineered her exit from public life, she allowed herself and Oliver Hoare to be spotted in her car, where they were seen to sit talking for an hour. A watching journalist wrote coyly that Diana's head 'rested trustingly on Mr Hoare's shoulder'. They had several safe houses where they could meet, so their rendezvous may have seemed risky, but it was also a way of them backing into the spotlight as a couple. This private meeting conducted in public seems to bear out the psychoanalyst D. W. Winnicott's wry maxim: 'It is a joy to be hidden, but a disaster not to be found.'

It now seemed possible for them to realize a future together. Yet that Christmas Diana made a brief appearance at Sandringham with the rest of the royal family before flying off to Washington to spend the remainder of the festive season with her friend Lucia Flecha de Lima and her husband Paulo Tarso, who had now been transferred to a diplomatic posting in America. Oliver Hoare was nowhere to be seen – at least in public.

During these few weeks it seems that Diana had strolled along a path familiar to so many star-crossed lovers and found herself in a sober place called reality. Practical matters had to be considered. At this point in her life money was an extremely sensitive issue – she was furious, for example, when a story appeared in early 1994 about her lavish annual expenditure on grooming. She still relied on her husband for finance and was very anxious to avoid adverse publicity that could substantially affect any divorce settlement, concerns that ultimately had a profound impact on her life. She was aware too that it was Hoare's heiress wife Diane who controlled the purse strings in their marriage. As Diana understood it, Hoare did not, at that time, have the means to keep her in the manner to which she had become accustomed. Of course, if she had really been serious about buying a place in Italy and settling down to raise a new family, then these considerations should have been irrelevant.

The real issue, though, was that the rules of the game had been altered. And she didn't like it. Until Oliver Hoare left his wife she had been able to play out a romantic drama of love and loss, hope and pain, without any ultimate commitment – just as she had with James Hewitt. However, once Hoare became available, the safe psychological boundaries that she had enjoyed were removed. 'She was terrified once he was free for her,' a friend of hers declared. Her reaction was by no means unusual. The Princess was, according to a relationship counsellor, behaving in the same way as many other women going through a separation. 'They enjoy a relationship with a man who is unavailable, usually married, so that they can enjoy and suffer the emotional highs and lows of a romantic entanglement without making the ultimate commitment.'

In January 1994, within five weeks of the Princess's famous speech, Oliver Hoare was back at home with his wife. Yet that did not stop Diana and the art dealer from continuing to see each other, meeting at their usual haunts, notably the Chelsea Harbour Club and, of course, Kensington Palace. In March he was photographed being driven into the royal apartment complex by the Princess after they had had a meal at a Chinese restaurant with Beatrix Flecha de Lima, the daughter of their friends Lucia and Paulo. While Diane Hoare was away in France, Diana paid a tearful ninety-minute visit to Hoare in late July, just as a newspaper was investigating claims that she had made silent phone calls to the Hoares' home. Even after the phone call scandal broke, in August 1994, they continued to see each other, the art dealer spotted one day in January 1995, climbing into the boot of the Princess's car.

Such exotic excursions aside, the sustaining, if mundane, reality of their relationship was the mobile telephone, her calls as frequent as they were intense. There were some days when she would call him twenty times on his mobile; a quiet day was just six or seven calls. If Oliver and his wife Diane were in the car together he would pull out the phone socket slightly so his mobile was effectively off the hook. 'I would say Diana has pursued Oliver every single day for three years by phone calls, by their meetings,' Barry Hodge, Hoare's chauffeur for ten years, claimed on television. 'But then it is not one-sided. Oliver pursued her.' When he was away on business in America, for example, Hoare sent her a string of loving messages on her pager.

There was a darker side, however, as periodically the Princess made silent telephone calls to Hoare's home, hanging up when his wife answered. This unnerving behaviour began in September 1992 – ironically at the same time as the Squidgygate tapes publicized the late-night conversations between Diana and James Gilbey. The calls continued for a year before Diane Hoare insisted that her husband instruct the police to trace them. In October 1993 the police equipped the Hoares' telephone with a special device that could trace calls. It was not long before some of the calls were tracked to the Princess's mobile phone and others to telephone lines inside her apartment in Kensington Palace and to public telephones in Kensington and Notting Hill Gate, not far from her London home. Shortly afterwards, the Princess discussed the matter with Ken Wharfe, but while she admitted making some calls, she insisted that she was not responsible for the majority.

Others were not so sure. The Princess was known to be a phone junkie, dependent on it to derive comfort from those closest to her, men or women. In the Hoare incident, her behaviour was markedly similar to the way she had acted during her relationships with James Gilbey and James Hewitt, the former army officer helpfully telling a Sunday tabloid that he too had suffered nuisance calls during his romance with the Princess. Even when it was James Colthurst she called (which could be as often as twenty times a day), if it was his wife Dominique who answered, Diana would hang up without identifying herself. 'It's important to realize that she telephones at times of distress, often in tears, and she only wants to speak to one person,' Colthurst explained. 'She would understandably feel embarrassed talking to someone who was not close to her. Everyone is aware of the loneliness of her position so we make allowances.'

This time she found herself exposed and publicly humiliated. In August 1994 the Sunday tabloid, the *News of the World*, splashed details of the 'cranky' calls across its pages and revealed that the police investigation had pinpointed Kensington Palace as the source. The Princess's attempts to disguise her behaviour only inflamed the furore. A clandestine meeting in her car with her friend, the *Daily Mail* journalist, Richard Kay, whom she regularly used as a conduit for her opinions, was photographed, effectively blowing her media cover. In his page-one story, headlined 'What Have I Done To Deserve This?' the Princess made a robust and defiant defence, asserting that there was 'no truth' in the allegations that she was a phone pest. For good measure she authorized the release of her official diary to prove her story. 'Somewhere, someone is going to make out that I am mad, that I am guilty by association, that the mud will stick,' she said. Foolishly, she rather undercut her case by claiming that she had no idea how to use a public phone box, a contention which was met with widespread ridicule. Conveniently, a schoolboy, who knew the Hoares' sons, was later fingered as the likely culprit and accused of using phone booths in central London to harass the art dealer's family. In fact, as the boy's mother pointed out, the teenager was away at boarding school at the time. A year later, when Diana made her famous television appearance on *Panorama*, she emphatically protested her innocence, denying that she had made the nuisance calls: 'But that again was a huge move to discredit me and very nearly did me in,' she insisted to the BBC presenter, Martin Bashir, asserting that she had 'found out that a young boy had done most of them'.

This claim, however, was exposed as a lie by her earlier confessions to Ken Wharfe as well as to a handful of her women friends, including Elsa Bowker, whom she told that she had called Hoare seventy times. Her actions, while on the surface resembling those of a teenager going through her first crush, were much more self-destructive, following patterns of behaviour established during her unhappiest time with Prince Charles. Then, at its most extreme, she had cut or marked herself to get the Prince's attention in a desperate plea for help mingled with self-loathing. Simone Simmons, her healer, maintained that she continued this practice of self-injury during her romance with Hoare, implying that she never progressed from the despair she felt during the first years of her marriage. 'Diana's arsenal lay within the kitchen cupboard, the slender tines of a fork her preferred weapon,' she declared, allegations subsequently repeated in some articles and biographies. Ms Simmons's claims, however, were flatly dismissed by Stephen Twigg, who worked on Diana's body from 1988 until 1995: 'There was never the slightest scratch on her body and, believe me, I would have noticed.'

While self-injury seemed to have been consigned to the past, Diana's emotional insecurity remained. Her emotional life had the quality of a self-fulfilling prophecy; she would desperately seek love, certain that she could not be loved, and if love was offered she would back away and even provoke rejection so that the relationship would end, confirming her sense of worthlessness. This would go towards explaining the silent telephone calls, which she must have known could only lead to rejection.

When Oliver Hoare, perhaps sensibly, declined to make any public statement either during the nuisance phone calls saga in August 1994, or when his chauffeur Barry Hodge went to the Sunday tabloid, *News of the World*, and sold his story about Hoare's relationship with the Princess, his behaviour only confirmed Diana's profound feelings of abandonment and rejection. 'She was willing to give up everything for him, so imagine her devastation when he didn't come to her assistance,' observed Stephen Twigg. When Hoare returned a pair of her father's cufflinks – she gave similar gifts to other men in her life – it was a recognition on both sides that the relationship was going nowhere. 'That man let me down very badly,' she commented bitterly – but in truth he had taken a considerable gamble to pursue and possibly cement their relationship.

'I bet I could get Will Carling to ask me out,' the Princess said in a light-hearted aside to her fitness trainer Carolan Brown as they worked out at the Chelsea Harbour Club, of which the England rugby captain was also a member. It was a few months before Carling's marriage to TV presenter Julia Smith in June 1994, and Diana was in a mischievous frame of mind. 'I might be able to stop that marriage happening,' she mused, giggling at the wicked thought. Her idle, rather juvenile, contemplation would lead to a further tarnishing of her image as a wronged wife, but at the same time it was a development in her character.

'She was young and naive,' commented Carolan. 'Basically living her life backwards because she had had no experience of the dating game. So she was flirtatious with everybody. Will Carling couldn't believe his luck. She was desperate to win his affection and would flirt outrageously with him. But when he asked her out, she said no. She was like a giggly girl, flirting like mad and then playing hard to get. It was playground stuff.' Those who had known her since her bachelor days agreed with the observation. 'She was whisked off into this marriage aged twenty.' Carolan continued, 'and has lived in a vacuum for ten years. Now she is taking up those feelings that she left off as a teenager. She has a lot of catching up to do.'

Diana's skittish behaviour was also a sign of the newfound confidence she felt in her body. Her training programme, based on ballet and step, ensured that she developed a long, lean shape, with an emphasis on standing tall and with confidence. In early 1994, after her morning workout she started seeing Carling for coffee and a chat. Soon after Jenni Rivett took over her training from Carolan Brown, who was then expecting her first child. Jenni Rivett placed a greater emphasis on weights to change the definition of the body. 'If you start to tone your muscles you feel good about your body and you feel in control of your life. That was very important for her,' she explained. 'She was inspired because she was getting so many compliments.' On a trip to the Council of Fashion designers in New York in February 1995, Diana felt so confident with her body shape that she wore a backless dress to a star-studded gala. 'Wait till you see how good I look,' she told Jenni.

Just how important her body shape was to her was demonstrated when the paparazzi took pictures that suggested that she had cellulite on her thighs. She was so upset by the implied insult that not only did she allow her trainer to put out a statement denying that she had cellulite, but she embarked on a ferocious detox programme just to make sure.

Her growing interest in physical fitness naturally meshed with Carling's own interest in the body beautiful; true to form with men she was attracted to, Diana immersed herself in what interested him. By his own admission he is an 'anorak' regarding weight training and exercise regimes. Soon the aggressive way Diana was pumping iron and lifting heavy weights concerned both trainers, who felt that she was becoming too Amazonian, forfeiting the lean elegant look she had worked so hard to achieve for an over-muscled appearance.

As a professional athlete, Carling took his fitness regime very seriously, regularly attending the BiMAL Medical and Sports Rehabilitation Clinic with his physiotherapist Alan Watson for a sophisticated breakdown of his body functions. Everything from lung capacity to heart rate was monitored and evaluated. Soon Diana followed suit and every Friday morning she too went along to the West London centre for a thirty-minute fitness check.

By now they had met for lunch a couple of times – on one occasion he and former Wales captain Ieuan Evans went to Kensington Palace – and Diana, as Carling wrote in his autobiography (imaginatively titled *My Autobiography*), was 'particularly interested to hear some rugby stories' and even asked him if he could arrange for her boys to attend an England training session at Twickenham. When the boys went to the headquarters of English rugby in March 1995, Diana came along as well. Besides showing a keen interest in his love of fitness and rugby, the Princess expressed concern about his marriage. Their conversations had progressed from light-hearted banter about astrology, the latest celebrity gossip and observations about world leaders – she considered Bill Clinton sexy but his wife Hillary rather over-ambitious – to affairs of the heart. Carling had not been married for a year and already the cracks were showing. When she asked him and he confirmed that he was very unhappy, the Princess proceeded to give him the benefit of her own experience in the rough and tumble of romance gone wrong.

It was not her abilities as a marriage counsellor that made the headlines, but as a marriage wrecker. Frequent telephone calls, specially installed private phone lines, secret meetings at Kensington Palace and fond nicknames – Diana would jokingly answer the phone as 'Mrs Carling' to the man she called 'captain' – these all made up some furtive agenda the Princess seemed to be pursuing. And, thanks to allegations made by Carling's former PA, Hilary Ryan, they were splashed over five pages of a Sunday tabloid, the *Sunday Mirror*, in August 1995. 'He did run around her like a puppy dog,' said his former employee. 'It was pretty pathetic.'

Others like the royal chauffeur Steve Davies, who caddied for Will Carling, took the same view, believing that she was simply toying with the infatuated rugby star. Carling, who had also made a habit of visiting Diana's office at St James's Palace, subsequently compounded his folly in early September by delivering rugby shirts for William and Harry to Kensington Palace after the scandal had broken, making himself an easy target for his detractors in the media. At the time the Princess was visiting her friend, Joe Toffolo, who was recovering in hospital after suffering a heart attack, and had become smitten with his surgeon, Hasnat Khan.

While the clandestine nature of the relationship between Carling and Diana bore a remarkable resemblance to her affair with Oliver Hoare, unlike Diane Hoare the media-savvy Mrs Julia Carling, formerly in PR, refused to remain silent. 'This has happened to her before and you hope she won't do these things again, but she obviously does,' she told the *Mail on Sunday*. 'She picked the wrong couple to do it with this time because we can only get stronger from it.'

Within a month, though, in September 1995, the Carlings had separated, the implication being that Diana had broken up the marital home. 'It hurts me very much to face losing my husband in a manner which has become outside my control,' announced Julia Carling, a standpoint that reinforced the headlines that were describing Diana as a 'homewrecker' and a 'bored, manipulative and selfish princess'. For his part, Will Carling argued that his marriage was effectively over before his friendship with Diana was made public. 'That assessment of our difficulties seems to me to be too glib, too much a convenient excuse,' he wrote later in his autobiography.

In this cat fight, Diana gave as good as she got, letting it be known that she thought Carling had been a 'fool' and that the collapse of his marriage had had nothing to do with her. In fact, she told Max Hastings, she saw him mainly for the sake of the boys. While Diana was said to have dropped Carling 'like a hot brick' as soon as the scandal erupted, months later she was still going to considerable trouble to maintain their friendship. Days after her groundbreaking TV interview on *Panorama* in November 1995, where the omission of questions about her relationship with Carling was cause for considerable comment, she came close to delaying her trip to Argentina while, as her private secretary Patrick Jephson acerbically observed, 'she scrabbled to find the right SIM card to go with the special mobile phone she had acquired to take Carling's calls'. By then, however, she had, for nearly three months, been secretly seeing the heart surgeon Hasnat Khan.

'She was the sort of person who didn't like being out of a relationship,' says Carolan Brown. 'She didn't like being on her own because she needed constant reassurance that she was loved. That was her ultimate dream – to find the perfect husband, have more children and settle down. She was looking for the right man.'

Certainly she had no shortage of suitors – flowers, invitations and gifts for her were arriving all the time at Kensington Palace. 'Naturally these attentions flattered her and at some level she enjoyed them,' said Simone Simmons. 'Sometimes she would spend a cheerful evening with one squire or another but it was to be a long time before she was ready even to consider a wholehearted relationship.' More than that, she was intimidated and nauseated if a man became too ardent and began declaring his undying devotion and affection. 'As soon as they say everyone is madly in love with you, it's instant rejection. It's absolutely repulsive,' she told James Colthurst, referring to one particularly devoted admirer.

Diana tended to put the men in her life into compartments, and she, her hairdressers and Paul Burrell light-heartedly devised a 'racecourse', picking out nine admirers, who – besides Hasnat Khan, who was always the front runner – included a musician, a novelist, a politician, a businessman and a lawyer. These they moved up or down the course depending on how she felt about them. For a time the American billionaire Teddy Forstmann was deemed to be well in contention. Their relationship not only had a suitably transatlantic flavour but earned the approval of Patrick Jephson, who felt that his money, kindness and common sense made him an ideal partner. He first met her in 1994 at an Independence Day dinner hosted by her friend Lord Rothschild (on the advisory board of Forstmann's company, Gulfstream Aerospace) at Spencer House (a magnificent eighteenth-century town house in St James's, London, built by the first Earl Spencer, and eventually acquired by Jacob Rothschild's company, which completed its restoration in 1987). Forstmann subsequently took her out to Le Manoir aux Quat' Saisons restaurant in Oxfordshire and she reciprocated with an invitation to Kensington Palace. Later that summer they played tennis together, in suitably matching outfits, while she was on holiday with her friend Lucia Flecha de Lima at Martha's Vineyard in the United States. Tongues really began wagging when Forstmann, who has also been linked to actress Liz Hurley, flew her, in October 1994, in one of his private planes from New York to Washington, where he was her partner at a movers and shakers dinner hosted by the late Katherine Graham, chairman and former publisher of the *Washington Post*. When the Princess returned to Kensington Palace she was on the telephone to her American hostess to discuss a surprise bouquet of fifty long-stemmed red roses – complete with an 'over-familiar' message which apparently came from Forstmann.

Besides Forstmann, Diana was linked to property developer Christopher Whalley, Canadian singer Bryan Adams – his Danish actress girlfriend Cecilie Thomsen accused him of having an affair with the Princess after her divorce – as well as the Asian electronics entrepreneur Gulu Lalvani and even an Italian count. There were plenty of other names mentioned, whether she had met them or not. As her friend Lucia Flecha de Lima cautioned when she spoke to TV producer Daphne Barak: 'She doesn't know who she can trust. And all the men they try to link her name to . . . *really*. Don't forget what this is about. It's obvious they are trying to connect her name to some man. This is a typical divorce struggle.'

While the thrill of the chase may have provided amusement and diversion, it did not entirely hide the desolation in Diana's soul, a sadness and isolation arising from her personality and her circumstance. 'She struck me as an incredibly lonely person,' Will Carling observed. 'She was able to alleviate emotional and physical suffering in so many people, yet retained a curious air of sadness herself.' It was a constant refrain from those who knew her well. 'She's alone and she's so lonely,' was Lucia Flecha de Lima's opinion. 'Everybody criticizes her when she makes a mistake, but these mistakes are the result of her loneliness.'

In her book, *The Impossibility of Sex*, Susie Orbach describes a personality type that she calls the 'vampire Casanova' because people of this personality follow a predictable pattern of pursuit, seduction and then indifference. It is the conquest that matters, but only in so far as it alleviates the 'dreadful emptiness' within. Vampire Casanovas are figures more to be pitied than judged; frightened and anxious characters who are emotional black holes. The parallels with the Princess and her romantic experiences are unmistakable.

While she could be consumed by her needs and passions, Diana gradually mastered the ability to stand back and examine, often with amusement, her life and position. But, as reported in the *Daily Mail* of 14 July 1997, she commented sadly to model Cindy Crawford, 'I have my picture in the paper every single day. Who would want to take me on?'

Following the Waleses' separation in December 1992, Diana began to see – alongside her idealized vision of living happily ever after, invariably abroad, with the man of her dreams, far removed from the everyday cares and constrictions of her existence – that she could use her position to do something worthwhile. 'Her head tells her that she would like to be the ambassador to the world, her heart tells her that she would like to be wooed by an adoring billionaire,' observed James Colthurst. A friend and counsellor of Diana's agreed with Colthurst's opinion about her 'head', but not about her 'heart': 'She was on a trajectory where she was going to do something in the world that was really valuable. Her ambition was not to chase every man in her life.'

As for being 'wooed', while she no doubt enjoyed it, 'It was bad enough getting to grips with being "Mrs W" ['Mrs Windsor'], never mind bringing another one up,' she said ruefully to James Colthurst.

Much as the Princess strove to come to terms with the past, inevitably the separation cast a long shadow over her life. She had greeted it as a step forward, but it hardly made her life any easier. She lived in a constant state of agitation and uncertainty, not only about the men she was currently involved with, but also about her husband, her fears and anxieties fuelled by speculation among her friends or in the media about what the Prince and his supporters might be plotting and planning. Yet, amidst the lurid headlines about silent phone calls and affairs with married men, it is easy to overlook the fact that she and Prince Charles managed their separation in a way that, though understandably edgy, defensive, and suspicious, was reasonably civilized. From a position where Diana could not bear to be in the same room as her husband, there came a time when she felt sufficiently composed to make regular visits to Prince Charles in his rooms at Colour Court in St James's Palace.

This was no ordinary separation. She had not only to cope with the emotional reality of the continuing place of Camilla Parker Bowles in Charles's affections, but she had to contend with the attempts to downgrade her royal status, the whispering campaign against her – 'Quite mad, poor dear,' one of the Prince's circle opined – and the ponderous hostility of her husband's family as a whole. Indeed, if her own experience had taught her anything it was that once women like herself, who had married into powerful families, were considered no longer desirable as family members they risked losing everything. Not only was that borne out by the ruthless despatch of the Duchess of York from the bosom of the royal family, but also by the treatment of other aristocratic friends of her generation. Diana felt an immediate fellowship with Annabel Goldsmith's niece, Lady Cosima Somerset, who found herself ostracized when she left her husband, the eleventh Duke of

Beaufort's youngest son, Lord John Somerset. 'We shared the experience of being separated from our husbands and uncertain about what the future held,' Cosima Somerset recalled. 'We had both broken away from large, powerful families and therefore had lost our protection. Both of us were considered "hysterical, unbalanced, paranoid, foolish".'

In contrast to her behaviour when in pursuit of love, Diana's conduct in relation to the Prince and his family was in many ways a triumph of restraint and shrewd counselling. She was quite aware that, as legal precedents for a divorced Prince and Princess of Wales were sketchy, the end game of her marriage would be played out in the court of public opinion. This meant, she knew, that the extent of her popularity would ultimately define the verdict, as the Duchess of York – 'the canary down the mine shaft' as Diana called her – had found to her cost. The Princess had witnessed the full weight of the Establishment bear down on Fergie in July 1993 when she accepted the post as a goodwill ambassador for the United Nations High Commission for Refugees, and had the offer quickly withdrawn. Diana, a woman now deemed mad, bad and dangerous to know, saw that she had to navigate her path with diplomacy and subtlety. 'She was very grown up about that part of her life,' Vivienne Parry noted.

The path she took was neither easy nor consistent. While the days of lurid imaginings that Camilla Parker Bowles was, in her words, 'a sexual machine' no longer held the capacity to torture her, she still pondered over her rival's astrological fortunes, gossiped about the supposed smell in her house, listened with anger and disbelief to the roll-call of those she had once called friends who had played host to the lovers and, on one occasion, laid out an Ordnance Survey map to plot the devious routes the woman she still called 'the Rottweiler' took on her journey to meet Prince Charles. So while Diana was upset when Camilla was present at the memorial service for the Earl of Westmorland on 3 November 1993, which she also attended, she was not as emotionally wrung out as she once would have been.

Paradoxically the emotional book-end to her obsession with Camilla came a few weeks after the separation. If the love letters from Camilla to her husband that she had read in August 1991 had confirmed the intensity of the older woman's longing for Prince Charles, so the late-night telephone conversation between the Prince and Mrs Parker Bowles, illicitly recorded and broadcast by radio hams and subsequently published in tabloid newspapers in January 1993, was undeniable proof that these feelings were reciprocated. The so-called 'Camillagate' tapes were deeply embarrassing for the Prince of Wales, containing as they did distasteful references to his desire to be a sanitary tampon inside his lover (which Diana described as 'just sick'). More pertinently, the tapes demonstrated just why the Princess had always been the third wheel in their marriage. Amidst her husband's self-absorption and fretfulness he mused that the whole reason for Camilla's existence was to validate his own.

'I'm so proud of you,' he tells Camilla.

'Don't be silly, I've never achieved anything,' she replies.

'Your great achievement is to love me,' Prince Charles answers.

In happier circumstances this could have been the Princess herself speaking.

As far as Diana was concerned, while Camillagate was traumatic it was also cathartic, and although she continued to keep track of Camilla's relationship with her husband, she was no longer totally consumed by thoughts of their affair. 'She had this torment going on in her head,' said a close friend. 'Now she doesn't care where he is and she isn't interested and she doesn't want to know.' She was now following the ups and downs of the liaison between Camilla and Charles with a kind of disinterested fascination, at times even feeling sorry for Camilla, who had waited so long for her prince who still couldn't make up his mind about their future together.

Diana felt a little sympathy for her husband too, conscious as she explored her own background in therapy, that his own bleak upbringing had made him the man he was. He had a 'tricky, very tricky' relationship with his father. 'He has to sort out his childhood before he can sort himself out,' Diana said to a friend. Likewise, as she began to make more public speeches, she began to appreciate the frustrations her husband felt when the press ignored or discarded his words for a picture of her on a shopping trip. 'He is so unhappy, he is suicidal,' she said to Penny Thornton. 'He has such a struggle that he cannot be taken seriously, he gets really hurt by it and I now understand.' She herself was so furious when a speech she made to the Red Cross in 1993 was only lightly reported that she tore up a note of explanation from Dickie Arbiter. Even though Arbiter was suspected of being a double agent by both sides because until December 1993 he was working as press secretary for both the Prince and the Princess, he later felt that the relentless war between what Diana called the A team (her side) and the B team (Charles's side) did scale down after the separation: 'I think she grew up. The Princess felt a weight had been taken off her shoulders. She was able to lead a life without living a lie, and could do her own thing.'

It was something of an illusion. If not quite all-out war, their armistice had the complexity of an armed truce, mutual suspicion punctuated by sporadic outbreaks of fighting. Both sides had their offices swept for listening devices, the Prince and his acolytes convinced that 'her side' were listening to their telephone conversations. Every move was watched with a doubtful beady eye. In November 1993, a month before she announced her decision to retire from public life, for example, Diana had an uncomfortable meeting with her husband who was irritated and fearful that he would catch the flak for her decision. He had, after all, told his circle that he wanted her 'completely removed from public life'. 'Charles has been whingeing that he wants the stage for his own; now he's got it. I'm going to find my own,' Diana told James Colthurst.

Prince Charles's decision, early in 1992, to allow the television broadcaster Jonathan Dimbleby to write his biography, and to make a two-hour ITV television documentary to accompany it, revealed the intricacy of the couple's relationship. Diana at once began fretting that he was making a 'huge mistake', worried that the programme would seriously undermine her position and concerned about the possible effect on the boys. This was somewhat disingenuous given her collaboration in *Diana: Her True Story*. But while her involvement with my book was still effectively camouflaged, she believed the documentary would carry greater weight as Prince Charles was very publicly involved. For two years the documentary loomed large in her life, her conversations with friends peppered with references to Dimbleby. She was worried that the film, ostensibly to mark the twenty-fifth anniversary of her husband's investiture as the Prince of Wales, would tarnish her reputation and would somehow be to the Prince's advantage in any negotiations surrounding their marriage.

Before the broadcast Patrick Jephson organized a lunch between the broadcaster and the Princess in the 'mischievous' hope that Dimbleby would see the 'real' Diana as opposed to the Diana in the stories relayed to him by Charles's circle. 'It was my intention to show him that large parts of it were demonstrably false or at least incomplete,' Jephson wrote in *Shadows of a Princess*. After the lunch Dimbleby wore the dazed look of so many middle-aged men, from newspaper editors to senior politicians, upon whom the Princess had turned her charm. Her magic had worked. Dimbleby departed saying to her private secretary something to the effect that he now doubted the stories he'd been told by the Prince's side (a contention that Dimbleby has since denied).

While the Princess was often accused of manipulating the media, during this entire episode she deliberately kept a low profile so as to leave the field open for her husband. At the time she was being courted assiduously by the veteran American broadcaster Barbara Walters, as well as by the talk-show host Oprah Winfrey, both of whom Diana eventually invited to lunch at Kensington Palace. She turned down their requests for face-to-face interviews as she did, reluctantly, when ITV producer Mike Brennan discussed an hour-long documentary about her charity work. 'It was the right pitch at the wrong time,' commented Brennan. 'It didn't help that the Palace continually tried to shunt the project into a siding.' That year, 1994, the Princess argued, was Charles's year.

On the night of the historic broadcast, 29 June 1994, the Princess, far from thinking of scoring points over her husband, was a bundle of nerves. She had a long-standing engagement to attend a dinner at the Serpentine Gallery of which she was patron, but would have much preferred to spend the evening on her own inside the four walls of Kensington Palace. 'How am I going to get through tonight?' she asked James Colthurst plaintively. Everything seemed to conspire against her. To her irritation the couturiers Valentino prematurely announced to the world that she would be wearing one of their gowns, so at the last minute she decided to wear something else and picked a flirty little number by Christina Stambolian. (This dress led to accusations from some commentators that she was seeking to upstage the programme about her husband.)

As the Princess strode confidently across the courtyard to shake the hand of her friend Lord Palumbo, few realized the effort of will she was making. In the event, the TV documentary, which in fact focused on the Prince's working life, was to be remembered only for his confession that he committed adultery and, subsequently, for initiating a debate about his fitness to be king. According to Dickie Arbiter, 'The programme was a complete whinge, a terrible own goal that not just affected relations between the Prince and Princess, but between St James's Palace and Buckingham Palace.'

Even though the media praised Diana's poise while heaping opprobrium on the Prince's head, there was little satisfaction in her triumph. She witnessed the fallout the very next day when she visited her boys at Ludgrove School and William, referring to the lurid headlines, asked her, 'Is it true that Daddy never loved you?' While she explained the statement away as best she could, she felt sufficiently aggrieved to write to Prince Charles's solicitors complaining about the programme's effect on the children.

It was noticeable that while Diana had a golden opportunity to drive home her advantage, she chose to blame the Prince's advisers, notably his private secretary Richard Aylard, for the débâcle rather than her estranged husband. Her magnanimous behaviour was part of a wider perception of a rapprochement between them, sustained by the mixed signals she gave out. She began to speak more favourably about his role as a father – although she and the boys were distinctly unimpressed when he kept them waiting two hours for a family picnic on Sports Day at Ludgrove School in June 1995. One of her friends, the motherly restaurateur Mara Berni, sincerely believed that Diana remained passionate about the Prince and wanted to effect a reconciliation, dreaming of the day he would come back on bended knee. And on several occasions James Colthurst asked her how she would react if Prince Charles threw his arms around her and told her how well she had done. 'I would be absolutely shaken and would forgive him,' was her reply.

These were romantic visions, however, and nothing more. As a close friend, with whom the Princess often discussed her true feelings for Prince Charles told me, 'The idea that she was still in love with him was never a plausible scenario. She was humiliated, ashamed, furious and hurt. Anybody in that situation wants the other person to see the light, but it is not the same as loving them. She felt contempt, sorrow and disappointment.' She only had to think for a moment that this was still the same man who took his own wooden Victorian toilet seat, towels and lavatory paper when he visited friends, and sent memos to hosts about the size and thickness of the sandwiches he required. Even his father, Prince Philip, according to one officially sanctioned biography, *Elizabeth: The Woman and the Queen* by Graham Turner, regarded him as 'precious and extravagant'. 'She loved him in an abstract sense but didn't want to live with him,' commented one of Diana's confidantes.

For all the profound differences between the Prince and Princess of Wales, their relations did thaw somewhat where their children were concerned. Even their staff were amazed by the civilized and composed way they arranged the times and dates to see the boys, occasions which were set in stone in their respective diaries. Given the high stakes and her own experience, it took real will-power for Diana to stay on an even keel. On the one hand, she wanted the boys never to feel the guilt or sense of responsibility that she, as a youngster, had experienced over her own parents' divorce; she was also acutely aware of her mother's searing experience when she had set her face against Established society. On the other hand, she realized that this was no ordinary divorce battle. Unlike a normal break-up, Diana's children were both her shield against her enemies, within and without the royal family, and her passport to achieving her wider ambitions. She knew that, as the mother of the future king, she could not be as easily marginalized as was the Duchess of York, whose daughters, Princesses Beatrice and Eugenie, were distant from the line of succession. As well as defining her own status, the Princess was utterly conscious of her responsibilities regarding their upbringing. She spoke often and seriously about her role when she was with her former detective, Ken Wharfe. 'The Princess believed that the preparation of William, and to a lesser extent Harry, for their public roles was her primary duty. She said repeatedly that the boys should be fully aware of what was expected of them but that they should also be allowed to develop as young men.' Whenever she dreamed of living in a far-off land, she knew in her heart she had to stay at home for the sake of her sons. 'I do whatever is best for my children,' she would say primly.

Understandably, where the boys were concerned, the climate could quickly change from thaw to frost, the Princess both jealously guarding their affection and protective of their well-being. Small matters took on a significance that outsiders found difficult to appreciate. So for example when Prince Charles's valet, Michael Fawcett, arranged the outfitting of the boys at his preferred West End tailors, the Princess's hackles rose. She was deeply suspicious of this powerful figure who had, as she saw it, an unhealthy influence over her husband. She felt that Fawcett, who could make or break a royal career with a well-chosen word in his master's ear, was now extending his considerable influence to include her sons, a suspicion confirmed when his understudy, Clive Allen, was appointed part-time valet to Prince William.

While Fawcett's interference was bad enough, the appointment of a nanny to look after the boys when they were staying with their father, common sense though it was, was deeply hurtful to her and made her bitterly resentful.

For, whatever the gloss and goodwill, the boys were at the epicentre of their struggle. The Princess sincerely and consistently believed that the man she had married, loved and lived with was not a suitable candidate for the throne. She felt that the crown should skip a generation and go directly to Prince William, the living embodiment, as she saw it, of her legacy and testament to her life. It was a view she expressed time and again in private.

'I am absolutely determined to see William succeed the Queen. I just don't think Charles should do it,' she told Max Hastings, a view she reiterated, if somewhat hesitantly, when she made her historic appearance on *Panorama* in November 1995. 'Because I know the character, I would think that the top job, as I call it, would bring enormous limitations to him and I don't know whether he could adapt to that,' she told the BBC's presenter, Martin Bashir. Inevitably, the interview, which sent shock waves along the red-carpeted corridors of the royal palaces, was seen as a stinging riposte to Prince Charles's documentary of the year before. But as remarked before, and as with so much in the Princess's world, nothing in Dianaland was ever quite as it seemed.

CHAPTER SIX

A Princess of the World

A s she settled into her coach-class seat on the North West Airline flight from Minneapolis to Denver, Mrs Heather Rodd was in reflective mood. If anything, she was feeling a little sorry for herself. She had left her two sons behind in England to spend Christmas with her in-laws while she joined a group of strangers at a luxury chalet for a week's skiing in Vail, Colorado. Hardly the ideal start to the New Year, especially after her plans to sun herself in Cape Town had been aborted because the Queen was due to make a visit to South Africa later that year. Even though she was officially separated from her husband, and thus from the royal family, 'Mrs Rodd', perhaps better known as the Princess of Wales, was still cocooned in royal red tape. During the long flight with her companion – her personal trainer Jenni Rivett, who had organized the stay with print tycoon Mike Flannery and his family in January 1995 – Diana quietly pondered her future, reviewing her own journey of exploration and discovery, a voyage that had tested her personal boundaries and the limits of her unique role.

On balance, while the absence of her boys clouded her horizon, the outlook was much brighter than at any time in her adult life. She was more in control of her body and her personal life, daring to revisit her past to understand her future, and, since her return to public life after her Time and Space speech in December 1993, was gradually exploring her gifts, her interests and her exceptional position as what the press liked to call a semi-detached member of the royal family. Since her brief curtain call in 1993, the Princess was now firmly established on the world stage as a woman of some substance.

Her international standing was reflected by the reception she received on both sides of the Atlantic before her skiing trip. When she attended a banquet in the Hall of Mirrors in the Palace of Versailles outside Paris in December 1994, she was accorded a standing ovation by the great and good of France; and, some weeks before, in October, she was treated like one of the family when she joined Washington's power elite at the dinner in honour of Katherine Graham. The transformation was almost palpable. Whereas she would once have been intimidated in the company of the then First Lady, Hillary Clinton, Katherine Graham and General Colin Powell, former Chairman of the Joint Chiefs of Staff (the nation's highest military post), now the Princess felt at home and among friends. 'This is a warm and welcoming city in a great country,' she told her American audience. 'It symbolizes hope and the promise of better things to come.'

That sentiment served as a guide for her own thinking. For a woman prone to self-doubt, whose life had been characterized by feelings of worthlessness and inferiority, she found herself regularly acknowledged and accepted in her own right and on her own terms, not just by the man-in-the-street but by the men and women in power. In short, she was beginning to feel validated not only as a public personage but as a human being.

From the great and the good to the unwanted and the unloved, Diana demonstrated time and again her uncanny ability to connect. Just days after the glamour of Washington, she was back in gritty reality, visiting special secure hospitals, mixing with the most dangerous members of society. One day she was swapping jokes with Colin Powell, the next sitting in on a meeting of a patients' council at the notorious Broadmoor high security hospital, surrounded by men who were locked away because of the danger they posed to the public. Her travelling companion on a subsequent trip to Carstairs secure hospital in Scotland was Jayne Zito, whose husband was stabbed to death on a London Underground platform by a schizophrenic and who has since campaigned for better community care for the mentally ill. These two visits reflected her public direction, seeking out hidden, neglected corners of society and illuminating them, not just by her position but also her presence. The Princess did feel a degree of trepidation at entering these hospital prisons, surrounded by barbed wire and high-perimeter fencing – nervousness which she offset by making rather feeble jokes about understanding these institutions because she had been in a similar one for most of her adult life – but courage was not something the Princess ever lacked.

When she returned from her skiing trip – 'What I liked about her was that she mucked in with everyone else,' Jenni Rivett later remarked – Diana capitalized on that upbeat mood by drafting out her own plans for her future in public life. Under her blueprint she envisaged cutting through the red tape surrounding royal visits, operating a streamlined office that would be under her control, while utilizing what she considered to be her 'healing abilities' on the global stage. Not so much the Princess of Wales, more a princess for the world, a roving ambassador for the downtrodden. If her musings did not quite amount to a coherent mission statement, her thinking was much more than a series of transitory New Year's resolutions. Indeed her thoughts formed the template for the unique union of the spiritual, political and humanitarian that her life had become geared towards. At least she was giving more consideration to her future direction than most, if not all, other members of the royal family.

While Patrick Jephson might have scoffed (though not in front of the Princess) at the contradictions and caprice in her plans, it was a genuine and significant progress from the days in the not so distant past when James Colthurst had been cajoling her to do something positive rather than always merely reacting to events. In fact, Diana and Jephson had parted company the year before over this very issue.

During early 1994 Colthurst had organized private meetings between the Princess and the American life coach, Anthony Robbins, to give her more formal training in the power of positive thinking. As Colthurst had now moved out of London, was busy in his own career and could no longer devote the time Diana required for advice and counselling, he felt that she needed more professional training to cope independently with the vicissitudes of her life. He believed that Robbins could provide the necessary psychological signposts, and he arranged a meeting between the millionaire guru, with his wife Becky, and the Princess at Kensington Palace. It did not take Robbins long to see that here was a young woman with tremendous untapped potential – and, for all the sadness and isolation, a strong, brave woman who had tackled many difficult issues head on. Diana, who liked his drive and energy, told him lightly that, while she woke feeling positive, by lunchtime she often felt 'lower than a cockroach in Bulgaria'.

Following this meeting, Colthurst arranged for the Princess to visit Robbins in Washington for private coaching. She could, he thought, stay with Lucia Flecha de Lima, but this scheme fell through. When another visit was arranged, this time to Houston, with a private jet and bodyguards laid on, Diana demurred, and Colthurst, realizing that she had got cold feet, sent her a note on the lines of 'carpe diem'. She excused herself by saying that the Foreign Office had warned her about a stalker on the loose in the States, and that at the time there would be too many senior royals out of Britain; adding for good measure, and bizarrely, that she had to deal with her profound feelings of anger before she could see Robbins. The implication was that she was apprehensive of moving on with her life, or, perhaps more accurately, did not want to take the road suggested by Colthurst. Following a tart forty-five-minute phone conversation, the old friends agreed to differ and a period of coolness, familiar to many of those who were close to the Princess, ensued.

A year later, however, Diana was doing what Colthurst and others, including David Puttnam and Patrick Jephson, had long counselled, charting her own course but on her own terms and in her own time. That she came to these decisions herself was a reflection of her growing sense of independence and authority, as well as her maturing self-belief.

For the coming year – 1995 – she had taken on more than 120 domestic engagements and embarked on no fewer than ten overseas visits, from Hong Kong and Japan to Argentina, Italy and, of course, America. They all followed the model that Diana, in her self-made role of independent ambassador for good works and causes, had worked hard to sustain, and each was a triumph of glamour meshed with compassion. Even Patrick Jephson was moved to describe her fund-raising trip to Hong Kong in April 1995 as 'the model of how her working life might have evolved'. On this occasion the Princess combined high-profile charity visits and a high-octane dinner with a woman whom she had always admired, the former Prime Minister Margaret Thatcher, who also happened to be visiting Hong Kong. Diana's performance during these trips was faultless and her appeal universal, proving time and again that she was not a loose cannon, much as the forces ranged against her at Buckingham Palace and the Foreign Office would have liked to believe. She was no Duchess of York or, for that matter, Duke of Edinburgh, prone to accidents and gaffes, and the thick file of congratulatory telegrams from British Ambassadors and Foreign Office officials underlined her international status.

At a gala dinner for the United Cerebral Palsy Foundation in New York in December 1995, she was hailed as a 'luminous personality' by no less a personage than the veteran diplomat Henry Kissinger. Presenting her with an award for her humanitarian work, he declared, 'She is here as a member of the royal family, but we are honouring the Princess in her own right who aligned herself with the ill, the suffering and the downtrodden.'

During her acceptance speech, in which she spoke of the need for 'kindness of heart, bearing and sharing the grief of others', the Princess even dealt deftly with a woman heckler who asked, somewhat incongruously, 'Where are your children?' Diana's calm reply – 'In bed' – earned her a standing ovation.

This year saw her coming of age on the international circuit. Now confident, self-assured and sophisticated, the girl who had once figuratively hid behind her husband on tours deliberately chose a pair of high heels for a visit to the Imperial Palace in Tokyo in February 1995, so that she would tower over the diminutive Emperor. 'Her four-day tour [of Japan] shows every sign of turning into a major step on the road to rehabilitation for the Princess's public image,' noted the London *Evening Standard*, an observation matched by what Jephson called the 'eulogistic terms' used by the British Ambassador to describe the visit when he reported back to the Foreign Office.

Perhaps the high-water mark of Diana's overseas work that year came in November during a visit to Argentina, a country where relations were still being mended following the 1982 Falklands conflict. It was a mission that perfectly encapsulated her thinking. While she had no interest in party politics, she saw the need to keep communications open between countries at loggerheads if only to facilitate humanitarian aid.

As Diana was regularly at odds with her own family, had little to do with other residents of the Kensington Palace compound and seemed to be entrenched in a duel to the death with her estranged husband, her aspirations to be a goodwill ambassador appeared to many to be both naive and disingenuous. But the Argentinian President, Carlos Menem did not see it this way. He expressed the utmost delight at her trip. 'Princess Diana managed to make her way to the heart of my people,' he declared as he hailed her visit as 'exceptional, absolutely positive'.

'I did my best,' she said modestly, knowing quite well that acquiring the approval of the Palace and Whitehall for that visit, and indeed other overseas trips, had involved much behind-the-scenes work to convince doubtful courtiers and suspicious diplomats of her worth. She had lobbied skilfully to achieve her position, not only maintaining diplomatic links with the Queen but also wooing and wowing politicians, senior media figures and high-ranking civil servants with an overwhelming combination of charm and flattery. As she had on so many occasions, Diana showed that she was shrewder than she looked.

On the home front, her friend David Puttnam joined her for a meeting with Sir Hayden Phillips, who in 1995 was permanent secretary at the Department for Culture, Media and Sport, where they spent several hours discussing ways and means of using her position more productively in Britain.

It was in Diana's role as a humanitarian ambassador, as she instinctively realized, that her true value and appeal lay. In the first months following her separation she joined with the then Overseas Development Minister, Baroness Chalker ('I look upon her as my favourite niece,' the minister said), on a visit to Nepal in February 1993 and made it her business to get to know her, staying on friendly terms throughout the term of that government. Besides seeing Chalker, the Princess met with the Prime Minister at least once a year and maintained amicable contact with the then Foreign Secretary Douglas Hurd, who described her as an 'invaluable national asset'. As he recalled in his memoirs: 'She looked to me for support in just one matter important to her: namely, her overseas work. I was glad, or more accurately, enchanted, to give it.'

Hurd made it clear, however, that given her uncertain position inside the royal family, she could not officially represent the nation even though when she visited a foreign country, ostensibly on charity work, the Head of State would invariably request a meeting. 'As far as I was concerned there was never any question of her having a formal appointment as a roving ambassador,' he wrote.

While Diana realized that there were formal limits to her ambition under the then Conservative Government, she discovered a greater rapport with the Leader of the Opposition, Tony Blair, now Prime Minister. As with so much in her life, she established this important political contact by chance. Maggie Rea, a member of her divorce legal team, is a friend of the Blairs and effected an introduction, which led to the Princess and the politician enjoying several unpublicized meetings at the homes of mutual friends from late 1994 and during the two years before the Labour Party's election victory of 1997. Blair immediately saw the potential in the Princess. 'Tony was very aware that she had this ability to make a direct connection with people by touching,' according to an aide. 'They talked very frankly, there was a real empathy. She was very indiscreet about the royal family and hilarious about Fergie.' Tony Blair was one of the first political heavyweights to recognize that Diana's humanitarian ambitions were informed as much by her sense of spiritual mission as by her public duty.

During one of their first meetings, Diana spent most of the evening talking about Alastair Campbell, then Blair's media spin doctor, who was waiting in a car outside. 'I've got somebody who wants to meet you,' he told Campbell as they were leaving. She was so impressed by the way Campbell was managing the Labour Party's image that she lightheartedly offered him the job of controlling the media for her.

As with the world of Westminster, she had tried to tame the big beasts in the media jungle herself, but had been badly mauled. She had hosted numerous lunches for editors and senior journalists, wooing both those who supported her and those who seemed never to have a good word to say about her. Most satisfying were those encounters where she managed to bring her 'enemies' to heel. Prickly characters like the columnist Paul Johnson and the humorist Auberon Waugh went away singing her praises, their innate scepticism set aside once they saw that she did not take herself too seriously, yet was serious about her purpose and position. At one lunch with the senior editorial staff at the *Sunday Times*, she was quietly amused to find herself intimidating a table full of bright men who behaved for the most part like tongue-tied teenagers. 'She held the ring in a way inconceivable just a few years before,' Geordie Greig, now editor of *Tatler* magazine, recollected. The Princess even spoke at a *Literary Review* lunch, organized by Waugh, where she told her delighted audience that she had written a limerick in honour of the occasion, in between, she said wryly, 'therapy sessions and secret trysts'.

Of course there is no such thing as a free lunch, and, at the lunches she gave at Kensington Palace, the Princess was pursuing her own agenda, frankly discussing her position and her problems with her influential guests. As Stephen Twigg observed, 'She was trying to create a real relationship with the public by using the media. She knew that the only power against the most powerful family in the land was the balancing power of the public.'

Andrew Neil, formerly the editor of the *Sunday Times*, who supported the publication of *Diana: Her True Story*, which he serialized in his paper, remembered a poised and confident young woman: 'She was talking about the future of the royal family and she was making sense.' By 1995 her attitude to her estranged husband, his family and his mistress was more nuanced than the media caricature of mutual antagonism. When she returned home from her skiing trip in January 1995 to find that Andrew and Camilla Parker Bowles had announced their divorce, her reaction surprised Stuart Higgins, editor of the *Sun*. 'I feel sorry for Camilla,' she said. 'The woman has lost almost everything in life and gained . . . what, exactly?'

She was now less overtly confrontational with her husband as film maker David Puttnam discovered when he organized a lunch at Claridge's Hotel for the Princess to meet media big hitters like Alan Yentob, then Controller of BBC One, and Michael Grade, at the time chief executive at Channel Four Television. They were enthusiastic about funding and promoting a Princess of Wales Foundation – a proposal I myself, Stephen Twigg and others had put forward in previous years – but, much as she liked the idea, she did not want to cause yet more conflict with her husband.

Throughout 1995 she could afford to be magnanimous. Her husband's attempt to celebrate the twenty-fifth anniversary of his investiture as the Prince of Wales the previous year had been an unmitigated public relations disaster. The two-and-a-half-hour ITV documentary was, as mentioned in the last chapter, only remembered for Charles's fleeting confession of adultery while Dimbleby's weighty biography of the Prince, published in November 1994, painted a picture of a man who had never loved Diana and was forced into marriage by a bullying father. Not only did this portrait upset and offend the Queen and Prince Philip, but numerous courtiers in the senior household at Buckingham Palace, along with senior government figures, including the Prime Minister, John Major, and Douglas Hurd, now felt more kindly disposed towards the Princess of Wales than they had ever been.

All of that year Diana occupied the moral high ground, not just in public popularity but in the skirmishes surrounding her and Charles's inevitable divorce. This fully justified the 'wait and see' policy advocated by her divorce lawyer, Lord Mishcon, a view which accorded entirely with her sentiments that, as Charles had been in love with another throughout their marriage, then it was up to him to ask for a divorce. 'She has always operated on the basis that it is not going to be her that causes the crisis because she feels that it would reflect badly on her,' noted James Gilbey. 'She has a pathological fear of being blamed.' On numerous occasions, in conversations with politicians, editors and others, the Princess stressed, rather disingenuously given her secret cooperation with my book and her own extra-marital affairs, that she had not wanted the original separation. She was at pains to point out that she had no plans or appetite for a divorce, not only for her own sake but for that of the children and the nation at large. Close friends like Lucia Flecha de Lima constantly reinforced her instincts. 'I told her they could lead separate lives but remain married. It was not like an ordinary marriage – she didn't have to ask him for money, or press his shirts or cook for him,' Lucia Flecha de Lima told the *Daily Mail* in November 2003.

For her pains, Diana was widely described as 'manipulative', a word she hated. The epithet stuck when she was photographed furtively getting into the car of the *Daily Mail* journalist Richard Kay, whom she regularly briefed so that he could write sympathetic stories. This meeting, in the summer of 1994, at the time when the nuisance phone calls to Oliver Hoare were being splashed all over the newspapers, served to undo all the quiet work she had undertaken behind the scenes.

While the Princess prided herself on being media savvy, she never really understood that she could never be the puppeteer when the mass media considered that they were the ones who pulled her strings. 'Was she Machiavellian?' asked Stephen Twigg, who went on to answer his own question. 'No. She wasn't that skilful at media manipulation. She was regularly desperately unhappy about how she was portrayed in the press. I remember when she came in to see me in floods of tears and complained: "Why can't they understand that all I want to do is love everybody." Now that seems a crass statement, but in terms of who and what she was, that's all she really wanted to do.'

Far from the sophisticated schemer of popular mythology, Diana frequently revealed herself to be rather unworldly and innocent in her dealings with the rest of humanity. Somewhat naively she believed, for instance, that she could have had a role as a peacemaker in Northern Ireland, as a frequent visitor of the victims of the sectarian bombing campaign over the years. As her friend Vivienne Parry, who helped her regularly with her charity work, remarked, 'If she had been a Miss World contestant, I am sure she would have said: "I want world peace, I want to end suffering."'

During 1994 and 1995 the Princess often left Kensington Palace and went to local haunts of the homeless, handing out money, food and advice; according to her butler, she even made it her business to try and help local prostitutes. She gave one woman, who had two children to bring up, money to buy herself a winter coat. On another occasion she threw her fur coat into a skip hoping that a tramp would find it. She was endlessly intrigued to see how the other half lived. In the autumn of 1995, for example, she spent an evening around the seedy King's Cross area of London in the company of a plain-clothes detective, watching drugs deals, albeit from a safe distance. 'I feel close to people, whoever they are. That's why I upset certain circles,' she told Annick Cojean in an interview, her last ever, for *Le Monde* in August 1997. 'It's because I'm much closer to the people at the bottom than the people at the top and the latter won't forgive me for it.'

This otherworldly quality, Diana's profound sense of spiritual mission, often dismissed as an interest in New Age mysticism, became more apparent as she explored the religious spectrum in the months and years following her separation. There was speculation that, like her mother, Frances Shand Kydd, Diana might convert to Roman Catholicism. While she enjoyed the bells and smells of High Church, numbered many Catholics among her closest friends, and had discussed the faith with her friend Rosa Monckton's priest Father Anthony Sutch, in truth she was eager to explore and discuss all creeds and spiritual ideas – with anyone at any time. So she sat cross-legged on the floor with Jimmy Choo, a shoe designer, and discussed his belief in Buddhism; spoke about God and the Devil with her local Kensington parish priest, Father Frank Gelli, over a cup of tea; and about the works of the New Age thinker, Deepak Chopra, whose writings she admired, when she visited another of her friends, the actor Terence Stamp, for a homemade macrobiotic lunch.

'She was very much into Eastern philosophy,' recalls the Californian lawyer Richard Greene, who gave the Princess voice coaching during the mid 1990s. 'She believed in reincarnation and felt that this was her last lifetime, that whatever mission she had, she was going to take care of it during this lifetime. She was on a spiritual mission.'

The Princess, who believed that in a previous lifetime she had been a nun, was thrilled to discover that she shared her spiritual journey with a Spencer ancestor. In the mid-1990s her friend and acupuncturist Oonagh Shanley-Toffolo gave her a pamphlet about her great-great-great-uncle, Father Ignatius Spencer, who is currently being considered for canonization because of his work during the Victorian era to try to unify the Catholic and Protestant churches, not to mention his selfless hard work among the poor and needy. He was ahead of his time. Cast out from his own family for converting to Rome and ridiculed by high society, Father Ignatius was viewed as either a prophetic rebel or a naive misfit as he tried vainly to create a movement for universal Christian unity. His treatment by his family and society together with his work for the sick and the poor, as well as his attempts to cut across religious boundaries, struck a deep chord with the Princess. 'She felt sympathy for him,' said Oonagh. 'She felt a sense of destiny that she was part of a similar line of people. It was the deep soul quality she admired. In his journey she saw something of herself.'

It was a journey Diana had begun as a young girl, feeling that she was different from others. She always felt 'very detached', once telling her father that she believed that one day she would have an ambassadorial role. At that time she thought she would be the wife of a diplomat. It would take her many years, though, before she began to realize and release her spiritual promise, restricted as she was by life inside the royal system. It was clear early on in her royal career that, while she conformed impeccably at formal events, she found them constraining and frustrating. 'From the first day I joined that family, nothing could be done naturally any more,' she told *Le Monde* in August 1997. Gradually, she began to shed the flummery and protocol, adopting a more hands-on approach, often literally. A decade earlier, when she shook the hands of an AIDS patient at Middlesex Hospital, Diana began to understand her potency as an international icon. More personally, it proved to her that this path of compassion and caring reflected her inner spirit, a feeling reinforced when she helped nurse her friend Adrian Ward-Jackson, who died of AIDS in 1991. 'I reached a depth inside which I never imagined possible,' she wrote to Angela Serota afterwards. 'My outlook on life has changed its course and become more positive and balanced.'

This gave the Princess the strength to undertake her work for the sick and needy outside her circle; consoling strangers during secret visits to hospices, holding and comforting the dying, gave her a sense of fulfilment. It was an exchange. In her world of doubt, deception and suspicion, where she trusted no one, she found complete integrity and honesty from those about to die. It was sustaining and nourishing. Diana herself said to James Colthurst, 'I love going round places like Stoke Mandeville Hospital. I'm not so gripped by those getting better. It's the ones on the way out that I feel a deep need to be with.' Little wonder that she completely agreed with a friend's comment that, in other circumstances, she could have been a nurse. 'I can't wait to get into it, it's like a hunger,' she told her astrologer Felix Lyle in 1991. 'I've opened up – this is an extraordinary path of transformation. This is only the beginning.'

Her intense feeling that she was on a spiritual journey was further confirmed in 1991 when her masseur Stephen Twigg gave her the book, *Please Understand Me* by David Keirsey. It contained the well-established Myers–Briggs psychology test, which gives an indication of personality types based on temperament. According to the formula there are four basic temperaments: guardian, artisan, rationalist and idealist. There are four sub-sections to each temperament type, so that, for example, the idealist temperament is divided into four other categories: teacher, healer, champion and counsellor. After answering seventy multiple-choice questions, Diana was defined as having an 'INFP' temperament, that is to say she was introverted and intuitive, a woman governed by feelings and perception.

Her temperament type, which applies only to one per cent of the population, showed her to be a healer with a capacity for caring not usually found in others. As Stephen Twigg read out the description of the INFP personality type, Diana mentally ticked off many of these qualities as those which she either exhibited or wanted to develop. She was astonished and amazed by its accuracy. 'This is me, this is me!' she said. Keirsey's analysis reads:

> Healers care deeply and passionately about a few special persons or favourite cause, and their fervent aim is to bring peace to the world and wholeness to themselves and their loved ones. They base their self-image on being seen as empathic, benevolent, and authentic. Often enthusiastic, they trust intuition, yearn for romance, seek identity, prize recognition and aspire to the wisdom of the sage.

The popular pseudo-scientific test, based on the theories of Carl Jung, reinforced her own instincts and belief that she had a healing mission in life. It was a significant building block in that it gave her further confidence to reach out, while in the process blurring the border between private emotion and public duty.

The Princess's first ever solo foreign visit – to Pakistan in October 1991 – gave fuller expression to her developing public and private persona. She was nervous before she went – a friend remembered giving her a Bach Flower Remedy to soothe her – but she had the encouraging words of Felix Lyle ringing in her ears: 'You need to see the world as your family. You want to go out and make the world a better place.' That visit had a profound effect on her, as she told James Colthurst. 'What is so ironic is that when I was supposed to go [the visit had been originally scheduled for 1990], mentally I could have done it but I would have skimmed through it.' During the trip she met children made homeless by regional conflicts and first became aware of the scourge of landmines, visiting the prosthetic centre in Peshawar, on the turbulent Afghan-Pakistan border, which had been set up by the former TV newsreader and war correspondent Sandy Gall.

A year later, Diana was further inspired following a visit to the hospices in Calcutta in India, run by Mother Teresa and her dedicated band of nuns. Her visit to the hospice where hundreds of desperately sick people spent their last hours had 'the greatest impact' as she realized that it was 'probably the first time in their lives that someone has cared for them'. In a letter to Oonagh Shanley-Toffolo, Diana wrote, 'The emotions running through the Hospice were very strong and the effect it had on me was how much I wanted and longed to be part of all this on a global scale.' She planned to take William and Harry to Calcutta to see Mother Teresa's work so that they could witness at first hand the grinding yoke of poverty that so many laboured under. From 1995 onwards she spoke with increasing frequency about setting up a network of hospices around the globe. 'Diana really wanted to change the world,' observed Oonagh. 'She felt very destined.'

It was perhaps inevitable that during her spiritual journey, her work with the sick and the dying and her vision of her humanitarian mission, Diana should be attracted to a man working in the caring professions. In early September 1995 the Princess received an urgent call from Oonagh, whose husband Joe had suffered a relapse following a heart operation. Her distressed friend asked Diana if she could visit Joseph at the Brompton Hospital where he was in intensive care. The following morning Diana entered Room 125, followed just five minutes later by Joseph's doctor and the surgeon, Hasnat Khan, with his team. They were concerned about his condition and asked for his wife's permission to operate once more. As Mr Khan (British surgeons are addressed as 'Mister' rather than 'Doctor') was discussing Joe's medical problems with Oonagh, she introduced him to Diana, who was standing quietly in the background. Not really recognizing who she was, he gave her the cursory nod of a man who had been up all night and had little time for social niceties.

Then, still with Joseph's blood on his medical boots, Khan left the room, leaving one heart beating much faster. Diana was smitten. 'He's drop-dead gorgeous,' were her first words. 'I would say it was love at first sight,' Oonagh said. 'She was so overwhelmed it can only have been a soul encounter.'

It seemed that Diana, seeing herself as an outsider and a healer, devoting her life to helping and comforting others, had found in

Khan a reflection of her own ideals and beliefs. Here was a man, from an ethnic minority – he was born in Pakistan – who dedicated his skills to saving lives. 'It was the first time in her life that she actually admired the man she was involved with for the work that he did,' Debbie Frank pointed out. 'He cared so much for other people – and that resonated very deeply with her.'

It was a relationship that began in disguise – the Princess visiting Joseph Toffolo more often than necessary in order to see Khan – and continued in great secrecy. Diana would combine her visits to patients at the hospital in the autumn of 1995 with assignations with the new man in her life. She visited the hospital casually dressed in jeans and a baseball cap, and sat with critically ill patients, some of whom were just coming round from surgery. Eventually the Princess's cover was blown, when she was photographed one night in November 1995 by paparazzi who were acting on a tip-off. To pre-empt the inevitable press stories, Diana took matters into her own hands, borrowing a mobile phone from one of the photographers. 'There are hundreds of patients who are there without their own loved ones and they need a human presence. I really love helping, I seem to draw strength from them,' she told an astonished Clive Goodman, at that time the *News of the World*'s royal correspondent, after the photographers who snatched her picture had identified themselves as working for that particular Sunday newspaper.

With this clever move, which made a virtue of her visits to the hospital while disguising her ulterior motive, Diana managed to put the media off the scent – at least for a while – and for the most part her two-year affair with Hasnat Khan was conducted in conditions of complete concealment, to the extent that Diana took to wearing some form of disguise whenever they ventured out together.

She would use a staff car and take circuitous routes to meet her new lover, often disguised in a wig designed by her hairdresser, Sam McKnight; sometimes she would wear sunglasses or glasses with plain lenses. The woman who had been entertained in the White House and the Palace of Versailles now dined with her boyfriend in an anonymous fish-and-chip shop near his flat in

Chelsea or, more frequently, at Kensington Palace. In the autumn of 1995, with the fallout from her relationship with England rugby captain Will Carling still reverberating, secrecy was essential not only to protect their privacy but also so that their friendship would not affect her delicate marital status. On one occasion, Diana climbed out of a ground-floor window when she was visiting Khan at Harefield Hospital, to the west of London, to avoid being seen. When he secretly visited her at Kensington Palace, Diana's butler was entrusted with the task of smuggling him into her apartment.

As with her other relationships, Diana threw herself into his life and interests. Certainly, as with her other romances, she made a particular point of being friendly with his family. Within the first few months of their romance she and Hasnat Khan had had dinner with his uncle Omar and his British wife Jane at their home in Stratford-upon-Avon. When she visited Pakistan, she made a point of going to see his parents.

Just as she had followed the activities and interests of James Hewitt, Oliver Hoare and Will Carling, the Princess now turned her attention to human anatomy, in particular the heart, so that she would more clearly understand Khan's work. For a woman who religiously watched the hospital soap *Casualty* every Saturday night and spent her life visiting hospital patients, her study of *Gray's Anatomy* was no real hardship – she passed an impromptu 'exam' conducted by a friend after just a few days' study. The workings of her own heart were rather more complex and contradictory.

At Kensington Palace the sound of choral music was replaced by the husky voices of Ella Fitzgerald and Louis Armstrong as Diana got to grips with Khan's love of jazz, even accompanying him, in disguise, to Ronnie Scott's jazz club in Soho, where she had the vicarious thrill of standing in line without being recognized. While she had already taken an interest in Eastern culture and religion, works on the Koran joined the small mountain of books in what she called her 'knowledge corner' in her sitting room, while her wardrobe was augmented by more than half a dozen bright silk shalwar kameez, the tunic and trouser ensembles worn by Muslim women. While he was serious about his own caring mission, Hasnat Khan was in many respects an incongruous suitor, being overweight, a heavy smoker and a beer drinker, with only a surgeon's salary to sustain him. For a woman who had passed muster as the bride of the future king because she was white, aristocratic and Protestant, the fact that she was seriously dating a Muslim whose family lived in Pakistan was a further sign of how far this young woman, who saw herself as a rebel, had travelled on her personal journey. 'It was a sign of her devotion,' noted Debbie Frank. 'The lenience of a woman in love.'

Diana's love affairs in the past had been about testing her own boundaries, enjoying the thrill and pain of romance without making the ultimate commitment; now she talked about crossing religious and racial borders by making a life with her Pakistani lover. The marriage of her friend Jemima Goldsmith, the beautiful daughter of Sir James and Lady Annabel Goldsmith, to the former Pakistani cricket captain and aspiring politician, Imran Khan, gave Diana a romantic signpost and the hope that one day she could follow a similar path. What particularly impressed Imran Khan about Diana was that she appeared quite unaffected by religion, nationality or colour: 'She seemed to be above all that. It was this combination of ingredients that made her such a great figure.'

Thus, by the autumn of 1995 her life, if not perfect, had its share of excitements and a sense of opportunity and chance of fulfilment that had eluded her for much of her adult life. For so long confused, isolated and directionless, Diana's life was beginning to make sense. Such was her popularity that she was edging towards her ambition of being made a roving ambassador, whatever the Palace or politicians may have wanted. Over and over again she had proved that her credentials were impeccable, however many obstacles were placed in her way. More than that, she was earning a grudging respect even among her enemies – a recognition that she had the courage, chutzpah and charisma to take on a significant and substantial role in national affairs. While she strode on towards the sunlit uplands, her husband was lost in the mists, seen as self-indulgent, introspective and lacking in judgement. Not only was she exploring and testing her personal limits, whether spiritual or political, but, by the autumn of 1995, she believed that she had found the true love of her life.

Within a few short months her reputation would be savaged and her position as royal Princess become perilous. The Queen's patience with her errant daughter-in-law would be exhausted, prompting her to write formally to Diana advocating divorce. At the same time, any remaining sympathy felt by courtiers was to evaporate, while government ministers would shake their heads in dismay at what was seen as a wilful act of self-destruction. What provoked this hostile response was her hour-long interview on the BBC's current-affairs programme, *Panorama*, in November 1995. The show, watched by half the British population, was both her soap box and her snare, the Princess left swinging in the wind by an unforgiving royal family, infuriated by her airing of yet more dirty linen in public, and an indignant Establishment who felt she had betrayed their faith in her.

Both her supporters and her critics scratched their heads in bewilderment. For the last year the Princess had conquered all before her, her standing with the public and the powers-that-be never higher. She was focused and in charge. Her timing could not have been worse. So why did she put the noose round her neck?

CHAPTER SEVEN

'They Want To Kill Me'

DIANA'S APARTMENT at Kensington Palace, with cream church candles burning in the windows and the smell of incense wafting through the sitting room, seduced her guests with its monastic calm. It was a quiet disturbed only by the sound of choral music or the soaring film scores of Vangelis, the composer of the *Chariots of Fire* theme music, played at high volume – sometimes to the annoyance of her neighbours. 'The music police are after you,' her immediate neighbour Dave Griffin would call out to Diana if he spotted her at her first-floor window. 'You've been murdering a tune for the last half-hour.'

On the surface, it seemed that at last life inside the combined apartments 8 and 9 was in harmony, enjoying a rhythm and routine that was much more peaceful than the discord of the Princess's married life. But behind that smoothly orchestrated royal existence lay a world of conspiracy and treachery. For much of her adult life, Diana lived in an environment of unease and apprehension, distrust and suspicion virtually incomprehensible to outsiders. At her door, no fantasy, no plot, no conspiracy, however absurd, was ever turned away and rarely a day went by without some alarm or plot to trouble her.

Diana was continually being buffeted by events, either real or imagined. A typical day might start with an urgent phone call from the Duchess of York passing on a doom-laden warning from one of her 'spooks' – the battery of mystics and soothsayers she consulted; or perhaps a rumour about an impending hostile story in the newspapers would make its way to the Princess's ears. Unsurprisingly, therefore, the Princess would begin her day on edge, anxious and apprehensive about what the hours to follow might have in store for her.

Then, if Prince Charles's private secretary Richard Aylard were to call unexpectedly to arrange a meeting she would be thrown into a state of agitation, wondering and worrying about a possible ambush 'the enemy' might be preparing for her, fearing it would be some proposal regarding the vexed subject of divorce. In the end it would, more often than not, concern some mundane administrative matter. This state of constant agitation was reinforced by her personality. Vulnerable, impressionable and unworldly, the Princess, who, as her astrologer Penny Thornton observed, loved intrigue and the excitement of cloak-and-dagger, was naturally predisposed to credulity. For Diana, her life was a melodrama in which she was a problem; first to her parents for being born a girl; then to her husband for getting in the way of his surrogate marriage; and later as an outsider challenging the Establishment. While her personality encouraged her sense of victimhood and her feeling that she was a martyr to dark forces ranged against her, this tendency in her was exploited by those who called themselves friends. For it was not only the 'men in grey suits' inside the Palace, or Prince Charles's circle of friends, who were working against her. They at least were easy to identify. But, the Princess eventually realized, even her closest friends, staff and advisers wanted her to remain weak and dependent so that they could be strong for her. In her uncertainty and insecurity lay their power.

She knew too that behind the ever-obliging veneer of life at Kensington Palace, every fragment of her existence was picked over, discussed or salvaged. In the early 1990s she bought herself a shredder because she suspected that the cleaning staff were picking through her discarded mail; she also had strong suspicions that members of staff were showing their friends and acquaintances around her apartment – for a fee. (These misgivings were well-founded – it later emerged in a Sunday newspaper that at least one member of staff was conducting private tours. 'For £200 you could get a guided trip around Diana's bedroom,' another member of staff told the *News of the World* in December 2002.) She also had concerns about Prince Charles's court, fearing that those close to the Prince were using him for their own ends.

Indeed, when the Duchess of York first joined the royal family the Princess suspected that her friend had been rummaging through her mail and then reporting her findings back to the Prince of Wales in order to curry favour. Diana passed on these concerns to her astrologer, Penny Thornton, who commented, 'Diana told me that Sarah had been doing things behind her back.' What is not in doubt is that the Princess trusted no one inside the royal world, for years keeping the famous letters from Prince Philip in a safe at the Brazilian Embassy. 'All sorts of people could come and go in her apartment,' as Lucia Flecha de Lima explained.

It is easy to understand Diana's caution. When she entered Buckingham Palace as a teenager she discovered that nothing in the Alice-in-Wonderland world of the royal family was as it seemed. From the early 1980s until Prince Charles publicly confessed his adultery in 1994, she had been at the centre of a web of deceit, organized and coordinated to cover up the Prince's relationship with Camilla Parker Bowles. As outlined in earlier chapters, everyone – bodyguards, butlers, courtiers, members of the royal family and friends, Diana's own grandmother, Lady Fermoy – was either actively or passively involved. Any questions she asked about her husband's relationship were dismissed as the ravings of a woman suffering from jealousy, depression or worse. 'Diana's unstable and Diana's mentally unbalanced,' she said of people's attitudes towards her within the Establishment. 'And unfortunately that seems to have stuck on and off over the years.'

What truly rankled with and upset Diana was that, while Prince Charles was protected by a discreet network of friends and safe houses to conduct his liaison in the time-honoured royal fashion, her own attempts to find happiness were doomed to exposure, embarrassment and heartbreak. During the 1980s not only was there a concerted plot to shield Prince Charles – but, or so it appeared to Diana, there existed a conspiracy to shackle her and condemn those who came too close to her.

She saw this the first time she enjoyed some kind of a relationship once it seemed to her that her marriage had broken down, shortly after the birth of Prince Harry in September 1984. Her instincts told her that Charles had, in her words, 'gone back to his lady', and not long after that she became close to Sergeant Barry Mannakee, who had joined her protection team in the late spring of 1985. He was a charming man with a roguish manner and jaunty sense of humour, and Diana immediately warmed to him, at first enjoying his joshing compliments about her appearance and later confiding in him. The father of two became a shoulder to cry on and a dispenser of worldly advice. She even consulted her astrologer Penny Thornton and asked her about his star sign – he was a Gemini – and whether it was compatible with her Cancerian sign. 'He really made her zing,' Penny recalled. Diana herself told James Colthurst: 'He meant an awful lot to me. He was my father figure, everything. He just looked after me.' Years later she went further, apparently confiding to the writer Anthony Holden that he was 'the love of my life'. There was a degree of romantic hyperbole about her statement; throughout her adult life she was rarely without a man who was 'the one' for her. At the time though their closeness did not go unnoticed by senior officers, and after barely a year, in July 1986, Mannakee was transferred to other duties, much to Diana's dismay. 'I was wearing my heart on my sleeve and everyone was talking about us and giving him a very hard time,' Diana said to Colthurst.

In a way the transfer came as something of a relief for Sergeant Mannakee who found her intense neediness difficult to handle. As a friend of his told me, 'He was a frightened man, not for his life but his job. He was only a temporary inspector and he was concerned that the "affair" would have implications for his job.'

Tragically, Mannakee died in a motorbike accident in May 1987, less than a year after being transferred. When Diana heard the news – while she and Prince Charles were travelling to the Cannes Film Festival – she was distraught. The Princess had been so fond of him that on the anniversary of his death she made a point of visiting the crematorium in Redbridge, where his ashes are scattered, hiding her face in a headscarf to avoid being recognized. Later, she used a clairvoyant to try to contact Mannakee in the spirit world. For a long time she believed that he had been assassinated by the secret services because of his proximity to her. Indeed, when I started work on Diana's biography in 1991, an early request from her was to find out more about the true cause of his death. As luck would have it, an acquaintance of mine, then a newspaper crime correspondent, had been on his way home to Loughton, Essex, and arrived at the scene of the accident moments after it had occurred. He was able to confirm that it was nothing more sinister than a tragic accident involving a novice car driver and a motorcycle, on which Mannakee had been the passenger.

Diana, though, was never truly convinced, for she breathed the air of a world suffused with plots, rumour and hearsay, a bewildering reality where, as nothing was as it seemed, then anything could be believed.

Following the occasion in late 1991 when my office was broken into, Diana, James Colthurst and I bought scrambler telephones – which, to be honest, rarely worked effectively – while the Princess brought in a surveillance company, recommended by Colthurst, to check her sitting room for bugging devices. This was the first of many occasions where she had the apartment at Kensington Palace 'swept' for listening devices, while she herself several times pulled back the carpet in her search for evidence. While nothing was ever found, the possible presence of surveillance equipment became a standing joke, the Princess peppering her conversation with light-hearted references to MI5 and MI6. On the telephone, whenever she heard any clicking on the line she would say, 'Hello, boys . . . time to change the tape.'

The Princess had been proved right about her husband's relationship with Camilla Parker Bowles, and the conspiracy to hide it from her, so perhaps she was correct in thinking that her telephones were or had been tapped. When, in June 1992, Prince Philip confronted her at Windsor Castle and told her, in the presence of the Queen and the Prince, that they had a tape recording of her telephone conversation with an unnamed man discussing the serialization of *Diana: Her True Story*, the logical conclusion was that her telephones were indeed routinely monitored and the contents of her conversations held on file.

It could perhaps have been an elaborate bluff, but it was possible that it indicated rather too much knowledge about the book for that. A few weeks later, in August, contents of the now notorious Squidgygate tapes, of Diana's late-night conversations with James Gilbey, illicitly recorded three years earlier, were published by the *Sun* newspaper. While the then MI5 boss, Stella Rimington, always officially denied any involvement with the telephone tapings, the fact that Camillagate – another late-night chat, this one between Charles and Camilla – and also a covertly recorded conversation between the Duke and Duchess of York, were published within the space of a year seems, even to the most credulous commentators, to be carrying coincidence too far. The only consolation for Diana was that the Camillagate conversation was proof to all and sundry that her suspicions about her husband were not the imaginings of a deranged woman.

Once the Prince and Princess separated in December 1992 matters took on a more sinister hue. Diana was alone, and acutely aware of the forces ranged against her. They may not have wished her harm, but they certainly did not support her in all that she wished for herself. Now, as though on cue, she began to hear all kinds of conjecture, from the apparently informed to the obviously spurious, that her life could be in danger.

In early 1993 Stephen Twigg heard from several of his well-connected clients that stories were circulating around their friends' drawing rooms that the Princess might be the focus of unwelcome attention from Britain's shadowy security services. 'It was quite possible that someone, somewhere, might, in the atmosphere of animosity and anger that prevailed at the time, try to do something as stupid as to make an attempt on Diana's life,' Twigg commented years later. 'It seemed that others felt as I did.'

He was sufficiently alarmed to tell Diana about these rumours during a massage session at Kensington Palace, and suggested that if she had any evidence that might be embarrassing to her enemies she should place it in the hands of someone she trusted, as insurance. Moreover she should let her enemies know what she had done. It appears she took his advice to heart, giving various letters to friends for safekeeping. 'In the climate at the time the idea she might be killed was not very fantastic and that remained the case, with various degrees of credibility, for the rest of her life,' Stephen Twigg said to me years later. 'She was aware of it. Her subsequent determination and drive to become the woman she wanted to be were all the more remarkable.'

Assailed on a daily, sometimes hourly, basis by all kinds of lurid stories, some true, most speculation, the Princess could do no more than check their veracity as and when she was able, however bizarre they seemed. Thus, after dinner one evening in 1993, she asked a nonplussed Max Hastings, then the editor of the *Daily Telegraph*, if he knew about a scheme funded by his acquaintance, the Canadian gold tycoon Peter Munk of Barrick Mining, to hire David Wynne-Morgan, the public relations expert, to 'get rid of me at any price'. This story, like so many, proved to be false.

While it became fashionable to dismiss Diana as paranoid or troubled, at the time she had perfectly legitimate grounds for concern. 'The remarkable thing is how sane she was,' Patrick Jephson maintained. 'Under the most extreme provocation, again and again I saw her keep her temper – and even raise a laugh – when lesser people would have thrown a royal tantrum, a habit she proudly refused to copy from her husband.'

If she was suspicious, then so were the majority of the British public. The belief that the security forces were guilty of taping the telephone calls was so widespread, that, in 1993, John Major, then Prime Minister, issued a statement declaring that the security services had no involvement in any interceptions of communications of members of the royal family. His assertion did little to stem the tide of speculation and rumour. A year later, in September 1994, the Labour Party demanded a parliamentary inquiry after a former Royal Marine claimed that he had led a surveillance operation which allegedly filmed the Princess and James Hewitt making love in the garden of the Devon home of Hewitt's mother. Former Colour-Sergeant Glyn Jones said that the operation, which took place in 1988, involved planting listening devices and cameras, which recorded the encounter. The Royal Marines – and Ken Wharfe, who said that the tiny garden made the alleged scenario a physical impossibility – dismissed Jones's claims as 'nonsense'. My own conversations with him make me severely doubt the plausibility of his evidence. None the less that did not stop the rumour mill working overtime, doubtless feeding Diana's anxieties at the time.

Over and over again, though, it was inexplicable events affecting not just the Princess but others as well, that caused her antennae to start twitching. While curious if isolated incidents made friends and staff pause before carrying on with their lives, the Princess, as the recipient of much of this disturbing intelligence, was able to see the bigger picture, an unnerving pattern of puzzling phone monitoring, covert surveillance and mysterious burglaries. Examples abound: a detective friend of James Gilbey found himself speaking to an MI5 officer, when, in an idle moment in 1993, he checked Gilbey's phone number against the police computer. The inference was that Gilbey's phone was already under surveillance. At Kensington Palace, most staff operated on the basis that all their phones were monitored, a belief reinforced one evening in the mid-1990s by the experience of a uniformed officer who was using the police box at the end of the Palace drive to call his loved one. After he had finished the call and put down the receiver, the phone immediately began ringing. When he picked it up he was to hear the conversation he had just finished playing back to him. It was an unsettling experience, and the officer was quick to warn staff in the Palace compound to be on their guard.

Burglary seemed to be an occupational hazard for friends and staff of the Princess. When her chef Mervyn Wycherley resigned in January 1995, his home in Shropshire was broken into within days of his departure from Kensington Palace. The offices of Fergie's divorce lawyers in London were burgled and files relating to her divorce tampered with, while the journalist Richard Kay, one of Diana's confidants, had two burglaries at his home, and suspected at least the second one to be the work of professional snoopers. He later employed a private detective when he found himself being followed on several occasions by the same car. James Hewitt, even after his affair with Diana had ended, complained to her bodyguard Ken Wharfe that he was being followed by strangers and, rather melodramatically, that he was afraid that, like Barry Mannakee, he was a target for elimination. (Even Wharfe, himself a police officer, was to wonder if he too might become a target. When he published his own memoir of the Princess, *Diana: Closely Guarded Secret*, in 2002, he was utterly convinced that on several occasions he was followed from his North London home by undercover police.)

It was hardly surprising then that the covert activities of the secret services were often mentioned by Diana in her conversations. Far from a symptom of paranoia they were simply a fact of her dislocated life. When I interviewed David Puttnam he recollected: 'It is absolutely true that on a number of occasions she spoke to me about being bugged, followed and that people were out to get her. She genuinely believed it. When someone chunters on about something a lot, you tend to dismiss it. It was far more paranoia than reality. Unquestionably though, her phones were tapped. That would get to her – and would get to me. She was probably being followed for her own good. So certain neuroses were being triggered by actuality.'

Puttnam was one of an ever-diminishing group of advisers, staff and friends surrounding the Princess. It was no coincidence that as her suspicions grew, her circle shrank, so that by 1995 she had pared down her staff to a handful of those she trusted, devising ever more convoluted tests to assess their loyalty to her. Perhaps the most bizarre was when she calmly informed Patrick Jephson that someone had taken a pot shot at her in broad daylight as she was driving through Hyde Park. The subtext was to see how seriously he would take her and how vigorously he would pursue the matter. Friends like Kate Menzies, Catherine Soames, Julia Samuel and others she had known since childhood fell by the wayside in favour of an eclectic, somewhat eccentric, collection of characters who danced attendance. 'She let false friends and fraudsters into her life,' observed Patrick Jephson, who argued that these dubious characters were filling the gap left by the absence of a husband or close family. That was not the whole picture, however. The Princess was also consulting, and captivating, worldly-wise, savvy and intellectual characters like Richard Attenborough, Douglas Hurd and Jacob Rothschild, as well as media figures like Clive James and David Puttnam. As Patrick Jephson noted, 'Some of the advice she sought and received was of the highest quality – wise, humane, patient, and delivered with a rare understanding of her isolated predicament.' All too often, though, their well-meaning advice was ignored, as the Princess relied more and more on her instincts, instincts which had proved accurate in the past, particularly with regard to her suspicions about Charles and Camilla. 'The frustration for me,' David Puttnam commented, 'was that she was so good at listening and taking advice from you, that the disappointment was all the greater when she clearly didn't. Personally I used to feel very let down.'

Inside Kensington Palace, her staff had also been gradually cut back so that by 1995 loyal retainers like the chef Mervyn Wycherley and before him the butler Harold Brown found themselves out in the cold. More and more, Diana's life revolved around one man, her butler Paul Burrell, on whose devotion and discretion she came to rely utterly. 'My role began to evolve in 1995 into personal assistant, messenger, driver, delivery boy, confidant,' he wrote in his memoir. 'I stepped in at times when she chose not to use her chauffeur, PR guru or private secretary because she didn't want professional eyes witnessing certain friendships, messages or private missions.'

Over the years he had gradually insinuated himself into her life so that by the mid-1990s he had become indispensable, their relationship unusually close and dependent. As Diana once told his friend, the lawyer Richard Greene, 'He's my everything. He knows who I am and what I want.' It was an association of mutual need. 'I couldn't imagine life without the Princess,' Burrell commented.

As Richard Greene observed, 'It's almost impossible to not develop some very powerful emotions when you are tucking somebody into bed every night. Paul was big brother, father, friend, and someone that she could safely flirt with because he knew how to keep the boundaries. When she wanted to feel like a woman and he was the only man around, he was there for her. She could be a little girl having a temper tantrum or be very strategic and focused.

Paul would accept her for who she was and support her in each one of those roles. He was a chameleon for her.'

Burrell is himself a complex character; sexually ambivalent (he has admitted to a gay past – but as his wife Maria told the press firmly, 'What's in the past is in the past'), and in some ways feminine, he was typical of many royal servants in that he became institutional-ized by the ritual and routine of royal life; but above all he craved the security of service. It was his profound need for security that impelled him to jump through any hoop, perform any service that Diana wanted, in order to remain in his post. Life with the Princess was uncertain – he saw all too many of the Princess's staff and friends fall out of favour with her, usually for some perceived disloy-alty, and either be dismissed from or leave her circle. Often though, Burrell was himself the architect of their departure, uncompromis-ing in guarding his terrain. Darren McGrady, a chef at Kensington Palace, reflected the views of several former Palace staff I spoke to when he declared, 'He [Burrell] was a shameless manipulator who would never hesitate to stab his colleagues secretly in the back if he thought he could sabotage their careers and further his own.'

Burrell himself had already passed the sternest, and possibly cruellest, of Diana's loyalty tests when she sacked his wife Maria, who had worked as her dresser for a year. While Maria left Kensington Palace in stony silence, her husband stood by the Princess. Over the years, his marriage and family life always came second to his unswerving faithfulness to Diana.

He was more than her servant, he became her shadow. Indeed, his invasive presence earned him the nickname 'Mrs Danvers', after the sinister servant in Daphne du Maurier's *Rebecca*, from other inhabitants of the Kensington Palace compound. More than that, he became the Princess's gatekeeper, filtering her phone calls and faxes, effectively manipulating and controlling her life through his own prejudices and perceptions. Thus her daily reality was dis-torted and coloured by Burrell, who was able to feed her existing anxieties, fears and worries with a word here and a warning there.

Ironically, Diana took immense satisfaction in the way she had pared back her staff, not realizing that by doing so she had merely concentrated power and influence into a handful of retainers. Her housekeeping practice was guided by her virtuous desire to place clear blue water between herself and Prince Charles. She had long been concerned by the sycophancy, size and self-serving nature of his court, continually astonished by her husband's many and increasingly eccentric indulgences. She was not the only one. As Max Hastings commented in *Editor: A Memoir*:

> If it had become publicly known that some other rich eccentric, such as Howard Hughes, had taken to carrying his own towels and lavatory paper to every house in which he stayed . . . it would be assumed that medical supervision could not be far off.

During their marriage Diana found it embarrassing that when she and the Prince of Wales went away he took more luggage than she did: 'I am always appalled that Prince Charles takes twenty-two pieces of hand luggage with him. That's before the other stuff. I have four or five.' After her separation she wore it as a badge of honour that her administrative staff numbered just four while, as Patrick Jephson noted, the Prince employed thirty-five people. (Now there are eighty-five, including nine gardeners, four valets, three butlers, four chefs and two drivers.) In this climate of extravagance, laxity and excess, it was perhaps inevitable that it would rub off on his staff. As early as July 1991 Diana was sent a confidential report by the Waleses' then deputy private secretary, Peter Westmacott, now Sir Peter and Ambassador to Turkey, about staff using the Prince's name or St James's Palace stationery to gain advantage. During his conversations with the Princess the name of Michael Fawcett, the Prince's valet, was frequently mentioned. Indeed, when Diana raised the topic with her husband she later remarked to James Colthurst that it was one of the first times Prince Charles had ever taken her seriously.

Diana initially found Fawcett, a self-styled Mr Fix-it, convivial and amusing company, who would helpfully use his contacts – and discount – at Turnbull and Asser and other tailors to obtain shirts, ties and other items of menswear that she could give as presents to friends and members of staff. Over time, however, his role as the Prince's gatekeeper, monitoring those who gained access to Charles – and that included the Princess – began to rankle. 'Oh, we will see what the Prince has to say about that' would be his stock reply to those who questioned him, a comment that displayed his proximity to the heir.

Fawcett had worked hard to reach such an exalted position. Like Burrell, he began life as a junior footman below stairs at Buckingham Palace, and he had battled his way to the Prince's side by force of personality and imagination, creating for himself a vivid past that did not bear too close scrutiny. He told stories about his father losing millions on the Canadian stock market and of his mother being a minor member of the aristocracy.

A single incident captures well his blend of camp joviality, avuncular condescension and underlying aggression. When introduced by Ken Wharfe to a new Scotland Yard recruit, he looked the young man up and down, put a genial paw on the sleeve of the recruit's rather modest acrylic sweater and said, 'Don't rub it, dear – you'll go up in smoke.'

In many respects, Fawcett, a theatrical, court-jester character with an unfortunate bullying manner, was in the mould of Charles's most famous valet, Stephen Barry, who worked for the Prince until 1981. Sociable, funny and frequently outrageous, Barry, who died of AIDS in 1986, was the only valet in memory to accompany the Prince on a royal walkabout, often gathering bouquets for his royal master. Like him, Fawcett did everything for the fastidious Prince, from drawing his bath, to laying out his large white towel lengthways so the Prince could wrap himself more easily, and even using the silver toothpaste-tube squeezer decorated with the Prince of Wales feathers to squeeze the royal toothpaste on to the royal toothbrush. He went one further than Barry, though. When the Prince broke his arm playing polo in June 1990 and was taken to hospital, Fawcett was given the honour of holding the royal bottle while his master provided a urine sample.

Diana began to feel that he had an unnatural hold over her husband, becoming increasingly concerned about the intimacy of their relationship. The Prince's one-time private secretary, Major-General Sir Christopher Airy, was as bemused about the Prince's relationship with Fawcett as the Princess. He could never fathom out why Prince Charles should be so much influenced by a man who was, in military terms, the equivalent of a sergeant. 'Diana couldn't work out what this relationship was between Michael Fawcett and her husband,' commented Ken Wharfe. 'She thought it was unhealthy. I think she firmly believed that.' It was her constant refrain, voiced to her family and friends, including Vivienne Parry who recollected that, 'Princess Diana would frequently say he's got something on Prince Charles. She certainly told enough people. She told members of the Spencer family. Diana seemed obsessed by her husband's relationship with Fawcett. My impression was that it was not a joke.'

Diana came to view Prince Charles's relationship with Michael Fawcett with a mixture of contempt, suspicion and gallows humour, but ironically it replicated her own bond with Burrell. 'I can manage without just about anyone, except for Michael,' the Prince once remarked, a sentiment that echoed his wife's words about her butler – 'He's my everything.'

'For a man of his age,' the writer Joan Smith commented when Charles's louche way of life came under the spotlight, 'the Prince leads a lifestyle which can best be described as infantile, depending on servants to perform the simplest of everyday chores. Fawcett was to Charles what Burrell was to Diana, a combination of flunkey, nanny and confidant.'

If the Princess came to see Fawcett as the fourth wheel in her marriage, once she and her husband had separated, and Fawcett, of course, had remained firmly by Prince Charles's side, she clearly felt that she need not make any show of friendliness towards him. After he had come to collect the Prince's personal effects from Kensington Palace, Diana apparently ordered the locks to be changed. As a former member of her staff, who regarded Fawcett as an 'affable and charming character', told me, 'She didn't trust him. She knew that everything she said would go back to the Prince.'

While the Princess was irked by Fawcett's power over the Prince's household and distrusted him deeply, she resented him less than she did Alexandra 'Tiggy' Legge-Bourke, daughter of a lady-in-waiting to the Princess Royal, who was appointed as nanny and companion for the boys. It was Tiggy's job to entertain William and Harry and organize diversions for them when they stayed with their father, but Diana saw things differently, feeling that Tiggy was usurping her most treasured and valued role, as the boys' mother. Certainly, staff at Kensington Palace knew they were in for a bad day if there was a flattering photograph of Tiggy in the newspapers. A picture of Charles embracing Tiggy at Harry's school, stories about how she had lost weight to please the Prince, her admission that, like Diana, she had nurtured a schoolgirl crush on the heir to the throne, and unguarded comments from her that the boys saw her as a surrogate mother, set tongues wagging and Diana's imagination racing. According to a friend of Tiggy's, quoted in the *Sunday Times* in January 1996, Tiggy, who grew up on a 6,000-acre estate in Wales, claimed that she gave the princes 'what they need at this stage – fresh air, a rifle and a horse. [Diana] gives them a tennis racket and a bucket of popcorn at the movies.'

The Princess was so sensitive to Tiggy's involvement in her sons' lives that she sent a note to her husband asking him to clarify the scope and extent of her duties. Staff at Kensington Palace knew that the trickiest phone call of the day was when Tiggy rang with details of the boys' movements. As the Princess refused to speak to her, Paul Burrell had to relay messages back and forth.

Undoubtedly, Tiggy's involvement with her children triggered profound feelings of insecurity in Diana, making her feel vulnerable and cornered. Over the years, her private secretary, Patrick Jephson, had seen her behaviour pattern at close quarters and observed that, 'As always, when forced on to the defensive, the Princess protected herself by lashing out. It mattered very little who was in the firing line.'

This was the scarred, suspicious landscape inhabited by the Princess, a bipolar world where she was celebrated one minute, consumed by plots the next; her home both a refuge and an open prison, into which male friends had to be smuggled to avoid prying eyes.

It had become a fact of her royal life, the climate becoming more malignant before the separation as Charles and Diana were consumed by the war of the Waleses. When they parted in 1992, their antagonism was recast in a different form, Diana's qualms and concerns fed by the fact that there were now officially two separate camps. From the autumn of 1995 there was a distinct transformation in her behaviour. Even though, as discussed in the previous chapter, she occupied the moral high ground in relation to Prince Charles, enjoyed a consensus of support inside and outside the Palace, was expertly exercising her dominion on the world stage and, after meeting Hasnat Khan, seemed to have found the love of her life, she was a woman living in fear.

Before the year was out, she genuinely believed that her life was in danger – so much so that she considered fleeing the country for safety and sanctuary in America. Patrick Jephson saw at first hand drastic changes in the Princess's demeanour. 'Her paranoia had reached new heights,' he wrote of this desperate time in the autumn of 1995. 'She saw plots everywhere.'

Diana was obsessed by the conviction that her apartment was bugged; she claimed to Jephson that an unknown and unseen assailant had fired a random shot at her in Hyde Park in broad daylight, and she suspected that the brake linings of her car had been tampered with at the behest of Prince Charles. Eventually she wrote a letter as 'insurance' to that effect. Most grotesquely, the Princess made a remark in public to Tiggy Legge-Bourke that implied that the nanny had had an abortion and furthermore that the baby had been Prince Charles's. It was a wholly unfounded and deeply hurtful allegation.

At the time Jephson thought that Diana must be going mad, her fears the figments of an overheated imagination. Either that, he wrote in the *Evening Standard* in January 2004, or by voicing these fears and assessing if he was taking them seriously, she was setting him the most twisted of 'loyalty tests' at a time when he was considering resigning. Yet, even with the benefit of hindsight, he now admitted that he could think of few examples of paranoid, even irrational, behaviour from her during the eight years he was by her side.

Since her death, the critical few months before she recorded her famous BBC interview in November 1995 have served to redefine her in the popular imagination as a tragic if unstable combination of drama queen and mentally flawed princess. This view played into the hands of those, mostly Prince Charles's supporters, who have always argued that she was beautiful but bonkers.

So was she mad or did she have evidence from credible sources to back up her allegations? The short but surprising answer is that she believed she had compelling proof, which she had, in the circumstances, to take seriously. Throughout 1995 she had been hearing all kinds of rumours about Prince Charles's relationship with Tiggy Legge-Bourke and had for some months believed that her estranged husband had loosened his ties with his long-time mistress, Camilla Parker Bowles, and was now intimate with the boys' nanny. Emotionally, Diana was not particularly perturbed by this turn of events. As friends to whom she confided her thoughts told me, 'She was more curious than hurt. She genuinely thought that she was having an affair with Prince Charles and that Tiggy occupied a place once held by Camilla. She had "known" about this for a long time. At this time in her life she was no longer obsessed by Camilla, so it was more a case of sniggering about it than worrying about what to do next.' If anything, Diana was more bothered about the impact on her children than on her husband, or for that matter herself.

None the less, it niggled, worming away at her sense of place and security. Hints and allusions in the media – which, for example, made much of an affectionate peck on the cheek on the ski slopes at Klosters, and at Sports Day at Prince Harry's school in June 1995, as well as headlines like one in the *Mail on Sunday*: 'Why do my teenage sons need a voluptuous young nanny to look after them?' – invited the public, and the Princess, to read much more into the relationship than actually existed.

Newspaper tittle-tattle and unsubstantiated conjecture from within her circle was one thing, however – detailed information from credible sources outside the royal court was quite another.

During the summer and autumn of 1995, Diana was told by apparently reliable sources that Tiggy had twice seen her gynaecologist, which had resulted in two separate stays in hospital for medical procedures that autumn. It seems that the same reliable sources also led her to believe that Tiggy had undergone a termination. As the Princess thought that her estranged husband

and Tiggy were having an affair, she now accepted as fact that Tiggy had aborted Prince Charles's baby. Trusting in the veracity of her sources, Diana approached Tiggy during a staff Christmas party at the Lanesborough Hotel in London, in December 1995, and made the now notorious remark: 'So sorry to hear about the baby.'

Tiggy was so taken aback by this vindictive utterance that she had to be helped from the room by Charles's valet, Michael Fawcett. Later her solicitor wrote to Diana's lawyers demanding a retraction of the 'false allegations'. The horrified consensus of opinion was articulated by royal biographer Brian Hoey: 'She is showing signs of paranoia. This is very, very nasty.'

An internal inquiry into the matter, undertaken by the Queen's private secretary Sir Robert Fellowes, confirmed the accuracy of Diana's source regarding Tiggy's medical history – she had indeed seen her gynaecologist and gone to hospital during the period in question – but it was for 'women's problems' rather than the malicious conclusion Diana had been led to believe. When Diana gave Sir Robert the specific date of the alleged abortion, he checked it to discover that on the day in question, Tiggy had been at Highgrove with the young princes. In a handwritten note, he urged Diana to withdraw her allegations saying that she had got the whole thing 'dreadfully wrong'. Even so, it seems that Diana never did apologize.

Until Sir Robert's intervention, however, the Princess sincerely believed the truth of the information she had been given. She felt that her husband was demeaning himself but she could understand it. Jaundiced as she was by Prince Charles's behaviour, and contemptuous and suspicious of his court, nothing could have prepared Diana for the story she stumbled across in October and November 1995. This was the allegation made by a junior servant employed by Prince Charles that he had twice been raped by a member of Charles's staff. More than that, he was to claim that he had encountered Prince Charles with a servant when he served him breakfast in his bedroom suite.

These seemingly preposterous allegations were made by an orderly in Prince Charles's household called George Smith, when the Princess visited him in the private Priory clinic in south-west

London where he was recovering from alcoholism. Diana, who often visited sick royal staff in hospital, had a soft spot for the former Welsh Guardsman whom she called Gorgeous George. Endlessly cheery and obliging, George Smith had fitted well into the royal household after he joined in 1987, his sunny disposition earning him the affection of the Princess of Wales and numerous members of staff, particularly the girls in the office. (Diana might have been less well disposed towards him had she known that her husband entrusted him with the organization of his clandestine meetings with Camilla.) Beneath the merry banter, though, Smith was a damaged character, severely traumatized by his experiences when he served in the Falklands conflict, and going through a particularly bitter divorce. A weak individual, he was easily manipulated and often drowned his troubles in drink. In November 1995, distressed and wayward, he voluntarily checked in to the Priory clinic, after a stay at the Prince's Highgrove estate in late October had failed to ease his psychological problems.

As with other members of staff who had been taken ill – Vic Fletcher, the Yeoman of the Silver Pantry, Diana's former body-guard Graham Smith, who eventually succumbed to cancer, and even Charles's former valet Ken Stronach, who had suffered spinal problems – Diana made it her business to visit Smith in hospital to cheer him up. 'You will get over this – I have been through worse,' she said, alluding to his alcoholism – and, presumably, her bulimia. There may have been another motive for her visit. Smith, who was in an extremely disturbed and distressed state, had made allegations about a senior member of Prince Charles's staff to at least one other member of the royal household. So when she visited him at the Priory with her secretary Victoria Mendham, he spilled out a horrifying story. It appears that he told the Princess that the real reason for his change of character was that in 1989, and then again in 1995, a member of the Prince of Wales's staff had raped him after plying him with drink. It is not clear whether at this first meeting he also confided an even more startling story – that he had witnessed an incident involving Prince Charlers and a servant as Smith prepared to serve breakfast. Certainly at subsequent meet-ings at Kensington Palace and his home in Twickenham, he unburdened himself of this extraordinary, scarcely believable tale to the Princess who, according to Smith's account, seemed 'shocked'.

Although she tried to calm him, she left the clinic troubled and concerned about him, and even more worried about her own well-being. It seemed to her that she was gathering too many dangerous and damaging secrets for her own good. She was so alarmed that in early 1996 she made a tape recording of Smith's allegations both as an insurance policy and as independent evidence of the seemingly debauched if unbelievable goings-on in the court of Prince Charles.

At this time, in October and November 1995, the Princess was, as Jephson observed, fearful of being watched and, ultimately, afraid for her safety. To her it seemed quite plausible that some attempt should be made on her life – perhaps by tampering with her car so that she might be involved in an accident. So when, that year, the Princess, according to Simone Simmons, had a minor accident in her car when her brakes failed while she was driving home from the Hale Clinic in Marylebone, she was understandably uneasy. While mechanics at her garage confirmed that the cause was simple mechanical failure, Diana was not convinced and took it to a different garage to be checked over.

In a letter that she apparently entrusted to her butler, Diana wrote of her suspicions of a plot to kill her:

> I am sitting here at my desk today in October, longing for someone to hug me and encourage me to keep strong and hold my head high. This particular phase in my life is the most dangerous. My husband is planning 'an accident' in my car, brake failure and serious head injury in order to make the path clear for Charles to marry.

The existence of this note and Prince Charles's alleged involvement in any plot was only revealed after the inquest into Diana's death was announced in January 2004. The letter was, claimed Paul Burrell, written in October 1996 – just ten months before her death – and given to him for safekeeping. There has been considerable debate about when the letter was written – friends suspect it was in October 1995 – for, by October 1996, Diana had left behind the anxieties of previous years, and was facing different issues and challenges. 'I saw her three times in October and each time she was in very good spirits and there was no great bitterness towards the Prince of Wales,' Rosa Monckton declared, while Richard Kay bumped into her in a restaurant and described her as being in 'sparkling form' sitting joking with her mother.

On the other hand, it is clear that in the autumn of 1995 she believed that there was a conspiracy to harm her. In the edgy world Diana inhabited, where everyone was suspicious of everyone else and everyone seemed to have something to hide, where her existing suspicions and fears were being fed by plausible outsiders and damaged insiders, she was running scared. As a confidante to whom she spoke regularly about these concerns remarked, 'She had the capacity for paranoia – who wouldn't in the situation she was in?'

The Princess was so certain that there was a plot against her life, that the 'enemy' was planning to harm her, that she considered fleeing the country. What intelligence had excited and provoked this sense of dread? At this critical period an unknown BBC journalist, Martin Bashir, had entered her life. The lurid stories he told her, together with the documents he showed her, filled her with fear and alarm. It is no exaggeration to say that the day he entered her world, Diana's life – and legacy – was changed for ever.

CHAPTER EIGHT

Fakes, Forgeries and Secret Tapes

H E IS NOW one of the biggest names in television with a roll call of major interviews, a number of them controversial, to his credit. But when Martin Bashir joined the BBC's flagship current-affairs programme, *Panorama*, in spring 1992, he was just a very small and unknown fish in a large pond teeming with big names.

Born in 1963, the son of an immigrant family (his parents had moved to Britain from Pakistan), Bashir had the drive to succeed, perhaps to over-achieve, typical of first-generation families. A troubled background – his father suffered from psychiatric problems and his brother died of muscular dystrophy – probably served only to strengthen his resolve, and he graduated with a top degree in English and History from the University of Southampton, even though, as he was fond of saying, the only book in their council home on a south London estate was the rent book. When he joined *Panorama*, Bashir, a former sports reporter, had a reputation as an 'obsessional loser', a Walter Mitty character chasing left-field ideas that rarely came to anything. In the predominantly white, middle-class milieu of the BBC, he was seen as an outsider and a loner. While he was respected as a smooth and clever operator he had, as the journalist Sonia Purnell commented in the *Independent on Sunday*, 'barely made a name for himself in nine years at the BBC'.

One story is typical of his ingratiating charm, a potent and winning combination of flattery, humility – and make-believe. When he first joined *Panorama* he made a point of buttonholing Tom Mangold, doyen of investigative reporters, in the BBC bar in west London. Deferentially, he approached him and asked to shake the great man's hand. He went on to tell him that when his brother Tommy was dying, one of his last wishes was that he, Martin, should emulate the veteran reporter whom, it went without saying, he considered to be the best in the world. Mangold, his ego stroked and heart strings pulled in equal measure by this touching story, immediately warmed to the rather lonely and forlorn figure. Mangold became more sceptical about a year later, when he was talking to John Humphrys, the grand inquisitor of Radio Four's *Today* programme, at a party. Humphrys, it transpired, had had precisely the same conversation with Bashir – and so, at a different time, had the highly respected TV war correspondent, Michael Nicholson. As one BBC insider commented, 'You've got to admire a guy like that. He's out of Hollywood. It tells you everything you need to know about him.'

Behind the meek exterior was an ambitious journalist who was keen to make a name for himself. His previous two programmes, in 1993 and 1994, about the former England football manager Terry Venables and his financial dealings, had attracted attention as well as a libel writ from Venables who complained, as part of his case, about the use of fabricated financial documents. Bashir, who made the show with a fellow producer, Mark Killick, had, it seems, used the skills of a graphic designer, Matt Wiessler, to recreate material that already existed, but which was not to hand, so that it could be used to illustrate the story.

In mid-1995, while he and Killick were dealing with the fallout from the Venables show, Bashir started to look into the whole idea of the relationship between the security services and the royal family, as well as the apparent 'dirty tricks' campaign being waged against the Princess by her enemies inside and outside the Palace. Like many others, he had not taken the soothing words of the Prime Minister and the head of MI5 at face value, and was keen to explore the story further. In 1995, when he began investigating the story, he was moving into a crowded field – and with few contacts or leads to help him on his way. 'We had some little insights, nothing of huge significance, but bits and bobs,' one of his colleagues at the time later recalled. I myself, as someone who was at the time the equivalent of one-stop shopping for Diana stories, had been contacted by numerous reporters, including other BBC journalists, for help on this subterranean issue. For example, a freelance TV company called 20/20, based in north London, had spent weeks investigating the origin of the Squidgygate, Camillagate and other secretly recorded tapes of intimate royal conversations. They had uncovered a seedy world in which thousands of modern-day radio hams spent their spare time scanning the airwaves in the hope of listening in to salacious chatter. Evenings were most popular as it was then that mobile telephone conversations became more intimate as lovers whispered sweet nothings to one another. At the same time the possible involvement of Britain's security services in taping royal conversations was such an accepted part of national life that a TV play based on the idea had been broadcast. In editorial terms, then, Bashir's investigation seemed to be an idea past its sell-by date.

And if Bashir had grander ambitions and wanted to snag an interview with the Princess, he was just one TV journalist in a line representing the *Who's Who?* of the international media. Rarely a week would go by without a big-name TV interviewer, usually American, calling me and asking me to use my influence with the Princess to gain access to her. The naivety of some in respect of royal protocol was breathtaking, and flattering. 'If we fly Concorde Thursday could you line up the Princess of Wales for Friday,' the producer for one American household name asked me. 'And would it be possible to see the Queen Mother on Sunday?' As the Queen Mother had not been interviewed since 1923, I told them that the prospects were not hopeful. Other media stars, notably Oprah Winfrey and Barbara Walters, were much more sophisticated and savvy. Oprah considered making and sending the Princess a videotape filmed at her ranch in the mid-west outlining why the people's Princess should sit on the couch with the queen of confessional TV. Eventually Oprah was invited to Kensington Palace for lunch with the Princess, who was somewhat in awe of the self-possessed and articulate TV host. Oprah Winfrey was not the only one trying to secure the interview of the decade. Already enamoured of all things American, Diana was now subject to the remorseless charm of Barbara Walters, who also had lunch with the Princess and earned the approval of her private secretary, Patrick Jephson. Discussions about donations to the Princess's favourite charities – the conventional ploy to snag a royal – were at an advanced stage. Not to be outdone, the CBS network offered the Duchess of York a lucrative contract – provided she could haul Diana into the studio. While the Americans were clearly front runners, in Britain Sir David Frost and Clive James, already a friend of Diana's, had invested much time trying to set up a chat with the Princess, James even arranging a secret visit for her to see a recording of his chat show.

While Martin Bashir, who was unknown to both the Princess and her circle, wanted to enter the race for the first face-to-face TV interview with Diana, he was in fact further handicapped by the fact that he worked for the BBC. The publicly funded broadcaster generated only negative thoughts in the Princess, who saw the organization as the media arm of Buckingham Palace, as the Establishment in a cathode tube. The fact that the Chairman of the Governors, Marmaduke Hussey was married to the Queen's lady-in-waiting, Lady Susan Hussey, meant that, as far as Diana was concerned, the BBC could not be trusted. Indeed, that consideration had weighed in my favour several years earlier when she was deciding to whom she should tell her story, as she had immediately discounted the BBC because of its formal and personal links with Buckingham Palace. As for the BBC's current affairs show *Panorama*, that did not even appear on her radar screen. Yet it was an unknown journalist from this flagship show who ultimately scooped the prize.

Without doubt Bashir was plausible and a smooth operator. As his colleagues testify he has an ability, described as 'genius' by his former *Panorama* colleagues, to persuade anyone to give him an interview, once he has got his foot in the door. But then there were many others as persuasive as him, and, quite frankly, American television networks, with years of dealing with Hollywood royalty, are much more sophisticated and resourceful when it comes to bagging the big interviews. When I was writing a biography of Monica Lewinsky I could only stand back and marvel at the slick yet friendly way Barbara Walters persuaded the former intern to grant her the first television interview. Every step of the way Walters had the money, resources and support of the ABC Television network. It was an overwhelming combination. The Princess of Wales would doubtless have had the same treatment. A show like *Panorama*, worthy, serious-minded public television, simply had no chance when it came to snaring the big hitters on the celebrity circuit. It neither was, nor is, part of its agenda. Yet within a few months of first looking at the subject of Diana, the secret services and the royal family, Martin Bashir was sitting with the Princess in the boys' sitting room at Kensington Palace secretly filming an interview that would change her life for ever. More than that, because of her premature death, it served as the fulcrum of her life. The interview and the bizarre events surrounding it, notably her perceived paranoia about her safety, are now presented as her abiding image and form a substantive part of her historical legacy.

But did Bashir achieve his scoop not only by force of personality, but by persuading Diana that she was being conspired against?

The stories Bashir apparently told the Princess, the documents he showed her, subsequently revealed as forgeries, and the deliberately cloak-and-dagger nature of their meetings and conversations – could they have convinced her that to fight back she would have to speak out publicly? In short, her famous BBC interview might not have been an act of self-indulgence as many, including the Queen and the rest of the royal family, senior courtiers and politicians, believed at the time – but, rather, a deliberate act of self-preservation. In the prevailing mood of instability and disquiet, when everything seemed larger than life, the Princess was truly frightened. The documents and any alarming allegations made by Martin Bashir were all the more disquieting because he was a believable witness, an outsider from an organization at the heart of the British Establishment, with powerful links to every institution in the land, including the monarchy. In the climate of dread he helped create and exploit, she spoke out to pre-empt any attempt to discredit her, or worse, by the dark forces that she now believed stalked and watched her. She was in actual fear of her life, feeling extremely threatened. Thus the idea of the television programme was to get a message across to the people before, as she now felt, some kind of violent physical action was taken against her. The irony is that after the *Panorama* interview was broadcast, many more people loved her. That, however, had not been her aim. It was, as far as she was concerned, to save her life.

Critical in creating this sense of impending doom was a set of forged bank statements Bashir had made up by a graphic designer friend. They were physical proof of the stories he was spinning, that she was under constant surveillance, and ultimately under threat, from Britain's secret services. She was shown the documents in October 1995, just before she agreed to give the interview. The appearance of this evidence tipped the balance. Whatever her misgivings beforehand, Diana was determined to go ahead with the interview. It seems certain that there would have been no *Panorama* documentary if she had not been shown these forged documents; indeed, her reaction to the documents, as related to me by those in her circle, was 'terror and horror'. In years gone by she would have crumpled in the face of the forces ranged against her, but now she felt stronger. As with harassment by paparazzi, she decided to fight – to take the battle to those who wished her harm. None the less, the existence of these documents added to her general sense of 'They're out to get me.' She felt paranoid and genuinely in fear of her life.

The path that led to this vortex of fear and paranoia began among the peaceful rolling acres of Diana's childhood home of Althorp in Northamptonshire. It is here in the summer of 1995 that Bashir first met her brother, Earl Spencer, whom he and his colleagues had correctly identified as his sister's gatekeeper. Gain his confidence and there was a good chance of reaching Diana. At the time the Princess was not the only member of the Spencer family living with the constant fear of phone taps, undercover surveillance and intrusion, either by the media or by other more sinister agencies. Crucially, Charles Spencer was as convinced as his sister that dark forces were at work in the country, and, had already felt the need to take robust action to defend himself and his family. A year earlier, in April 1994, in an off-camera conversation with a television producer, Jackie Donaldson, he said that he knew that he was being bugged and who was behind it. His comments came at a time when he was defending both his reputation and his privacy. After a two-year fight he successfully sued the *Daily Express* in 1996 for a series of articles which suggested he was suspected of having been used to launder the proceeds of a multimillion-pound fraud by his friend and best man, Darius Guppy. Earl Spencer won £50,000 damages and an apology. At the same time, and more significantly in the light of subsequent developments, he took out a High Court injunction against his former head of security, Alan James Waller, forbidding him from disclosing information about his private life and that of members of the royal family. His writ followed the publication, in March 1994, in the now defunct *Today* newspaper, of a letter he had written to Diana in December 1993 warning her that her public appearances were damaging her popularity, which Waller was suspected of having sold to the paper.

So when the young earl agreed to meet Bashir to discuss his suspicions about the involvement of the security forces, he had his own fears and theories. At the time Bashir was telling colleagues that he had a contact within MI5, the British security service, who was giving him information. By the end of August Bashir had met Charles Spencer at Althorp and told him that it was his understanding that the security services were indeed targeting the Princess. It is unclear what evidence he gave the Earl to underpin this assertion, but Spencer, a former correspondent with NBC television in America and therefore likely to be sceptical, found it persuasive.

In the meantime Bashir's editor, Steve Hewlett – no doubt having seen other similar *Panorama* investigations peter out – was concerned by the slow progress and urged Bashir to aim for the stars, or rather the star, and press for an interview with the Princess. At one of several further meetings with the Earl, it seems that Bashir persuaded Charles Spencer to speak to his sister and arrange for Diana to meet Bashir secretly. Presumably he wanted to outline his knowledge about the hidden forces ranged against her face to face.

By now the plausible Mr Bashir had won the endorsement of her brother, which familial vote of confidence would have gone a long way to allay any doubts Diana may have had about Bashir's motives. An unforeseen by-product of the involvement of Charles in the early stages of this venture was that it helped to reconcile brother and sister after a couple of years of coolness. 'She was longing to reignite her relationship with her brother,' asserted Diana's circle, with whom she had discussed in detail what was happening. 'It meant a lot to her.'

While memories differ regarding the fateful first meeting between the Princess and the TV reporter – one account says it was mid-summer, another late September – all their encounters were characterized by secrecy and a theatrical atmosphere of intrigue that served to heighten the tension, and perhaps to bring the Princess and Bashir closer together, the conspiratorial feeling increasing her trust in the young reporter. It was a technique that became Bashir's trademark. By September 1995 Bashir had built up a considerable rapport with Diana. 'He's not had an easy life; I enjoyed talking to him,' the Princess told her butler after one of their hush-hush meetings. The first furtive encounter took place at a friend's London apartment, another, like a scene from the movie, *All the President's Men*, apparently occurred in an underground car park. Most, however, were at Kensington Palace. Paul Burrell would pick Bashir up from BBC Television Centre in west London and drive him, usually hidden under a green tartan blanket, to Diana's apartment. 'This passenger seemed to enjoy the cloak-and-dagger operation more than most,' he wrote in *A Royal Duty*.

In the autumn of 1995, soon after she began to see Bashir regularly, the Princess became far more fearful for her safety, her customary suspicions and warnings now suffused by a genuine sense of dread, verging on the paranoid. 'She was off on her own bat, having had her various insecurities fed by Bashir very cleverly,' noted her American biographer Sally Bedell Smith. Bashir apparently convinced her that her apartment was bugged, something she had long suspected – she had in fact had it swept for listening devices before, but now she seemed even more anxious than usual, summoning her private secretary to join her in a search of her apartment. He had already noted with concern her heightened state of paranoia, and here was another example of it.

According to Diana's confidant, who spoke to her during this period, the Princess had been given the information about Tiggy Legge-Bourke and her hospital visits by more than one significant source. That Tiggy had been to hospital several times was shown to be true, but whether Diana jumped or was led to the hurtful conclusion, later proven to be wide of the mark, that the nanny had had an abortion is uncertain. The source of these stories must have been very credible to Diana to lead her to make the extreme and uncharacteristic accusations against Tiggy.

When, that autumn, Diana heard from the lips of Prince Charles's orderly George Smith the tale of an alleged male rape by a member of the Prince's staff, she feared that her knowledge of Smith's claims might be dangerous. All was clearly far from well in the royal households – and then along came Martin Bashir, a credible witness, an outsider but also representative of the media establishment, amplifying and anchoring all the lurid stories she had heard about the shadowy security services. 'Fear of the security services was one of the emotions driving Diana's secret cooperation with the film,' noted a *Sunday Times* article on the eve of the broadcast. The piece, 'Diana's Prime Time Revenge' by Nicholas Hellen and Tim Rayment, continued, 'When she learnt that Martin Bashir, the *Panorama* reporter fronting the project, was investigating the role of MI5 in her long nightmare of tapped telephone calls and tabloid tip-offs, she wanted to know more.' Bashir's initial claim that he had a contact inside MI5 who was supplying information that showed she was under surveillance was one thing – now he apparently told her that he had documentary evidence to back his contention in the form of bank statements. Not only did these statements show payments to Earl Spencer's former head of security, but they also showed payments made by a shadowy offshore company. Could it be that he told the Princess that this company, Penfolds Consultants, was in reality a 'front' for a secret-service operation? While exactly what was said is unlikely ever to be revealed, it is known that Diana was sufficiently alarmed to discuss the possibility of her leaving the country for a place of safety. As a former *Panorama* colleague of Bashir's commented: 'He is a good operator. If he wanted to give the impression that he was so close to MI5 that he was getting bank statements from them, *I* would take him seriously.' Additionally, when the Princess talked about this, she expressed her belief that Prince Charles and the Duchy of Cornwall, his hereditary estate, were in some way involved. Where did she get that idea? In speaking to her circle, the Princess was not specific with details of the role of her husband or those around him. Plainly though, she was extremely concerned, especially in view of the lurid accounts she was now hearing about the goings-on inside the court of Prince Charles. 'That,' Diana's friends said to me, 'is why the whole thing is so sinister.'

Whatever the tale Bashir told the Princess, it is the firm and forceful contention of Diana's circle that he did show her bank statements – denied by both Bashir and the BBC – which verified his assertion that he had a source who could obtain such confidential material. What the Princess did not know at the time was that they were forgeries.

In keeping with the undercover nature of the operation, the forging of these bank statements was as clandestine and covert as the filming of the programme. When Matt Wiessler, a graphic designer, was contacted by Bashir in early October 1995 about a 'rush job', the impression he got was that Bashir was at the heart of some dark mystery. Wiessler, who was struck by the way Bashir was 'playing the super detective', later recalled that, 'He was very excited and told me that if he got this wrapped up it would make his career.'

What Bashir wanted Wiessler to do was to use his computer wizardry to fake two bank statements. Using information Bashir supplied, Wiessler worked through the night creating the statements, dated March 1994 and June 1994, for a National Westminster Bank account apparently held in Brighton. They showed a £4,000 payment purportedly made to a joint account ostensibly held by Earl Spencer's former head of security, Alan

Waller, and a former business partner of his, Robert Harper, by News International, owners of *Today* newspaper – which had printed the purloined letter from Charles Spencer to Diana in 1994. The other statement showed £6,500 supposedly paid to Waller and Harper by a Jersey-based company, Penfolds Consultants. (Strangely, the company name Penfolds made an appearance in Bashir's inquiry into Terry Venables, the name even appearing on screen during the report.)

It is not clear what role was assigned to the offshore company in the narrative Bashir relayed to the Princess, but could he have passed the company off as a front for a secret-service operation to monitor the Princess? It might even, given Diana's conversation about the Prince of Wales and the Duchy of Cornwall, have been given some sinister royal connection. During the two hours or so that he spent with the graphic artist, Bashir, who had a very clear idea of what he wanted created, talked about the background surrounding the bank statements. 'He said that it had to do with surveillance about her [Diana], that someone was being paid to keep an eye on her, check her movements, report on what she was doing,' Wiessler recollected. 'I was under the impression that these bank statements suggested that somebody was getting money to watch Diana. I can't remember if it was MI5 or MI6.'

At the time, Wiessler did not think that he was doing anything underhand or illegal, as in the past they had faked material based on real documents in order to create leverage that would encourage people to talk on camera. It was only after the interview was broadcast that he worried about the morality and legality of their actions. 'All I know is that Bashir said that if he showed these to this person [whom he did not name] it might lead to something that is going to have a real effect,' Wiessler recalled. 'He said he was going off to South Africa and that this might lead to a programme – she [Diana] might agree to something.'

After their conversation, Bashir left Wiessler working furiously to meet the deadline. At 7 a.m., tired but proud of his work, Wiessler handed over the completed documents, for which he was paid £250, to a BBC driver in an envelope addressed to Martin Bashir. The driver was told to meet the reporter in front of the

Sock Shop store at Heathrow's Terminal 2. It is not clear who saw these forged bank statements at this point, although many journalists believe Bashir showed them to Charles Spencer. An article in the *Independent on Sunday* on 9 February 2003, for one, suggests that he could have used them to gain the Earl's confidence:

> Controversy may still swirl around the exact details of the lead-up to the Diana interview . . . (There remain unanswered questions, for instance, as to why Bashir falsified bank statements relating to Diana's brother's head of security. Did he do this to worm his way into the bosom of the Spencer family?) But what is certain is that Diana talked to Bashir . . . It was a mutually beneficial relationship and he had made himself her friend, her confidant. 'Bashir worked on Diana for years, also getting close to her brother, Earl Spencer,' says one former BBC colleague.

Unfortunately, like Bashir himself, the Earl has remained tight-lipped about this vexed affair and has refused to be interviewed either for this book or elsewhere. As a former *Panorama* colleague of Bashir's, who has seen the original documents, told me, 'These are first-class documents. If you saw them you would think you were looking at genuine bank statements. So why work up these documents to broadcast quality? He was meeting someone at the airport that was crucial. My guess is he met Charlie Althorp [Earl Spencer] and says to Charlie: "Your man has been on the payroll, I have more of this stuff, Diana's under surveillance, I can reveal it all to her. Here's the proof."'

It was only six months later, in April 1996, that the existence of the forgeries become public, following a Sunday newspaper investigation into the methods Bashir used to obtain his TV scoop. In the story, in the *Mail on Sunday*, the supposed joint bank-account holders, Waller and Harper, and the account holder for Penfolds Consultants, all confirmed that the bank statements were false. Waller and Harper stated that they had had a bank account in Brighton but it had been closed in March 1994, three months before the alleged June payment from Penfolds Consultants. Inside the BBC there was the growing feeling that the interview had been obtained by underhand means and that the bank statements had been used in some way to persuade the Princess to agree to speak out. In the two internal BBC investigations into the affair, Bashir contended that the bank statements had never been used to obtain the interview and that he had had the documents made for an earlier story he was working on about members of the royal family.

A BBC statement backed their reporter to the hilt, declaring:

> The draft graphic reconstructions on which this story [in the *Mail on Sunday*] is based have no validity and have never been published. They were set up for graphics purposes in the early part of an investigation and were discarded when some of the information could not be substantiated. They were never connected in any way to the *Panorama* on Princess Diana, and there was never any intention to publish them in the form we believe they have been leaked. Their use would never have been sanctioned at a high editorial level and if they had been transmitted it would have been a clear breach of our editorial guidelines.

As Richard Lindley, the author of a history of the programme, *Panorama: 50 Years of Pride and Paranoia*, remarked, 'But if that was the case, what exactly had they been intended for? The press release did not say.' At the time the TV critic Paul Donovan noted that the BBC had studiously refused to report on the growing disquiet. 'By the BBC's own admission it paid money to fabricate bank statements for what precise reason it will not say and we do not know,' he commented. 'Is that really a legitimate use of licence payers' money?' (It might be noted that the BBC's statement, although it says that the bank documents had nothing to do with Diana, does not say that she was *not* shown them, but only implies that she did not see them.)

As the documents were faked in October, just a few days before Diana gave the go-ahead for the interview, which itself took place on 5 November, the BBC's argument that they were forged 'in the early part of an investigation' seems disingenuous, even more so in the light of Bashir's comments to Matt Wiessler. Certainly, Diana's circle have firmly and consistently disputed the claim that the Princess was never shown the bank statements. Diana actually discussed them with her friends *before* the programme was broad-cast in November 1995 – and long before the documents became public knowledge in April 1996.

More than that, the Princess discussed with her friends the pro-posed format of the programme in the weeks before the November interview. In the early days of her conversations with Bashir, the Princess had spoken of making a documentary divided into two parts, the first part dealing with her fears about the involvement of the security forces in her life, confronting head-on the role of Prince Charles's circle and senior Buckingham Palace figures in the machinations against her. She was also going to talk about the constant media harassment she faced, she said, harass-ment which prompted her to talk about the need for a privacy law when she encountered Lord Wakeham, then chairman of the Press Complaints Commission, at a dinner party held, ironically, just before the broadcast.

No longer a victim, Diana intended to take the fight to those whom she called 'the enemy'. She reasoned, according to her circle, that if she made public the secret campaign against her, it would forestall any prospective, possibly critical, moves against her. In the interview as it was broadcast, while it dealt substantially with her own problems, both medical and marital, the Princess also made frequent references to the forces arrayed against her. She realized that if she was viewed as a problem when she was inside the royal family, now on the outskirts, she was perceived as a con-stant menace. 'I was the separated wife of the Prince of Wales, I was a problem, full stop. Never happened before, what do we do with her?' she was to say to Martin Bashir, adding, 'They [the royal household] see me as a threat of some kind.'

The second part of the documentary was intended to be a more traditional royal film about her changing role, detached but still linked to the royal family. It was to concentrate on her charity work, particularly with the Red Cross, and refer to her ambitions to be an ambassador for the country at large. This too appeared in the broadcast, remembered especially for her desire to be the 'queen of people's hearts'. It seems that, in the course of discus-sions with Bashir, the scope of the programme was widened to embrace all aspects of her life. Indeed it was a concern of those BBC executives who were now in the loop, Richard Ayre, for instance, that the interview should not be seen as a propaganda exercise for the Princess, which would compromise the reputation of *Panorama* for producing impartial, hard-hitting broadcasting.

As the Princess nervously mulled over the prospect of unburdening her thoughts in a TV confessional, she took soundings from more than just her close friends about the advisability of her dramatic course of action. She spoke to media-savvy characters like Clive James and David Puttnam about appearing on television. During their conversations she never revealed the underlying fear for her life that impelled her forwards. All those she consulted were aghast at the idea, believing that she would lose the moral high ground she had occupied ever since Prince Charles's Dimbleby interview in 1994. 'On two occasions,' David Puttnam remembered, 'she told me that she had been given the opportunity to put her side of the story and asked me what did I think. I said it was the worst idea I have ever heard.' Even Diana's confidant was unsure about her course of action, believing that the Princess overestimated her ability to weather such a daunting hour-long interview: 'She had zero control and there were zero rehearsals. She was a very smart woman but stupid enough to think that she could discover something [about herself] in an interview.'

In keeping with the clandestine nature of the operation, Diana's private secretary, her press secretary, her family, apparently even her brother and her butler Paul Burrell – who had acted as unwitting go-between – were kept completely in the dark about the interview. Once she had made the decision to go ahead she did not want to be stopped either by her own officials or by Establishment figures inside the BBC. She was particularly concerned that if the BBC Chairman, Marmaduke Hussey, heard about the interview he would contact Buckingham Palace and she would be prevented from telling her story to the world.

Inside Television Centre, once Diana had given Bashir the green light, the editor of *Panorama*, Steve Hewlett, several senior BBC executives and Bashir himself met secretly to structure the interview. The BBC Director-General at the time, John Birt, was concerned that the questions should be well-phrased, but otherwise he did not interfere. One omitted area of questioning concerned the Princess's relationship with Will Carling. It was on Bashir's original list but, according to the then BBC Head of Weekly Current Affairs, Tim Gardam, they felt that as they were already asking about Oliver Hoare and James Hewitt, they did not need to include him – they did not want the interview to be just about her boyfriends. 'I remember feeling a fool afterwards,' Gardam later commented ruefully, about omitting Carling.

They all knew, however, that even with the 150 or so questions they had composed they were handling potential dynamite. 'This could bring down the BBC or the monarchy or both,' said Richard Ayre, BBC's Controller of Editorial Policy, only half joking.

On 5 November 1995, Martin Bashir, a cameraman, Tony Poole, and the producer, Mike Robinson, drove into Kensington Palace and were personally greeted by the Princess, who showed them into the boys' sitting room where the interview took place. In keeping with the intense secrecy surrounding the project, Diana had made sure that all her staff, including Paul Burrell, were off the premises. As it was a Sunday there did not seem to be anything unusual in their being given the day off.

Once the interview was complete, the master tape was copied in a BBC studio in London and put into a bank vault. Then Bashir and his team moved into Brock House, a disused BBC building in central London, to begin editing. After a couple of days, fearing the project could be exposed to prying eyes, they decided to decamp to a hotel in Eastbourne to complete the editing process. As Richard Ayre explained: 'It may be paranoia but we became increasingly uneasy.' They hired the Duchess of York Suite, appropriately across the corridor from the Windsor Suite, where they blacked out the windows and continued editing the interview. The watchword was secrecy. When a trio of BBC executives, including Richard Ayre, travelled to Eastbourne to view the finished film, they did so in separate cars and by different routes. Diana's so-called paranoia was catching. It was worth the journey, though.

Although the Princess had known the question areas in advance, there had been no rehearsals and no arrangements about the kind of replies that would be acceptable to the programme makers and the Princess. As a result, the overall effect was one of breathtaking honesty. 'Here was a royal talking like a real human being with all the traumas of a real person's life,' observed Tony Hall, BBC's Director of News and Current Affairs. 'I was bowled over by the frankness of it.'

After the film ended, Gardam broke the stunned silence in the BBC studio, commenting, 'He'll never be able to marry Camilla now.' As a piece of film-making it was very clean, the documentary needing only a couple of editorial cuts. One, made later by John Birt, was to protect the sensibilities of Princes William and Harry about unspecified remarks made by Diana, the other was when the Princess would not be drawn into answering Bashir's questions about the Queen Mother's role in orchestrating the marriage and the help, or lack of it, she gave when Diana first entered the royal family. While she was critical of the Queen Mother both in private and when contributing to her biography, during the TV interview the Princess was much more circumspect, saying that the Queen Mother had been 'very busy and did not have much time to help'.

For the Princess, the interview had been the easy part. Now came the difficult bit – speaking to the Queen, who had just returned from an official visit to New Zealand, and other senior royal figures about her secret decision to appear on television. As, at the time, courtiers did not know the full extent of Diana's close involvement with *Diana: Her True Story*, the *Panorama* programme was ostensibly her first foray into the world of the public confessional. Her only stipulation to the *Panorama* team was that she wanted to tell the Queen herself about what she had done before they announced the programme to an unsuspecting world. The Princess was determined to accept responsibility for her actions, and in mid-November, the week before the programme was broadcast, went to Buckingham Palace, where she saw the Queen's private secretary Sir Robert Fellowes. According to BBC sources, he asked her innocently if the interview she had given was an insert for the charity programme, *Children in Need*. 'No,' she answered. '*Panorama*.' His one-syllable reply said it all: 'Oh.'

As soon as the Queen had been informed, Diana telephoned Bashir to let him know that the BBC could now announce the interview. Inside the corporation they had their own difficulties, having been forced to stage their equivalent of a palace coup. The Director-General, John Birt, only told the BBC Chairman, Marmaduke Hussey, as the story was being released to the media – on 14 November, which just happened to be Prince Charles's forty-seventh birthday. Birt, aware that Diana was 'terrified' that Hussey might use his authority inside the BBC and the Palace to gag her, delayed his move for as long as possible in order to forestall any possible intervention. As it was, the programme caused an irreversible rift between the Director-General and the Chairman as well as rupturing relations with Buckingham Palace.

Diana's own resolve was tested to the full as she refused to divulge any of the contents of the programme either to the Queen and her courtiers, Prince Charles, her own private secretary, Patrick Jephson, and even her divorce lawyer, Lord Mishcon, who had built up a warm paternal relationship with his royal client. Mishcon tried everything from 'avuncular sympathy to dire legal warning' to encourage her to reveal all – but without success.

The Princess spent the days before the broadcast bravely assuring her friends and supporters that they would be proud of her, saying over and over, 'Everything will be all right.' But behind this apparent confidence she was anxious and uncertain. Just before the broadcast she telephoned Debbie Frank, and in breathless, apprehensive tones told her about the interview. 'She was terrified before the programme came out,' Ms Frank recollected.

The Princess had lit the fuse when she sat down with Martin Bashir at Kensington Palace on the anniversary of Guy Fawkes's attempt to blow up the Houses of Parliament. Just two weeks later twenty-three million people tuned into their television sets to watch the resulting explosion.

CHAPTER NINE

The Long Goodbye

WITH ITS GREAT LAWNS, secret walled gardens, sunken ponds, and cobbled courtyards, the Jacobean country house that forms the core of Kensington Palace seems to be many miles away from the hustle and bustle of Kensington High Street just down the road. Certainly the animal life to be found in the grounds – for a time a pair of 'married' ducks appeared at Princess Margaret's doorstep every morning to be fed – adds to its rural feel. The poet Leigh Hunt captured the non-regal character of the seventeenth-century building when he said, 'Windsor Castle is a place to receive monarchs in, Buckingham Palace to see fashion and Kensington Palace seems a place to drink tea.' However, the first thing new members of staff learn is that the assorted dukes, duchesses, princes and princesses who inhabit what Edward VII once called 'the aunt heap' are rarely minded to drop in on one another for afternoon tea; communication between royal neighbours tends rather to be carried on through memos between private secretaries. In all the time that Diana lived at Kensington Palace she never entertained her neighbours, Prince and Princess Michael of Kent.

Over the years, though, she did build up a rapport with her other near neighbour, the resident of number 1A Clock Court, Princess Margaret, occasionally going to the theatre with her and, in a daring breach of royal protocol, even travelling to royal engagements with her. After the Waleses' separation, Princess Margaret wrote to Prince Charles and informed him that she was going to continue the association with his estranged wife. For her part Diana always spoke fondly of the Queen's sister, telling James Colthurst, 'I've always adored Margo, as I call her. I love her to bits and she's been wonderful to me from day one.' So her shock was all the greater when she received a 'wounding and excoriating' letter from the Princess, following Diana's appearance on *Panorama*. From that day on Princess Margaret wanted nothing more to do with her. She turned against Diana so vehemently, in fact, that she went round her apartment turning over the cover of any magazine that featured Diana on the front. Her children, Viscount Linley and Lady Sarah Chatto, who had previously enjoyed a warm friendship with Diana, realized that, in their mother's eyes, she was now an untouchable. David Linley, who had gone skiing with the Princess and had written her warm and affectionate letters, now hid behind the garage wall at Kensington Palace when he was tinkering with his sports car rather than acknowledge her presence. 'He went out of his way to avoid her,' recalled Princess Margaret's chauffeur, Dave Griffin. And when Diana bought a present for Lady Sarah's first baby, Samuel, who was born on 28 July 1996, the Princess, now fully aware of the social difficulties, handed it to Griffin to pass on to Lady Sarah.

(There was no thaw even after Diana's death. Princess Margaret argued that she should not be allowed to lie in the royal chapel or have a royal funeral, and it was noticeable that, on the day of the funeral, Princess Margaret merely nodded in the direction of Diana's cortège when it passed the Queen and the rest of the royal family outside Buckingham Palace. The other royals followed the Queen's example and bowed firmly. When suggestions were made about replacing the statue of William of Orange, which stands out-side Kensington Palace, with one of Diana, Princess Margaret resolutely opposed the idea. 'I'm not having that woman outside my bedroom window,' she told her staff.)

As far as the Queen's sister was concerned, Diana had exceeded the bounds of propriety in agreeing to talk publicly on television about her marriage and her royal life. At that time she, and other members of the royal family, had their suspicions about, but were not fully aware of, her complicity with *Diana: Her True Story*. As with so much in royal life, they had collectively chosen to turn a blind eye to her behaviour, especially as she had never publicly admitted any collaboration with me. So, as far as they were concerned, Diana's candid TV interview was the first time she had ever made her views known in public, and as such her TV confessional was both shocking and unforgivable.

In the wide-ranging interview with Martin Bashir, the Princess, wearing striking black eye make-up that gave her a haunted look, discussed her failed marriage, her eating disorders, her attempts at self-harm, her post-natal depression, her husband's adultery – using that famous phrase, 'There were three of us in this marriage so it was a bit crowded' – as well as admitting her own infidelity with the Life Guards officer James Hewitt. 'Yes, I adored him, yes, I was in love with him,' she said, adding that she had felt 'absolutely devastated' by his betrayal when she heard about the book he co-authored.

The most withering assault though, she saved for her husband, casting doubts on his fitness to rule even as she spoke of her own ambitions for the monarchy as well as for herself. 'I would like to be the queen in people's hearts . . . someone's got to go out there and love people and show it,' she argued, her choice of phrase seen as a sly swipe at the Sovereign's chilly style. As for those she considered her enemies she was defiant. '"She" won't go quietly, that's the problem,' she said. 'I'll fight to the end, because I believe that I have a role to fulfil and I've got two children to bring up.'

It was seminal television; the Princess, confident and eloquent, speaking over the heads of the Establishment to the man and woman in the street – as she had in her Time and Space speech and, indeed, for *Diana: Her True Story*. As Andrew Neil, the former editor of the *Sunday Times*, who serialized the Diana biography, commented: 'It is the video of the Andrew Morton book and much, much more.' At the time it was seen as a devastating riposte to Prince Charles's Dimbleby interview, a fatal ratcheting of the couple's tit-for-tat behaviour that finally prompted decisive action by the Queen. To friends and enemies alike, the Princess's behaviour seemed in keeping with her character: reckless, heedless of advice, leading by her heart not her head, impulsive, playing the victim while desperate for the love of the public, manipulative, contrived, self-indulgent, vengeful, unstable . . . but great theatre. 'Like an ageing, isolated Hollywood star, she sought the love of an amorphous "public", and no one around her seemed capable of restraining her growing need for popular adulation,' wrote her American biographer Sally Bedell Smith disdainfully.

In the eyes of the royal family and many in the Establishment, Diana was now beyond the pale. Princess Margaret's view echoed that of the House of Windsor, in believing that she had behaved inexcusably by questioning Prince Charles's right to be king as well as challenging the Sovereign herself. In their eyes, there was only one queen and she had served the nation impeccably for fifty years.

Royal relations with Diana, already frosty following the separation, went into deep freeze after *Panorama* was broadcast. Prince Andrew, who had known Diana from childhood, would have nothing to do with her and fell out with Fergie, suspecting that she was instrumental in encouraging Diana to reveal all on television. Most woundingly, Prince William himself refused to speak to his mother for several days because of the way she had talked about James Hewitt. In the months to come it would be the one element of her interview she regretted, admitting that she only spoke about her lover because of the 'cue' given by her husband with his own confession of adultery on the Dimbleby documentary.

Even the Princess's below-stairs friends in the Kensington Palace 'village' were dismayed by the show. 'I said to her that that was the biggest mistake you have made because in your silence was your strength,' Dave Griffin said. 'She didn't like me saying that.' Other supporters, outside the royal condominium, were equally disappointed. 'It was unutterably damaging,' according to David Puttnam, who, along with media heavyweights like Clive James and Max Hastings, had counselled her against, in her words, 'putting her side of the story'. Later Diana wrote him a 'sweet note', saying that she thought she had let him down. Puttnam, who sent her a long letter advising her how to mitigate the fallout, was just one in a long line of allies who condemned her television appearance. 'It was Diana at her worst,' wrote her friend Rosa Monckton, while the Princess's former astrologer, Penny Thornton, considered her performance 'contrived and insincere'. The word 'psychobabble' was used a lot by friends and enemies.

While Diana never breathed a word to Puttnam, Thornton or anyone else about the driving imperative behind the interview or of what she had feared might befall her had she not gone ahead, at the time the more perceptive commentators tried to divine the motive behind her actions. The veteran journalist, Lord Deedes, who was to become friendly with Diana during her landmine campaign, wrote in bewilderment:

> So what was the inner driving force behind last night's sad performance? Considering the risks incurred, it must have been very strong. She has grievously upset the Queen by plotting with the BBC behind her back – she has played false by her own personal staff and will not be readily forgiven for that. All this to what end?

In groping for an answer, he suggested, as did the majority of commentators, that she was competing for status and ascendancy over her husband. It became the agreed view in both the pro-Diana and the anti-Diana camps. Not surprisingly, the pro-Prince Charles lobby, whose party line was that she was mad and sad and therefore bad, were perplexed. 'When the interest in Camilla's divorce was past, the fuss over Dimbleby long gone, and life was pleasantly uneventful, the Princess of Wales released another Exocet which took everyone back to square one,' wrote Charles's biographer Penny Junor in baleful tones.

As for conspiracies, Jonathan Porritt, Prince Charles's friend and adviser on green issues, was mystified: 'Some of these stories of the sort of uncaring, unfeeling, almost a sort of plot against Princess Diana, seem very strange.'

Of course neither he, nor Deedes, nor any of the twenty-three million people watching the show (the greatest number of viewers ever to have watched a *Panorama* programme before or since) knew anything of allegations of MI5 surveillance backed up by bank statements, apparently genuine, or of the Princess's fear that her life might be in danger. There was the usual harrumphing against the BBC, but even the government could not find fault with the corporation; indeed two Tory whips told a BBC executive that it was 'blatantly obvious that Diana emerges as the villain and not the BBC'.

In the offices of *Panorama*, though, worried colleagues of Martin Bashir were not so sure. The story of the forged bank statements was now emerging. There was concern not just that Bashir had used the statements in order to snag the interview with Diana, but that the use of the name of Penfolds Consultants, which was central to the inquiry into the football manager, Terry Venables, could jeopardize the impending Venables legal case. More than just Bashir's career was at stake.

Three senior *Panorama* journalists – Mark Killick, who worked with Bashir on Venables, the producer Harry Dean and the TV veteran Tom Mangold – attempted to question Bashir about the bank statements. He refused to speak to them, referring them to the programme editor, Steve Hewlett. At an acrimonious meeting, Hewlett told them that it was none of their 'f—king business'. It might just have been coincidence, but a few weeks after the broadcast, the first-floor apartment of Matt Wiessler, the graphic designer who had forged the bank statements for Bashir, was broken into. Nothing was stolen – apart from the green computer disks containing details of the forged bank statements. Wiessler was now very concerned as the implications of his own actions began to sink in. 'The little bastard,' he said of the thief. As a senior BBC producer told me, 'The BBC found itself with a substantial dilemma. The story [of the forgery] was essentially true. So here was this enormously successful programme, and if it turned out that lying, cheating and deceiving had taken place, the feeling was that things could go pear-shaped for the BBC.' The reaction was to close ranks and blame 'jealous colleagues'.

In the event, Diana came to the rescue. The show's producer, Steve Hewlett, had told his boss, Tim Gardam, that he could provide proof that there was nothing wrong with the interview. Shortly before Christmas 1995 a handwritten note from the Princess arrived by courier. In it she had written that she was happy with the way she had been approached and the manner in which the interview was conducted. Of course, at that time she fully believed that the bank documents were authentic, and that she was under MI5 or MI6 surveillance. In short, she did not realize that she had been duped. As the journalist Richard Lindley wrote in his history of *Panorama*, referring to the Bashir affair, 'In the absence of any plausible explanation, he was wrong to do what he did. That cannot detract from the brilliance of his interview with which Diana expressed herself completely happily.'

After such a tortuous journey and controversial outcome, why did Diana write about the interview in such glowing tones? A friend of the Princess, one of the handful who knew about the genesis of the programme, explained to me: 'If you are in a paranoid state of mind and something comes out that you think is OK, the original reason for doing it is not in your mind at all. You are on a different plane. Her mood had moved on. People saw her in a strong, dignified way standing up for herself. It was a triumphal moment.'

In the immediate aftermath of the broadcast, Diana was on a high. 'I'm on top of things at the moment. I'm fine and I'm strong and I'm looking forward to whatever the future brings me,' she said. Haunted, anxious and scared beforehand, the Princess now felt vindicated and safe, the immediate danger past. More than that, she felt intensely grateful to Bashir for having provided the means for her to articulate her message. In fairness to Bashir, even though the methods he used to bring Diana in front of the camera were highly questionable, if not duplicitous, it was Diana who bore full responsibility for the way she answered his questions. He did not put words in her mouth. She took control of the narrative of her life, telling her story in the way she wanted it told. As Stephen Twigg remarked, 'It was another example of her growing confidence in herself to take control of her own life without reference to others.' When she doubted herself she was nourished by the mountain of mail which she had received since her *Panorama* confessional. In just a few days, some 6,000 letters from distressed women who suffered from eating disorders, loneliness or who were desperately unhappy with their lives, arrived on her desk. They had recognized something in Diana's emotional openness on TV that reflected their own sadness, pain and isolation. 'I'm overwhelmed by the response. Amazing,' she said, adding that she would try and meet some of those who had written to her.

This reaction, by both the Princess and the public, echoed the response provoked by my book three years earlier. As she had been then, she was nervous before going public, but felt relaxed and vindicated when she was handed the first batch of letters from people who had genuinely connected with her. Perhaps the most touching was from a young woman in Perth, Western Australia, who said that she had been abused as a child, anorexic as a teenager, and as an adult had never learned to read or write properly. Inspired by Diana, she had decided to go for medical help and enrol on a literacy course.

What Diana had not expected was that so many people would be surprised by her opinions, particularly of Prince Charles, as she had tried to prepare the ground beforehand. In many respects the interview was an abbreviated version of *Diana: Her True Story*, and it told those in her circle, and on its fringes, little that they had not heard many times before. The parade of newspaper editors and TV correspondents who had dined at Kensington Palace or entertained the Princess in newspaper boardrooms had listened to her talk much more frankly about her doubts concerning Charles and her aspirations for the future than she had on television. 'No views were expressed that I didn't know already,' commented her butler, a view reflected by others in her circle. Submerged in the immediate commotion was the constrained and contained way she talked about her eating disorders, her post-natal depression, her self-laceration and even Camilla Parker Bowles. The impression she gave was of a woman discussing a persona she had left behind. Her message was plain: 'I have moved on.'

When I listen to the tapes made in 1991, of Diana talking about that period in her life, which she called 'the dark ages', the difference is striking. Back then she spoke with a breathless haste, her tone urgent, emotional and at times even frenzied. It was the voice of a woman who, beneath the banter and laughter, had little sense of self-worth and was groping, almost shamefully, towards articulating her dreams of a life beyond the royal world.

In 1991 she had still been the fairy-tale princess who saw herself as, and indeed was, a prisoner inside the royal redoubt. Her television interview some four years later revealed a calmer, more controlled character, a woman who now had a clear sense of herself rather than one who was defined by others, notably the monarchy and the media. Here was a woman who was focused, self-reliant, articulate and emotionally literate, unafraid and unembarrassed to talk about her problems. 'I think every strong woman in history has had to walk down a similar path, and I think it's the strength that causes the confusion and the fear,' she said defiantly. The Princess was effectively bidding farewell to the old Diana as she essayed her curriculum vitae for her future role in the nation's affairs. Nevertheless, the overall effect of the interview was to prove very negative for Diana's image, ambitions and legacy.

That Diana would one day have given a TV interview is not in doubt. In 1994 a three-pronged assault, from myself, Colthurst and the *Daily Mail* journalist Richard Kay, came close to persuading her to appear on an ITV documentary about her life. She herself was very keen to do an interview about her charitable work, but her senior staff, particularly her press secretary Geoff Crawford, opposed it. As a secret compromise, the Princess agreed to be surreptitiously filmed visiting down-and-outs on London's South Bank. There was never any question that she might give the sort of explosive interview that appeared on *Panorama*.

So why did Diana choose to give this interview just when everything seemed to be going her way? The answer seems to be that she only agreed to the interview at this time because she was fearful of various conspiracies against her – fears that had been enhanced by her conversations with Martin Bashir and by the forged documents he had shown her. If Diana, who was much smarter than her opponents gave her credit for, had been able to choose the appropriate moment for a TV interview it would have been after her divorce when she was an independent woman, free from the constraints of royal protocol and able to talk openly about her life and ambitions. If she had lived, it would have been just the first in a series of TV interviews with big names like Barbara Walters, Oprah Winfrey or Clive James. While Bashir is now a star in his own right, his career has been dogged by controversy, particularly over his interview with singer Michael Jackson, which Jackson called 'a deception and betrayal'. Even the *New York Times* was moved to call Bashir's show 'callous self-interest masked as sympathy' for the way he seemed to have duped the superstar. The Duchess of York drew parallels between the Jackson show and the Diana interview, claiming on the *The View* TV show that the Princess would never have said all the things she did if he hadn't 'tricked' her – a claim he denied. A BBC executive who worked with Bashir noted after the Jackson row: 'The dodgy graphic seems all of a piece with the Michael Jackson stuff.' Diana's premature death means that her only TV interview is both her testament and epitaph, the interview's timing setting off a chain of events that are felt to this day.

On 29 November 1995, just nine days after Diana's appearance on television, she and Patrick Jephson drove into Buckingham Palace to face the fallout from her fireworks display. The consequences of her actions were not long in coming. At a meeting with the Queen's private secretary, Sir Robert Fellowes, and the Queen's press secretary, Charles Anson, the Princess nominally agreed to accept the smothering bear hug of Buckingham Palace – an arrangement Jephson had wanted for some time – and allow them to organize her life, both financially and administratively. The grudging umbrella currently offered by her husband, who still paid for all her household and office expenses, would be withdrawn. Buckingham Palace was, however, only lukewarm about the scheme and Jephson, who was behind the plan, soon realized why. The Queen's private secretary and other senior royal officials were busily pursuing a very different agenda.

Even as they discussed her future role, soundings were being taken at the highest level about a royal divorce. Nicholas Soames, the Armed Forces Minister and a close friend of Prince Charles, had already contacted Downing Street and asked the Prime Minister, John Major, to speak to the Queen about the matter. The Archbishop of Canterbury was also quietly canvassed. Soames, who, after watching the *Panorama* interview accused Diana of displaying the 'advanced stages of paranoia', publicly urged the couple to divorce 'promptly'. 'It is plain that the marriage has broken down irrevocably . . . and that divorce is inevitable,' he said bluntly. The historian Lord Blake, who advised Buckingham Palace on constitutional issues, lent his authority to moves to prepare the nation for the sad ending to the fairy-tale marriage. 'The present situation in which they seem to be giving a sort of tit-for-tat, running each other down, really has become almost intolerable,' he said.

The moment arrived sooner than Diana expected. While the Princess was in New York, where she received a humanitarian award on 12 December, the Queen had taken matters into her own hands and informed the Prime Minister that she would write to the couple and ask them to agree to 'an early divorce . . . in the best interests of the country'. It was a sign of just how intractable and how damaging the continued dispute was to the fabric of the monarchy that the Queen, whose natural instinct is to avoid confrontation and not to interfere in the lives of her children, had, however reluctantly, become involved. The marital dispute was the talk of polite and impolite society not just in Britain but beyond our shores. As the former American Ambassador to Britain, Raymond Seitz, remarked of those days in his memoir, *Over Here*, 'There was the party of the Prince and the party of the Princess, one demanding loyalty and the other sympathy, one describing the Princess as cunning, manipulative and publicity-hungry, and the other calling the Prince naive, whimsical and self-pitying.'

Diplomats and historians agree that the fallout went way beyond the personal breakdown between the Prince and Princess of Wales. The timing of the Queen's historic letter, just days before the traditional royal family's Christmas gathering at Sandringham, as well as her decision to become personally involved (admittedly encouraged and supported in this by the Prime Minister), reflected the genuine sense of crisis and exasperation felt by senior courtiers inside the beleaguered institution.

That frustration was directed not only at the Princess but also at her vacillating husband and the BBC, courtiers feeling pained by the lack of trust the public broadcaster had shown in the Palace.

As the Queen's biographer, Sarah Bradford, told me, 'The Wales divorce was undoubtedly the most damaging event since the abdication of Edward VIII in 1936. It brought into question the reality of the monarchy and the Queen's personal attributes as a mother and as a monarch.'

Diana, however, did not see it that way when, on 18 December, the handwritten note from the Queen – the first letter, the Princess observed ruefully, she had ever received from the Sovereign – was delivered by uniformed courier to Kensington Palace from Windsor Castle. She was shocked, angry, tearful and indignant. Three weeks earlier, the Princess, presenting an image of strength and self-possession, had told the world that it was 'not her wish' to divorce; now she was being asked, nay ordered, by her mother-in-law to end her marriage. To add insult to injury the Queen had discussed the matter with the Prime Minister, the Archbishop of Canterbury and others, without conferring person-ally with her daughter-in-law. Once she had calmed down, Diana realized that the Queen, whom she well knew preferred to put her head in the sand during domestic disputes – what the royal family call 'ostriching' – truly meant business.

What is more, the Queen had the law on her side. As Diana had been aware since the separation, she herself had fewer rights under law, particularly with regard to her children, than any other woman in the land. The Queen has under common law absolute right and authority for the care and education of her two grandsons, in particular Prince William, the heir presumptive. This right was last recognized in 1772 and the law has not been altered since. In theory, indeed, the Queen could at any time have overridden the wishes of their parents with regard to the boys' education and how and with whom they were to be brought up.

No sooner had Diana digested the contents of the Queen's note than she received another letter, this time from Prince Charles, personally requesting a divorce. In the letter, which began 'Dearest Diana', the Prince described the failure of their relationship as a 'national and personal tragedy'. However, he used the same phras-ing as the Queen in referring to the 'sad and complicated situation' of the royal marriage, which led Diana to suspect that the

Windsors were acting in concert against her. In typical fashion – Diana always prided herself on replying promptly – she sent the Queen and her husband handwritten letters almost by return, after first consulting one of her divorce lawyers, Anthony Julius. In her responses she was non-committal, saying that she would need time to reflect and that she would 'consider her options'.

Even though the Princess was shocked and wrong-footed by the Queen's intervention, tactically it had inadvertently played into Diana's hands. Ever since the separation she had had a fear, verging on the pathological, that she would be blamed for the divorce and had always played the waiting game. Now that that threat was lifted, the Princess had a genuine opportunity to make good her great escape. At the same time the Queen's pre-emptive strike had neatly let Prince Charles off the hook as the apportionment of blame would be more limited. The Queen's letter, which was leaked to the mass media within days – 'For once they can't blame me,' said Diana – meant that the public perceived that it was the Sovereign who was, quite unusually but properly, taking the initiative in order to protect the institution of monarchy.

There were immediate practical issues to be attended to, most notably whether the Princess should accept or decline the Queen's invitation to join the royal family at Sandringham. Before the separation she had found family gatherings difficult. In the last few years she had avoided them as far as possible. While her *Panorama* interview may have, in her mind, ended the chance of any real threat to her, that did not mean that the hostility felt by 'the enemy' had abated. In her mind, Sandringham was enemy territory, a feeling underscored by Prince Margaret's hostile letter and by the almost tangible antipathy of other members of the royal family. An off-the-cuff comment made by Princess Margaret to a titled lady friend at the time seemed to encapsulate the family's attitude: 'Poor Lilibet and Charles have done everything they can to get rid of the wretched girl, but she just won't go.'

Diana was already anxious and uncertain about spending Christmas with 'the leper colony' as she disparagingly called the royal family. The divorce letter from the Queen finally decided her – even though it meant leaving the boys, she would not go to

Sandringham. 'I would have gone up there in my BMW and come out in a coffin,' she remarked afterwards. Instead she spent Christmas Day on her own at Kensington Palace before flying off for a Caribbean holiday. In the days before her holiday she twice visited her therapist Susie Orbach and had time to phone her friend, the magazine editor Liz Tilberis, who had been her honorary lady-in-waiting in New York, to encourage her in her fight against cancer, as well as contacting a family in Lancashire whom she had befriended, who had lost their daughter to the disease.

The Princess's decision to decline the Sovereign's invitation, normally viewed as a command, to spend Christmas at Sandringham proved to be a momentous judgement, marking the nadir of her relationship with the Queen. For the first time in her royal career Diana had placed herself in direct conflict with the head of state. Since the separation Diana, who sincerely believed in the monarchy, had carefully maintained their relationship and remained somewhat in awe of a woman who, while not beyond reproach, commanded her complete respect. So, however compelling her reasons, this was, as far as the Queen was concerned, an affront too many. From now on Diana found that the Queen was not available to take her telephone calls and that meetings with Her Majesty's courtiers were cool, brisk and formal. While the Queen ensured that the door to her daughter-in-law remained open, the Princess discovered that the hinges were much stiffer and she had to push much harder to get what she wanted. As she later remarked, 'The only thing we had in common was Charles, and now I didn't have Charles any more.'

Diana's problems were coming not as single spies but as a platoon. Not only was she now fast-tracked on a divorce, but she found her staunchest allies were deserting her. At a crucial moment in the divorce negotiations, in early January 1996 her private secretary Patrick Jephson resigned, ostensibly because of the *Panorama* interview and the Tiggy Legge-Bourke incident. While Jephson's departure left her bereft for a time, in truth it was remarkable that he had tarried for six years given that his long-term agenda for Diana – as some kind of saintly dowager princess doing good works from inside Buckingham Palace – fundamentally conflicted with her emerging vision of herself as an independent princess for the world. In fact, he had first considered resignation in 1993, following Diana's Time and Space speech, and later sounded out David Puttnam about a job in the film industry. When Diana heard of these plans, she refused to speak to Puttnam for several months because of his perceived 'disloyalty' and never fully regained her trust in her private secretary. 'It was the most ridiculous thing,' commented Puttnam.

It seemed to Diana that the circle of people she could trust was ever decreasing. At this critical time she felt that even her own family were deserting her. In early April, when divorce negotiations were delicately poised, she received a coruscating letter from her brother, accusing her of 'manipulation and deceit', adding that he hoped she was getting 'appropriate and sympathetic treatment' for her mental problems. While the origins of the row are unknown – it coincided with the revelation in a Sunday newspaper that month that Martin Bashir, the man Spencer had introduced to his sister, had forged documents – it added further pressures on the Princess. (In typical Spencer style, they healed the rift later in the year, the Princess visiting her brother in South Africa when he had his own marital difficulties.)

The question of whom she could trust was always on her mind and in this deteriorating atmosphere of acrimony and mutual suspicion she was at pains to exert more day-to-day direction of her affairs. Her links with her managerial staff became looser and more distant, as she sought to hire outsiders who were untainted by the Palace culture. The downside of this was that they lacked the experience to find a way through the labyrinthine maze that was Palace politics at this critical moment in her life. Additionally, they were hired very much on the Princess's own terms. For example, when she appointed a media adviser, Jane Atkinson, a few days after Jephson's departure, it was as a consultant rather than as a member of staff, a signal that the appointment did not carry much weight. Atkinson soon found that the Princess, who relied on her instincts more and more, worked to her own agenda whether it was right or wrong. Often Atkinson's advice was ignored, and while she was ostensibly Diana's official mouthpiece, the Princess, having taken spoonfuls of medicine from the media, was determined to be her own spin doctor, using her secretary, Victoria Mendham, and butler, Paul Burrell, to place stories anonymously in the newspapers.

Since the success of her television interview, Martin Bashir had also joined Diana's circle, helping to draft her speeches, much to the chagrin of the journalist Richard Kay who had acted as her unofficial mouthpiece for several years. Even when, in April 1996, the *Mail on Sunday* revealed that the bank statements Bashir had shown her were forgeries, the Princess kept faith in him. At the same time, she was regularly in contact with various Fleet Street editors, notably tabloid rivals Stuart Higgins (editor of the *Sun*) and Piers Morgan (editor of the *Daily Mirror*) as she attempted to ride the media bronco.

While this ad-hoc approach inevitably met with mixed results with the media, in other respects a more flexible arrangement served her well. Trust, loyalty and control were her watchwords. In 1995 she personally contacted Princess Anne's former close-protection officer, Colin Tebbutt, who had retired from the Metropolitan Police, and asked him if he wanted to work as her bodyguard-cum-driver. 'Are you still a rebel?' she asked gaily. 'Come and join the rebels.' Their relationship meant that she employed him or a member of his freelance team of drivers as and when she wanted, not because she was obliged to. (Contrary to public belief, when she was out and about in London and elsewhere she was often accompanied by a driver who was also trained in close-protection work.) The retired bodyguard became so close to the Princess that he and her butler Paul Burrell were the only mourners outside her immediate family to be invited to attend her burial on the Althorp estate.

With a small and inexperienced crew Diana entered the fray of divorce negotiations, relying on her own instincts and resources. She now understood that the Queen was, uniquely, as much a party to the divorce negotiations as Prince Charles. Indeed, the game plan of the Princess's lawyers, Lord Mishcon and Anthony Julius, was to resolve what they called 'the Queen problem', namely

Diana's future title, her continued residence at Kensington Palace and the custody of the children, before negotiating the financial settlement with Prince Charles. A satisfactory outcome of discussions with the Queen would have a considerable impact on 'the Charles problem'. At a meeting at Buckingham Palace in February 1996 the Queen assured Diana about the custody and care of her boys and indicated that it was 'unlikely' that Charles would marry Camilla Parker Bowles. On the vexed issue of her future title, one report says that the Queen suggested that she should be known as 'Diana, Princess of Wales', while the Princess herself later told friends that she offered to give up her title because she assumed that that was the wish of the Sovereign.

The issue remained uncertain until the Princess had met with her estranged husband a couple of weeks later. In a note to Diana before the meeting on 28 February, the Prince said that they should let bygones be bygones. 'Let's move forward and not look back, and stop upsetting one another,' he urged. While that may have been the spirit at the start, by the end of their forty-five-minute meeting alone together, the old suspicions crowded in. Diana was determined to issue her own statement before, as she saw it, her husband's side beat her to it.

She made it clear in her statement in February that it was Prince Charles who had requested the divorce. Not only had she agreed to his demand, but she had decided to give up her HRH title and be known as Diana, Princess of Wales. The Queen and Prince Charles were dismayed at her unilateral action, the Palace making it clear that the Princess's 'decisions' were as yet no more than requests. It seemed that Diana and Charles even disagreed about reaching a final agreement. This was perhaps a suitable epitaph for their marriage.

Irritation turned to anger when it appeared that Diana was briefing the media to the effect that she had been pressured into relinquishing her title. In response the Queen authorized her spokesman to state publicly and categorically that the decision was made by the Princess alone. 'It is wrong that the Queen or the Prince asked her,' said Her Majesty's spokesman. Now everyone knew. It was the Princess that did away with her title, stabbing herself in the back with her own knife. In many respects, the mixed messages she conveyed about the loss of her title symbolized her ambivalence about saying farewell to her old life, an understandable mixture of disappointment, resignation, sadness and regret for missed opportunities.

While Diana's title was within the purview of the Queen, discussions about the financial settlement were with the Prince and his lawyers. In the cut-and-thrust of offer and counter-offer, Diana was doubtless eager to explore every avenue to gain the upper hand. Her unsettling conversation with the former orderly George Smith and his allegations of male rape had preyed on her mind. In the spring of 1996, with negotiations delicately poised she decided to see him once more and this time tape his shocking story. While her attempts at being her own private eye were not entirely successful – she had to visit his home in Twickenham for a second meeting when she discovered that her tape machine had not worked – she now had the evidence that she could conceivably use as a bargaining chip if the divorce discussions turned nasty. Whether she was seeing Smith for his or for her benefit is open to debate. Indeed, it is worth noting that it was not until the autumn of 1996, after the divorce had been finalized in late August, that Diana first informed her ex-husband of Smith's allegations. If she had been truly alarmed she would have alerted him months earlier.

Unsurprisingly, the very fact that the information came through Diana served to devalue the currency of Smith's claims. Inevitably, Smith was pitied rather than believed; the Prince, his staff – and even Hounslow police, to whom he also reported the alleged offence, in October 1996 – giving no credence to his account. As the Prince's press secretary, Sandra Henney, observed, 'All we had was one poor, sad individual making an allegation of assault some years before to the Princess, who, at that time, quite frankly wanted to find ways of embarrassing her husband.' Indeed, the Prince's senior protection officer, Chief Inspector Colin Trimming later admitted that he had dismissed the allegations out of hand mainly because Smith's cause was being championed by the Princess.

Eventually, it was decided that the only sensible course of action was that Smith, who continued to have treatment for his personal problems at a private clinic, should be let go. In December 1996 he was given a £38,000 settlement. Fiona Shackleton, then the Prince's solicitor, told an internal household meeting that she had been ordered to make the problem 'go away' and confessed that an encounter with the distressed orderly was 'one of the lowest points in my professional career'.

By the end of the divorce negotiations, the Princess had become a very rich woman in her own right. She might have lost the title of 'Her Royal Highness' but she had found £17 million as compensation. As for the title . . . 'Don't worry, Mummy. I will give it back to you one day, when I am king,' William told her.

While Diana now faced the prospect of curtsying to junior royals like her neighbour, Princess Michael of Kent, whom she dubbed 'The U-Boat Commander', she was buoyed by a supportive letter from that lady telling her that it would cause her 'great embarrassment' if Diana even considered curtsying.

Diana used the loss of her title as a convenient excuse to relinquish her patronage of nearly a hundred charities – although she had in fact written her letters of resignation weeks earlier and kept them in the safe in her offices at St James's Palace before the decision was finalized in July 1996. She did, however, keep formal affiliations with six charities that reflected her current interests in AIDS, the homeless, sick children, leprosy and, thanks to the last-minute suggestion of her media consultant, the ballet. 'It will give you something light-hearted to do,' Jane Atkinson told her.

While this move came as a considerable blow to a number of very deserving charities, realistically it was no great surprise. The Princess had stepped back from her charity work at the end of 1993, and as she was trying to define her new style and life, it was as well that she should make a clean break with the past. What she failed to mention was the fact that she now resented working on behalf of a family she had little sympathy for and even less in common with. It says much about her residual bitterness towards the institution which made her, tried to break her in and finally released her, that while watching a phone-in television debate on the monarchy, one evening in early 1997, Diana made several anonymous phone votes in favour of Britain abolishing the monarchy and becoming a republic – with her eldest son, heir to the throne, stretched out on the rug beside her.

That said, whatever she thought in private, in public she was scrupulously supportive. She infuriated her friends, the fashion designer Gianni Versace and the singer Elton John, when she belatedly withdrew a foreword she had written in July 1996, just as her divorce was being finalized, for a book of photographs to raise money for the singer's AIDS Foundation. The book, *Rock and Royalty*, juxtaposed suggestive images with pictures of the royal family, which she felt would offend the Queen.

Doubtless she was concerned too that it could affect the detail of her divorce settlement, which was finalized a few weeks later on 28 August 1996. 'It's a tragic end to a wonderful story,' her brother-in-law, Sir Robert Fellowes, said to her in a phone call of support. Diana was resolutely upbeat. 'Oh no, it's the beginning of a new chapter,' she replied.

It was her son William who helped her write the first page of that new chapter in her life. While the Princess was, by force of circumstance and design, reshaping her office to reflect her distance from the Palace machine, her older son suggested a scheme that practically and symbolically signalled a long goodbye to her old life. In July 1996, just after her divorce settlement was agreed, Prince William had the brainwave that she should sell her royal gowns for charity as a way of saying a farewell to her royal life at the same time as doing some good. It was an inspired idea, capturing his mother's imagination, and very much in the spirit of her desire to free herself from the ghosts of the past. She chose seventy-nine of her favourite dresses, including the gown she wore at the White House when she danced with John Travolta, and joined in enthusiastically in the seven-month process of cataloguing, photographing and eventually auctioning her eventful royal history, appropriately, in New York, which she considered to be her second home. The auction, conducted by Christie's, raised $5.7 million for the Royal Marsden Hospital, which specializes in the treatment of cancer, and the AIDS Crisis

Trust – much to the outrage of the virtually bankrupt National AIDS Trust, of which she was still patron.

The whole process was a joyous release, and the Princess responded with the kind of energy and eagerness that summed up the essence of her personality. During that time Christie's creative director Meredith Etherington-Smith watched the new Diana emerging from the shackles of her royal past. 'The Princess is very energetic. She doesn't amble, she swoops and she's fast,' she noted. 'It became quickly apparent that she was very funny.' As she got to know Diana she began to 'glimpse the down-to-earth person behind the princessly chimera', a woman who was not exactly larger than life but 'somehow brighter, more luminous'. When the Princess suggested that a fresh set of photographs should be taken of her by a new fashion photographer, Etherington-Smith had the idea of using the Peruvian cameraman, Mario Testino. 'I want you to photograph her as a person, not as a princess, and I want you to capture her fun and her huge energy,' she told him, an editorial direction that, given how tragically soon the Princess's life would end, was unwittingly inspired. The photo shoot, in a disused schoolhouse in Battersea, was a memorably creative day, the high-light being an impromptu sashay down a make-believe catwalk by a barefoot Princess and her new best friend, the photographer from Peru. When she looked at the finished work, which eventually went on show at the National Portrait Gallery, Diana said, 'But these are me. Really me.'

It had been a long hard road. For the first time since she was a teenager sharing a bachelor apartment with three girlfriends, the Princess was free to be herself. In the winter of 1996 she went to a dinner party with her friend Lady Cosima Somerset, who had also weathered a high-profile divorce. 'As we drove there, I felt a sense of two women who had finally broken free of other people's rules,' recalled Cosima. 'Diana showed everyone, and especially women, that freedom has its rewards.'

CHAPTER TEN

The Crowning of the Queen of Hearts

L IKE A SCENE from a romantic Hollywood movie, a young well-heeled couple stood arm-in-arm on the deck of their luxury yacht watching the blood-red sun sink slowly into the Mediterranean. In the background the haunting refrain from the hit movie *The English Patient* played, the lush soundtrack interrupted only by the sound of popping champagne corks. The young woman, lithe, beautiful and carefree, raised her champagne glass in a toast. 'This is a special occasion; it's the anniversary of my divorce!'

It was 28 August 1997, exactly a year after the decree nisi of Diana, Princess of Wales was agreed and announced. On that day in 1996 she had been so overwhelmed with sadness and loss that Lucia Flecha de Lima had flown in from Washington just to be by her side. 'She was in need of comfort,' Lucia recalled. Later Diana had lunch at the home of her other surrogate mother, Lady Annabel Goldsmith, where she had a tearful encounter with her friend Lady Cosima Somerset. 'I put my arms around her and held her. We did not say anything,' Cosima Somerset remembered.

Now, twelve months later, she was in the arms of her host and new lover, Dodi Fayed, the son of the Harrods owner Mohamed.

She was, she told her friends, 'blissfully happy'. Talk of marriage was in the air. When she saw pictures of the two of them together, Diana's former astrologer, Penny Thornton, observed, 'You could see quite clearly that she was not only in love but in lust. Every woman in the world could see that she was having great sex.'

In celebration of her anniversary, Dodi handed out twenty-dollar Cohiba cigars to the crew on board the 180-foot *Jonikal*. Then they headed for the beach on Sardinia's stunning Costa Smeralda, where the couple enjoyed a romantic barbecue and drank vintage wine in the shimmering moonlight, and the yacht's captain, Luigi, serenaded them with a Gipsy Kings song.

It was an appropriate choice given the seemingly peripatetic and restless nature of Diana's life. In her first year of freedom she had made more than twenty overseas trips and spent twelve weeks away from London. It seemed that she was roaming from country to country in search of her personal Holy Grail – peace of mind. While few begrudged her a taste of happiness, many questioned the price she was paying, feeling that she had too readily exchanged the majestic pools of monarchy for the shallow springs of international celebrity, leaving herself open to dismissal, ridicule and vilification. For a woman trying to cultivate a serious global persona, she appeared to be indulging in incongruous frivolity.

Just a few days before, she and Dodi had used the green and gold Harrods helicopter to fly to the modest Derbyshire home of her psychic, Rita Rogers, for a reading. Even Dodi's indulgent father, Mohamed Fayed was bemused. 'I couldn't understand it,' he said.

At first glance it seemed that the self-styled queen of hearts had abdicated her throne. She survived with just a skeleton staff, her charitable commitments were pared to the bone, while what passed for her court had become the caricature of a Ruritanian folly, reduced to butler, cook, a couple of faith healers and an ever-diminishing circle of friends, many of whom were outsiders from overseas who had little appreciation of English society.

Like Edward VIII, who gave up his throne in 1936 for the woman he loved, Diana increasingly faced social if not physical exile from high society. As one of her closest friends explained, 'It was difficult for the Princess. Everyone says that she was the one who fell out with people. That is not entirely true. After the separation and certainly after the divorce, she was rejected by that tightly knit group, the English aristocracy. They were afraid of Prince Charles and the royal family and were uncomfortable having her around. The only place for her to go was abroad.'

Cast out, like her own mother, from British polite society, she was now dating a Muslim millionaire whose father, for all his wealth, could not buy himself a British passport. Her dislocation from the life she once led was symbolized by the fact that as she stretched out on the deck of the £15 million yacht, Prince William was spending his day crawling through the heather at Balmoral, doing what his father, grandfather, great-grandfather and great-great-grandfather had done for more than a century – stalking deer. Or, as his mother said bluntly, 'killing things'.

As with so much of Diana's life, first appearances were deceptive. In the last year she seemed to have come into her own, a woman who had glimpsed light at the end of a long, dark tunnel. She had proved to the world that it was possible to combine glamour with integrity, happiness with compassion, without the necessity of sacrificing her life on the altar of duty and propriety.

The Princess was determined to make something of herself, and her position, that would have a real impact on the world. As Debbie Frank observed, 'She could have ended up doing nothing with her life, she could have been so beaten down by the system that she gave up. Instead she really found a purpose in life and you have to admire her spirit.'

Far from abdicating, Diana had enjoyed her coronation just a couple of months before. The woman who had her own personal trainer and therapist – and did not conceal the fact – was crowned, appropriately enough, at the hairdresser's, where she was watching television. 'Yes,' she cried, punching the air in delight as, on 22 May 1997, she watched the then Foreign Secretary Robin Cook announce on the news that Britain would enforce a ban on landmines.

That was a moment of great triumph for the woman now lounging on the deck of a playboy's yacht. A fashionable icon embracing an unfashionable cause, she had produced some of the most powerful images of the decade when she consoled the victims of landmines in Bosnia and nervously walked through a recently cleared minefield in Angola, a powerful juxtaposition of beauty with the beastliness of war. 'Her crusade has captured public attention over a weapon that strikes hardest at civilians,' wrote Robin Cook in the *Daily Mirror* at the time.

Diana's interest in landmines was inspired, as so often was the case with her, by personal contacts. As early as March 1995 Mike Whitlam, then CEO of the British Red Cross, was sending her material – videos, books, briefing papers – about the issue of landmines. Her interest was further whetted by her conversations with Simone Simmons who, in the early summer of 1996, had visited Bosnia. She returned with horrific accounts and photographs showing the devastating effects of anti-personnel landmines, which kill and maim indiscriminately. The Princess was shocked by the terrible effects of these weapons on civilians, particularly women and children, and wanted to do something to help. At the time in the middle of helping to organize the sale of her royal dress collection, in the autumn of 1996 Diana invited Mike Whitlam to tea at Kensington Palace to consider the matter further, the couple discussing possible visits to Angola, Afghanistan and other lands scarred by the curse of landmines.

It was not until December of that year, however, that she formally agreed to visit the African country. In the same month, too, she accepted an invitation to attend the première of Lord Attenborough's movie, *In Love and War*, based on Ernest Hemingway's novel about the folly of conflict. The evening was in aid of a British Red Cross appeal to help the victims of landmines.

For the last few years Diana had had an ambivalent relationship with this venerable charity. When she and Charles first separated in 1992, courtiers felt that the Red Cross was an ideal umbrella organization to shelter her from the storms she would inevitably face as she strode out on her own. Diana was never wholly convinced, feeling that because of its long-established links with the royal family – the Queen Mother and the Queen had for decades been associated with the charity, and the Queen has been patron and president of the British Red Cross since 1952 – it was the monarchy under an assumed name.

Yet, even after her Time and Space speech in December 1993, Diana maintained her links with the Red Cross, agreeing to become vice-president and then joining a special Geneva-based commission to discuss refugee problems in Rwanda. It quickly became apparent that, while she aspired towards a more serious image as a working royal, sitting in rooms discussing strategy was not her forte. Her view was that as a frontline figurehead her image and personal skills could illuminate an issue more brightly than any number of worthy reports. The landmine campaign then was the right issue at the right time.

Once Diana was committed she made it clear that this was no passing fancy, as the landmine campaigner, Chris Moon, himself a landmine victim, observed after meeting her at Kensington Palace: 'She was genuinely committed from the humanitarian point of view. She thought landmines were simply wrong and knew she had the profile to bring the issue to world attention.' Diana's South African friend, Jenni Rivett, remembered how 'passionately' she spoke about the issue. 'The Princess felt very strongly about getting involved in something that wasn't a ballet charity,' Jenni said. 'She believed that landmines were a subject simply being ignored by people.'

After some discussion with Mike Whitlam and much soul-searching, the Princess decided that her first visit would be to Angola. She realized that this campaign marked a change in her approach to humanitarian issues. Not only was it an international movement but the issue was high-profile, highly charged and highly political. It was, as she would say, 'very grown-up', the Princess impressing even hardened journalists by her obvious commitment and hard work, and not just her charisma. The *Sunday Times* Africa correspondent Christina Lamb admitted that she had been cynical about Diana's motives before the tour but became deeply moved as she watched her at work, Diana never flinching from the gruesome sights she witnessed in the hospitals and clinics she visited. 'She had something I had only ever seen before – from Nelson Mandela – a kind of aura that made people want to be with her, and a completely natural, straight-from-the-heart sense of how to bring hope to those who seem to us to have little to live for.'

Diana agreed to be photographed walking through a recently cleared minefield, knowing that the image would be more powerful than any number of petitions, though she was acutely aware of the possible physical risks, and was genuinely scared. Millions of television viewers saw the Princess's walk, which, as she had recognized, did more than anything else to draw the public's attention to the issue. Once again she was pushing back the boundaries in her life, testing herself physically and emotionally.

While Diana had finally found 'a role', as Lord Deedes, her companion on several of her visits, noted, she had had to tiptoe gingerly through her own personal minefield, not only confronting her doubts and qualms but also in avoiding booby traps set by the Palace, politicians and diplomats. When during her four-day visit to Angola in January 1997 she was informed that Lord Howe, who had been a junior defence minister in the Conservative government, had labelled her a 'loose cannon' because of her naive interference in a complex matter, she was bewildered and reduced almost to the point of tears. David Puttnam dismissed Howe as a 'Prince Charles groupie', but the Princess was clearly flustered, protesting her innocence in a remark filmed by TV cameras: 'I only want to help. I am a humanitarian. I always have been and I always will be.'

Diana received a much warmer reception from the next government, elected in May 1997, her groundwork with the new Prime Minister paying instant dividends. During that summer she took William along to Chequers, the Prime Minister's official country retreat. While the young prince played soccer with the Blair boys, she spent several hours with the Prime Minister discussing her future role. Blair was very taken with the fact that the world's most famous and widely acknowledged woman was British and that her international stature should be utilized. 'I think at last I will have someone who knows how to use me,' she said later. (The Prime Minister intended to speak to the Queen about her role, but Diana died before a firm commitment could be made.)

Diana had come a long way from the days when she accepted her first charitable patronages because they were safe, mainstream, and uncontroversial. As the feminist commentator Bea Campbell said of the Princess at this time in her life, 'She found purpose by lending herself to philanthropy, but by now philanthropy had been politicized, good works were often dangerous works. Servicing the poor was radical, affirming people with AIDS took guts and campaigning against landmines took on the warmongers, the arms trade and of course the Government itself.'

As part of her renewed focus on humanitarian work Diana, using Martin Bashir as a ghostwriter, planned a charity book, provisionally titled *In Faith and Hope*, to point up her renewed commitment to global causes. Everything had been planned in outline right down to the launch party at Claridge's, although, typically, Diana was worried as to whether she had the intellectual ability to write a book – even with a co-author. The literary agent Vivienne Schuster recalled the discussions about the projected book: 'Under the terms of her divorce settlement she couldn't – wouldn't – talk about her marriage and divorce and the boys. But she did want to talk about the way ahead, and how she saw the future.'

An integral part of that future was her landmines work, the Princess having decided to throw herself into the issue. During the summer of 1997, she made two speeches on the subject, one in London, the other in Washington following an earlier meeting with Hillary Clinton. She had pencilled in a visit to Cambodia ('She was terrifically excited,' David Puttnam recollected) as well as trips to Iraq, Afghanistan, India and China. Diana was due, too, to make a speech in Oslo, Norway in September 1997, a week after her tragic death, in which she would propose bold new moves to render harmless minefields around the world, but her usual approach was to the people, not political.

Diana's visit to Angola in January 1997 made a profound and enduring impression. 'Those limbless children, I can't get them out of my mind,' she told friends when she arrived home, recalling how she had sat and held the hand of a little girl, Helena Ussova, whose insides had been blown out by a mine. 'Is she an angel?' the youngster asked shortly before she died. During her visit to Sarajevo in August, Diana impulsively hugged a woman who was tending to her son's grave in a local graveyard, a victim of the conflict, a young woman reaching out to another human being. 'I pay a great deal of attention to people, and I remember them,' she told the French newspaper *Le Monde*. 'Every meeting, every visit is special.'

As Tony Blair had observed after their first secret meeting, Diana was one of those rare public figures – he included former American President Bill Clinton in that category – who could communicate effectively by a gesture. 'Yes, I do touch,' Diana declared in her last interview. 'I believe that everyone needs that, whatever their age. When you put your hand on a friendly face, you make contact right away; you communicate warmth, show that you're close by. It's a gesture that comes to me naturally from the heart.'

Her favourite picture of herself showed her tightly holding a blind boy, whom she knew was going to die, when she visited the Shaukat Khanum hospital in Lahore, Pakistan, in February 1996. Her trip was in response to an invitation from the former Pakistani cricket captain, Imran Khan, who had raised funds for the hospital. She was so taken with the hospital's work that she flew over to Pakistan again in May 1997.

These visits were not, however, solely to support a deserving cause. Even after Diana's BBC interview and the tumult over the divorce, the man who occupied her thoughts throughout this time was Hasnat Khan. He was, in her eyes, her salvation and her future, and Diana saw her visits to his homeland as much a chance to get to know his culture and family as to support Imran Khan's project. She met Hasnat's parents, and other members of his family, declaring on her return home, 'They loved me, they really did love me and they didn't mind at all that I'm not a Muslim. Now there is absolutely no reason why we can't get married, I'm so happy.'

Diana was now talking about marriage, children, and a new life with Hasnat, either in Australia or South Africa. There was even a suggestion that she might consider converting to Islam in order to facilitate their union. She formally introduced him to William and Harry at Kensington Palace, all the while harbouring dreams of becoming 'Mrs Khan' and, according to one report, of having a 'beautiful brown baby girl' she planned to call Allegra, a name suggested by Annabel Goldsmith. Diana naively believed that the baby girl, being of mixed race and with parents of different religious backgrounds, would help unite the world and aid in peace making.

The Princess certainly saw the relationship as a true partnership, believing that with Mr Khan by her side she could achieve her dream of opening hospices, modelled on Mother Teresa's work, on a worldwide scale. 'She felt that this could happen and that together, she and Hasnat could change the world. Diana was very serious as she was aware of her power by then and knew that the money would be there,' asserted Oonagh Shanley-Toffolo.

At the same time, Diana actively pursued new avenues to help her lover advance his career abroad, either in South Africa or in Australia. She was so smitten with him that she accepted an invitation to attend a ball in October 1996 in support of the Victor Chang Institute in Sydney, named after a surgeon who had trained Hasnat Khan. A few days before, at a humanitarian conference in Rimini, Italy, she charmed the South African heart transplant pioneer Christiaan Barnard and discussed the work prospects for Khan in South Africa. 'She was just using me to get her boyfriend a job,' complained the veteran surgeon. Several months later, in March 1997, she paid her first visit to Cape Town to get a taste of the country for herself, meeting South Africa's President Nelson Mandela and enjoying a reunion with her brother Charles who, despite their previous differences, became her closest family ally during her last year.

While the prospect of making a new life existed as a tantalizing if unobtainable vision, Diana's single-minded focus on the object of her love was unnerving. Intense and obsessive, Diana's neediness was as demanding as it was compulsive. A certain 'Dr Armani' would bombard Khan with telephone calls while her butler was regularly sent to the hospital with letters and told to deliver them to the surgeon in person. Her demands began to interfere with Khan's work, and on several occasions she became distressed and tearful because he couldn't come to the phone as he was in the operating theatre. As Simone Simmons observed: 'She was besotted with him and I think his rather reserved manner made it worse.'

Khan's work meshed with her own interests and it was not uncommon for the Princess to follow him on his rounds while he was on duty at the hospital late at night. She even watched him perform heart operations. Unfortunately her chance presence at one operation exposed her to ridicule and mockery. The Princess, wearing gown and mask as well as black mascara and earrings, was captured by Sky TV watching a heart operation which, it so happened, they had arranged to film. She spent four hours watching Khan's boss, the leading heart surgeon Professor Sir Magdi Yacoub, operate on a young African boy, seven-year-old Arnaud Wambo, who had been flown to Harefield Hospital in April 1996 by the Chain of Hope charity, which had invited Diana to attend.

Afterwards she was not only criticized for being present in the operating theatre but, the *Panorama* interview still fresh in the public mind, she was also accused of staging a photo call to enhance her caring image. Sir Magdi Yacoub's valiant defence of her presence – 'The Princess comes to see sick people at other times, she supports them, she talks to them.' – was lost in the cacophony of censure. Condemnation from the media, and especially a cruel parody by the satirist and impersonator Rory Bremner, deeply distressed Diana who felt what she saw as her 'work', that was so much at the heart of her true spirit, was being wilfully misunderstood, that the wrong motives were being ascribed to her.

While Hasnat Khan did his best to comfort her, he recognized this as a vivid example of what lay in store for him should they ever marry. His first real taste of media scrutiny was when the *Sunday Mirror* broke the story of their romance in November 1996. Diana promptly used her journalist friend Richard Kay to denounce the tale as 'bullshit' and state that the notion was 'laughable', but Khan felt that her denial rather debased him and their relationship. She was, after all, now divorced and entitled to admit to an adult relationship with a new man. That their romance continued in hiding diminished and demeaned them both. At the same time, however,

Diana gives a speech for the charity Centrepoint in 1995 (*above left*). As her independence grew, so too did her desire to forge a unique role for herself on the world stage – she used her charity work to facilitate this. During this time the Princess enjoyed a fulfilling relationship with Dr Hasnat Khan (*above right*). The Muslim doctor, who has never betrayed Diana's confidence, fuelled the Princess's growing interest in medicine (*below*) and religion.

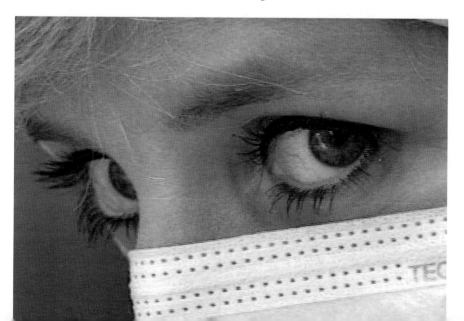

ABOVE: The Princess in Pakistan with Jemima Khan, the English wife of the Pakistani politician and former international cricketer Imran Khan. With Hasnat Khan an increasingly important figure in her life, Diana was encouraged by the success of their mixed-race marriage and developed a strong friendship with the couple.

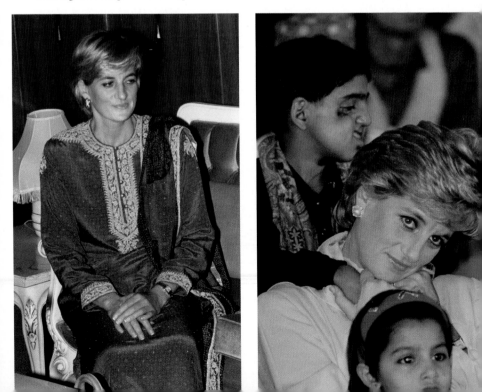

ABOVE: The Princess with a group of Hindu schoolchildren in London, demonstrating as ever her remarkable rapport with children, which was apparent throughout her life.

FACING PAGE, BELOW LEFT: Diana in traditional Muslim dress in Pakistan. Though ostensibly in the country for her charity work, it is known that she took the opportunity to visit Hasnat Khan's parents and hoped that they would approve of a marriage between herself and their son.

FACING PAGE, BELOW RIGHT: The Princess on a visit to a Pakistani hospital. From the millions of photographs taken of her, this was among Diana's personal favourites.

ABOVE: The Princess with her mother, Frances Shand Kydd, at Wimbledon in 1993.

BELOW: Diana shares a joke with her sisters, Lady Jane Fellowes and Lady Sarah McCorquodale. As the youngest sister, Diana would often turn to her elder siblings for their worldly-wise advice.

Diana with her beloved sons, Princes William and Harry, at the Head of State ceremony in 1995. Harry leans in to listen closely to his mother, as she carefully gives advice to the future King, Prince William.

LEFT: The Princess with her stepmother Raine, Lady Spencer. Although Diana hated the woman as a teenager, cruelly dubbing her 'Acid Raine', she found strength in putting her bitterness behind her and eventually forged a friendship that lasted until her death.

BELOW: Post-divorce, Diana and Charles meet at William's 1997 confirmation at St George's Chapel, Windsor Castle (William and Harry shake hands with the clergy in the background). Hesitantly relaxed with each other, the picture shows their increasing civility as well as their mutual determination to support the fractured family unit.

iiling and content, a divorced Diana attends a charity event in May 1997. She exudes a rarely
en peace and tranquillity, appearing confident and relaxed with her new found autonomy.

RIGHT: At Prince William's suggestion, the Princess celebrated the start of her new life by auctioning off the trappings of the old – her formal dresses. The New York event raised an astonishing $3.25 million for charity. Diana is pictured here at the glamorous pre-auction reception in June 1997.

BELOW: The Princess in New York, at a charity gala in 1995. Increasingly, Diana spent more and more time in America, where she was adored by both the public and the celebrity set, and readily embraced in their hearts.

ᴠᴇ: Diana breakfasts
the then First
, Hillary Clinton,
ashington DC.
shared the rare
ion of being
rful female figures
could really make
ference on the
al stage.

ᴛ: The Princess
s with Henry
inger, Colin Powell
Barbara Walters
ew York's United
ebral Palsy Awards
995. Diana was
ed Humanitarian
e Year at the
tigious ceremony,
ly recognition
er increasingly
ortant humanitarian
 across the world.

FACING PAGE: Diana in Bosnia (*top left*) and Angola (*top right*) during her 1997 campaign against landmines. Landmines were a highly sensitive political issue, and the Princess used her special abilities to gain global recognition of the widespread problem, simultaneously comforting the victims in her own unique way. It was perhaps the most significant work she ever undertook, leading to a change in international law.

During her campaign the Princess also agreed to walk through a recently cleared minefield (*below*), a brave yet typically 'Diana' thing to do. Her own vulnerability immediately highlighted the plight of millions.

RIGHT: Diana on her thirty-sixth birthday in July 1997. Accomplished, self-assured, respected and admired, seemingly poised for a bright future founded on her terms alone.

ABOVE: As this 1988 picture of Diana and Dodi Fayed shows, the pair were known to each other long before their whirlwind romance in the summer of 1997.

BELOW: Nearly a decade after they initially met, the playboy and the Princess embark on a passionate affair, sparking a paparazzi rush to secure that first, lucrative shot of them together, as they holiday in St Tropez.

ᴠᴇ: Lady Diana Spencer was, before her marriage, a swimming champion and diver
aordinaire. Shown here on holiday in 1997, the thirty-six-year-old Princess displays the same
eticism and spirit of her youth, delighting in her skill as she executes a perfect dive into the
diterranean.

ᴏw: The Princess and Prince Harry enjoy the water sports on offer in St Tropez. Diana
dayed with both her sons in the summer of 1997 and displayed time and again her distinctive,
loving approach to parenting, which she felt was so important to their future roles.

ABOVE: Saturday 31 August 1997, and Diana and Dodi leave the Ritz Hotel in Paris by the back door, th[e] moment captured by CCTV came[ra.] Ever since their romance had been splashed across the tabloids, pursu[ed] by paparazzi was ever more freque[nt.] Henri Paul (*left*) confidently assure[d] the couple that he will out-drive th[e] persistent photographers.

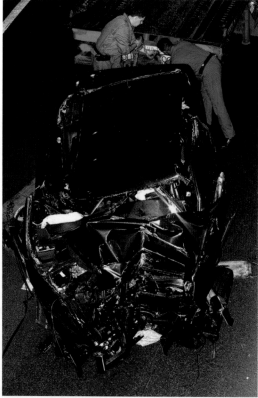

LEFT: The drive is short-lived. Shown here is the stark and horrif[ying] wreckage of the black Mercedes, annihilated in the crash that ultima[tely] proved fatal for Diana's lover and chauffeur – and herself.

RIGHT: The Princess's coffin lies at rest in the Chapel Royal, St James's Palace, ahead of her funeral in Westminster Abbey, London. No photographers were allowed inside the chapel, but an illustrator from the British newspaper *The Times* was granted leave to record this sad testament.

BELOW: Queen Elizabeth and Prince Philip inspect the masses of floral tributes to Diana laid outside Buckingham Palace. The global outpouring of grief following Diana's death was unprecedented.

Gone but not forgotten – Diana's legacy still flourishes, even seven years after her death. The Princess's family erected a memorial to her on the Spencer family estate (*left*); while the Princess of Wales Memorial Fund donates to those vulnerable and marginalized causes which Diana championed in life – for example, this struggling hospital ward in Afghanistan (*below left*). Diana's friends must remember her too – here Rosa Monckton (*below right*) lays the first stone of the Hyde Park Diana Memorial Fountain, a lasting monument to this very special, unforgettable Princess.

as Debbie Frank recollected: 'He wasn't at all interested in being a celebrity and would get very annoyed if things came out in the press about them – and he would accuse Diana of leaking it.' Diffident and unassuming, the surgeon would rather be sipping a pint of Guinness in the Anglesea Arms public house near his apartment than appearing on the front pages as Diana's latest escort. He wanted to follow in the footsteps of his mentor, Sir Magdi Yacoub, and become a medical professor. The limelight was not for him.

'Everyone knew she wanted to marry him,' Hasnat's mother Nahid told the Pakistan *Daily Times*, 'but he felt that a marriage would be impossible. "If we marry," he said, "we will not be able to go anywhere together. The two cultures are so different."' Given the success of the marriage between Imran and Jemima Khan this argument was somewhat disingenuous, masking more fundamental difficulties that separated them. For it was becoming increasingly obvious that he felt constrained not only by the curse of celebrity, by the conflicting demands of Diana and his career, and by the cultural and religious divide between them, but also perhaps by his own fear of commitment. Hasnat Khan, two years older than Diana, had already been engaged twice before, to distant cousins, but each time he had called off the nuptials.

With a weary inevitability, the couple drifted apart, friends dating the end of their two-year affair between May and July 1997. While there was undoubtedly a large room in her heart set aside for the reserved Mr Khan, the Princess was moving on. Now independently wealthy, she was determined to be in hiding no longer; during the early summer of 1997 she enjoyed lunch dates with Christopher Whalley and went dancing with Gulu Lalvani. At a gala dinner at the Tate Gallery, which coincided with her thirty-sixth birthday, she was, according to her brother, on 'sparkling form', still glowing from the triumphant sale of her royal dresses in New York. In a pointed reference to the life she felt she had left behind, she wore jewellery given to her by the Queen and Prince Charles.

In the last five years Diana had travelled far, faced many demons and slain numerous dragons. When she heard that Prince Charles was hosting a fiftieth birthday party at Highgrove for Camilla

Parker Bowles, she might have merely gritted her teeth, but she made light of it instead: 'Wouldn't it be funny if I popped out of the birthday cake?' It had not been an easy journey nor was it over. But Diana was a victim no more – she was a strong, independent woman displaying a robust confidence as she tried to make sense of her mission in life. Her desire for a new man, and one day a new family, did not dominate her thinking. As she had said in her *Panorama* interview: 'You know, people think that at the end of the day a man is the only answer. Actually, a fulfilling job is better for me.'

The Princess's diary for the summer of 1997 perfectly captured the spirit of freedom, pleasure and commitment of her new life. As well as her landmine trips to Bosnia, Cambodia and Vietnam, and her speech in Oslo, Diana planned to enjoy a little retail therapy and culture with her American friend, the business executive Lana Marks, in Milan in late August. Before that she had another girlie week to look forward to, a few days' island-hopping in Greece with Rosa Monckton. As the lawyer Richard Greene, who was in contact with Diana frequently at this time, observed: 'It was a great period of discovery and exploration for her. Diana was enjoying life, playing and wandering with more impunity. There was the sense of a kid in a candy store about her.'

Before that, in mid-July, her heart still fragile after the end of her relationship with Hasnat Khan, Diana was looking forward to a week's holiday with the two young men who had never let her down and whom she loved unconditionally, William and Harry. As they grew older it was, as every parent of teenage children knows, increasingly difficult to find destinations that would keep them amused.

Her one-time American boyfriend, billionaire Teddy Forstmann had solved her annual summer time dilemma for her, inviting her and the boys to choose between his mansion in the Hamptons or his home in Aspen, Colorado. The Princess picked the Hamptons and was looking forward to another stay in her home-from-home, the United States. As she would be travelling with the 'heir and the spare' she needed clearance from the security services before she could go. In what turned out to be a tragic twist of fate, the security services – Forstmann's friends are not sure whether it was the American or British side – vetoed Diana's holiday plans. They had doubts either about the security surrounding the billionaire's hideaways or perhaps a possible threat from elsewhere. Ironically, this decision by the security services, perhaps more than any of their perceived plotting in Paris, was what led to Diana being in Paris on 31 August.

While it was a blow for the Princess, for once she had a back-up plan, and she accepted a standing invitation to join Harrods owner Mohamed Fayed and his family at their beach-front St Tropez complex in the South of France in early July. It was safe, secure – and promised to be fun. In truth, with the landed gentry firmly on the side of the royal family, she did not have too many options concerning the people with whom she could safely and comfortably spend a holiday; this left her reliant on the largesse of rich outsiders in her own country or wealthy foreign friends and acquaintances. As the immediate heirs to the throne were involved, the Queen, Prince Charles and the Foreign Office were consulted. All gave their formal consent.

While Fayed cut a controversial figure, especially given his part in a bribery scandal involving Conservative Members of Parliament, as far as Diana was concerned he was first and foremost a family friend who had known her father and stepmother for years. He shared her penchant for off-colour jokes, and 'They got on like a house on fire,' as Countess Spencer recalled.

This time, as Diana and her sons boarded the Harrods executive Gulfstream IV jet bound for Nice with Mohamed, his wife Heini and their four children, it was Diana's life that would be changed for ever. She had shown, time and again, how much she yearned for home, hearth and family – now she was being welcomed into what Andrew Neil, a friend of the Fayeds, described as 'the warm embrace of the extended Arab family'.

While William and Harry raced each other around the bay at St Tropez on powerful jet skis, frantic photographers were in full pursuit, desperate to snap the royal party. Soon boatloads of media people were bobbing about near Fayed's beach, much to the annoyance of Diana's children. Typical of her robust policy towards the media, Diana did not avoid the photographers – she confronted them. Wearing just a one-piece leopard-print swimsuit, she zoomed out in a speedboat for a showdown with a boatful of British pressmen. 'How long do you intend to keep this up?' she asked. 'We've been watched every minute we've been here. There's an obsessive interest in me and the children.' She complained that her older son, who made no secret of his dislike of photographers, was 'freaked out' by the attention.

Before she left the press pack, she added cryptically, 'You're going to get a big surprise with the next thing I do'– a statement variously seen as signifying her intention to convert to Islam or to move to America. Much more likely though is that it was simply a throwaway remark that has gained greater resonance because of subsequent events.

While the media focused on her intriguing payoff line as well as the running comparison between Diana on holiday and the imminent fiftieth birthday party for Camilla, the arrival of Mohamed's son Dodi passed without notice or comment. His father summoned him from Paris where he was staying with his fiancée, the model Kelly Fisher, and asked him to join the royal party. Fayed, a furiously determined man who had built his empire from nothing, harboured dynastic ambitions for his son. As Dodi's step-uncle Hassan Yassin observed, 'Any father would like to see his son get into the best circles, so he did what he could.'

At first glance, Dodi and Diana were an unlikely match. Generous, undemanding, and lethargic, Dodi was known for his beautiful manners and his collection of high-powered cars. At the age of fifteen he had his own chauffeured Rolls-Royce and bodyguard and spent a short while at Sandhurst, the officer training school, before working as a film producer in Hollywood. Like his father, Dodi lived a life of exaggerated security, surrounding himself with surveillance cameras and bodyguards. He and his father carried their precautions to such an extreme that before they had a meal, they had their plates wiped with lime to detect arsenic poisoning.

'He was nice, polite but monumentally unserious,' was the opinion of David Puttnam, who worked with him during the filming of the Oscar-winning movie *Chariots of Fire*. 'He couldn't focus or concentrate. Unutterably superficial in a way that frustrated his father.' On one occasion Puttnam threw Dodi off the set for offering cocaine to the staff. Others, mainly women, saw him differently, viewing him as a rather immature, somewhat damaged young man living in the shadow of his dynamic and overbearing father. 'Kind', 'thoughtful', 'sweet' and 'sympathetic' were epithets used by his female admirers, who included the actresses Brooke Shields, Joanne Whalley and Mimi Rogers. Hassan Yassin confirmed the general opinion: 'He was a loner, very shy, better in the company of women. An introvert. Dodi was somewhat undefined. He was a late starter who wanted to live without being bothered.'

He seemed an unlikely suitor for the Princess. Certainly the contrast with her previous lover, Hasnat Khan, was marked; one a serious, career-minded surgeon who hated the limelight, the other a wealthy party animal who only dabbled in his work as he did in drugs and women. Apart from their Muslim heritage, their only shared characteristics seemed to be erratic time-keeping and an aversion to physical exercise. Unathletic and at 5 feet 9 inches, two inches shorter than Diana, who liked men taller than herself, Dodi, then forty-one, was pleasant but not exceptional. He was, apparently, also engaged to be married in four weeks' time to Kelly Fisher. This came as a surprise to Hassan Yassin, who had met the couple on numerous occasions. 'He was always surrounded by models from the fashion industry,' he said, shrugging.

Dodi and Diana had met several times before – at a film pre-mière, a polo match and at a dinner party given by Raine Spencer in the spring of 1997. While they had rubbed shoulders, there was no obvious spark between them, Dodi politely treating the Princess with the deference due her status.

That was certainly the feeling on board the *Jonikal*. 'They got on well enough, but I didn't think anything of it,' recollected the steward Debbie Gribble. An unlikely food fight where the couple chased each other around deck like a couple of kids ended with them talking rather than teasing one another. From then on the crew often caught them deep in conversation, either alone or with his father.

It seemed that Diana was enjoying herself, free of the emotional turmoil of the last few months, protected and safe within a stable family which was so important for her. She liked the fact too that her boys warmed to Dodi, who had rented a disco in St Tropez on a couple of nights so that the party could have fun in peace. Her parish priest, Father Frank Gelli, later recalled, 'She told me how fond Dodi was of her children and how much they enjoyed his company. That meant a lot to her.'

A couple of days later Kelly Fisher flew down to join her fiancé, but instead of staying in the villa, she was installed on board the Fayeds' schooner, the *Sakhara*. For the rest of the holiday Dodi commuted between the villa, the schooner and his father's yacht, spending the day with Diana, his nights with his fiancée. It was an unusual arrangement for a couple supposedly due to marry in just a few weeks. And they did display the trappings of a couple about to wed: Dodi had bought them a home, a $7 million estate in Malibu, California, once owned by the actress Julie Andrews; and he had presented Kelly, then thirty-one, with a £130,000 sapphire and diamond ring as well as a generous allowance. They were also talking about starting a family; according to Fisher, Dodi wanted two boys. 'I had no idea what was going on,' Kelly said later. 'Dodi kept leaving me behind with the excuse that the Princess didn't like to meet new people.'

She left after a couple of days for a modelling assignment in Nice. By the time she returned, Diana had gone, telling her host that it had been her 'best holiday ever'. When the Princess arrived back at Kensington Palace there were four dozen roses and a £6,000 gold watch waiting for her – a gift from Dodi. A week later, at the end of July, she agreed to join him in Paris, ostensibly for a private viewing of the Villa Windsor, owned by his father, where the Duke of Windsor and Wallis Simpson spent their years of exile. During their whirlwind weekend, Dodi and Diana dined together at a three-star Michelin restaurant but she slept alone in the Imperial Suite at the Ritz hotel while he retired to his apartment. Curiously, it seems that Diana, who made a point of spending as much time as she could with her boys, left them in the care of her staff at Kensington Palace while she was away.

With her apartment about to undergo redecoration she impulsively accepted another invitation from Dodi, this time to join him alone on board the *Jonikal* for a week's Mediterranean cruise in early August. This time the Princess suggested that the boys head to Balmoral a few days early to join their father.

While the couple were initially assigned separate cabins, it was during this holiday in early August that the famous long-range 'kiss' pictures were taken by a well-informed paparazzo, who snapped Dodi and Diana embracing in the shallow waters at Isola Piana at the southern tip of Corsica. The photographs, taken just five days before Dodi was apparently due to marry, earned the photographer Mario Brenna and his partner Jason Fraser a substantial six-figure sum, in the process alerting the world – and Dodi's bride-to-be – that the Princess was in the middle of a summer romance. 'Locked in her lover's arms, the Princess finds happiness at last,' was the headline in the *Sunday Mirror*, which devoted a further ten pages to exploring the nuances of the budding relationship. Indeed, if the publicity-shy Mr Khan had felt any pangs of jealousy as a result of the publication of the pictures, he would have been grateful for the quiet life after seeing how his fellow Muslim was treated for daring to romance an Anglo-Saxon Princess. The early stories about Dodi being 'sensitive, gentle and caring' soon gave way to barely disguised racism as details about his past lovers and his drug abuse came to light. When a tearful Kelly Fisher paraded before the cameras claiming a broken engagement, Dodi soon went from 'Mr Perfect' to an 'oily Egyptian bedhopper'. 'You Dodi Rat', yelled the *Daily Star*.

It was a scenario Diana had long anticipated and feared – 'Who would take me on? Anyone who takes me on has to accept that they will be raked over in the papers.' But the evening after the story of their romantic cruise became headline news, Diana had supper at Dodi's Park Lane apartment in central London, on what would have been the night before his wedding, while fifty photographers waited outside. For once she seemed supremely unconcerned about the furore.

That the couple had made a genuine connection was apparent to their friends and family. Dodi's worldly-wise step-uncle, Hassan

Yassin, who was fond of Dodi but realistic about his shortcomings, had phoned him a couple of times during their cruise. He jokingly told Dodi that he had just been called by Buckingham Palace and warned that if Dodi married Diana, he, Hassan, would be obliged to marry the Queen Mother. For a moment Dodi was nonplussed and took him at his word before realizing that he was joking. Hassan Yassin, who had watched his nephew drift through life, sensed a change: 'He was very happy and I thought that he had found someone. For the first time in his life he was blossoming.'

In a later conversation Hassan issued his nephew with a benign warning to take 'this golden girl' seriously. 'You've got to settle down,' he said with mock gravity. Dodi replied, 'I am going to.' Dodi had made similar comments when he met medium Rita Rogers during a flying visit to her home in Derbyshire. She had earlier performed a reading for him via satellite telephone while he and Diana cruised alone on the *Jonikal*, and told him that he would never have another girlfriend. 'I know. She is the one,' he had replied.

Diana seemed equally smitten. Just before she went on holiday with Rosa Monckton to Greece, she spoke for an hour on the telephone to her stepmother, Raine Spencer, who was staying with friends in Antibes in the South of France. 'She was blissfully, ecstatically happy, having really one of the best times in her life, and Dodi was very much part of that,' recalled Raine Spencer. 'One of the reasons Diana fell in love with him was because he was such a sweet, thoughtful person and he thought all the time about her. This she told me only a few weeks before she died. She said to me, "I'm so happy, at last here is somebody who thinks about me."

'If you see it in the context of her having become this person who is looking after sick people in hospitals, making speeches, it's very rewarding but very draining. Sometimes you feel that people are draining you of your life blood. This is what happened to Diana. She was exhausted by people draining her. She needed a bit of time to build up her own self and I think Dodi helped her very much.'

Open, affectionate, kind and protective – qualities which she had been searching for in a man for much of her life. Diana, by turns needy and demanding, insatiable in her yearning for affection, was now with a man who had all the time in the world for her. In many ways it was her first grown-up relationship. 'She liked the feeling of having someone who not only so obviously cared for her, but was not afraid to be seen doing so,' said Rosa Monckton. The woman who had longed for appreciation now found herself indulged by a cosseting lifestyle, showered with expensive gifts and constant attention. It was a seductive combination. 'I have been so spoilt, so taken care of, all the things that I never, ever had,' the Princess told Lady Elsa Bowker.

When the proposed trip to Milan with her American friend Lana Marks was cancelled because of the death of Lana's father, Diana found herself at a loose end. Rather than stay at Kensington Palace, she accepted another invitation to join Dodi on board the *Jonikal*, arriving in Nice on 21 August. It was a blissful time, soaking up the sun, cruising from port to port, insulated from the rest of the world within the luxurious bubble of their yacht. When Dodi ordered her a ring from Alberto Repossi's store in Monaco, there was speculation that they were to marry. The name of the range of rings, 'Tell Me Yes', added to the frenzy.

The more sober of her friends, however, described Diana's infatuation as a 'summer fling', reminding the more excitable that they had only known each other for six weeks, and had spent only twenty-five days alone together. But neither, unfortunately, had she spent much time alone with Prince Charles. Indeed the two romances that form the book-ends of her life, the one with Prince Charles and the one with Dodi Fayed, were not only the shortest and most famous but both had parental figures in the background. The first was presided over by the Queen Mother and Lady Ruth Fermoy; the second had Mohamed Fayed pulling the strings.

Diana first started seeing Prince Charles at Balmoral in August 1980 and famously complained that they were never really alone during their courtship. Yet six months later, in February 1981, she accepted his offer of marriage.

During her romance with Dodi she was saying to friends like Lady Annabel Goldsmith that she needed another husband 'like a bad rash', while the possessive Paul Burrell was already voicing his disapproval. As she and Rosa Monckton prepared to depart from

Kensington Palace in August for their holiday touring the Greek islands he said to Rosa conspiratorially, 'He's not right for her, you know that.'

The subtext was that Dodi was not right for the butler, who saw his position increasingly under threat. During Diana's last summer, Burrell had sensed the way the wind was blowing and concluded that it was not in his favour. Even before she met Dodi, the Princess was spending less and less time at Kensington Palace. In fact, during her last year, she performed more official engagements abroad than at home – a trip to Leicester in April 1997 was her first home engagement outside London in eighteen months. The successful sale of her royal dresses was an obvious sign of the way she was clearing the decks of her royal life. In reality, Paul Burrell, her 'rock', was the only relic from an unhappy time in her life – and their bond was rapidly crumbling. 'At the time of her death the relationship between Diana and Burrell was at its lowest ebb,' stated her friend Vivienne Parry, a view endorsed by several Kensington Palace staff, including the chef Darren McGrady. Now, their already highly charged association was further threatened by the presence of the Fayeds, who had their own butlers and domestic staff.

Concerned about his future with the Princess, Burrell had registered with several employment agencies and had made overtures to various Americans, notably Tom Hanks, with whom he had struck up a friendship. Even Donald Trump was interested in 'Di's Guy'. As Burrell's one-time agent, the lawyer Richard Greene commented, 'He felt that his time was coming to an end and that she no longer needed him. During that last year Paul was looking for work outside. He wanted to take care of himself and his family. Her dalliance with Dodi provoked genuine fears.'

For the last few years, 'Abroad' had become a familiar conversational thread, as much psychological as geographical, the Princess seeing America in particular as a place of 'options, optimism and openness'. During the last year of her life she made around twenty overseas trips and was away from Britain for more than twelve weeks.

Her references to moving to Australia, then to South Africa and finally the States were part of a wider disenchantment with British society, a disillusion fed by her own experiences as well as the commercial success of the Duchess of York, who had reinvented herself to an appreciative American audience. David Puttnam had long conversations with Diana about her buying a home in Martha's Vineyard where she had enjoyed a summer holiday. 'She felt that she could recreate her life in America,' he remembered. 'She liked the way she was treated by press, liked the people, and the sense of freedom.' While she had turned down a proposal from Revlon to represent them, and laughingly rejected Kevin Costner's offer of a part in the sequel to *The Bodyguard*, it was clear that the trajectory of her life was moving away from Britain. 'She loved Americans and loved America,' said Richard Greene. 'She felt a sense of freedom in America and was thinking, Why not America? The whole of life was opening up for her.' Certainly her brother Earl Spencer believed that one day she would have ended up in the States.

As the Princess wearily told the media during the first days of her holiday in St Tropez, 'My boys are urging me continually to leave the country. They say it is the only way. They want me to live abroad. I sit in London all the time and I am abused and followed wherever I go. I cannot win.' It was significant that she mentioned the boys, the anchors of her life, as giving her the go-ahead to look elsewhere. In earlier complaints about harassment she said that it was only the boys who kept her in Britain. Now those ties were loosening.

When the Princess started poring over architect's plans for Julie Andrews's former house in Malibu the alarm bells really started ringing. She had even chosen rooms for the boys. The fact that the house was now owned by Dodi made it an even more serious proposition. Before, she had merely dreamed – of opening a riding school with James Hewitt; buying a farm in Tuscany with Oliver Hoare; settling into a home in Cape Town with Hasnat Khan. For the first time she was looking at a place that existed outside her imagination.

Was she going to marry? It is a question that is as intriguing and contradictory as the lady herself. Dodi's father contended that his son had proposed, and claimed that he had sent three cases of champagne to Kensington Palace to toast the bride-to-be.

However, his assertions of a dynastic union are diluted by the fact that he also ardently believed that Diana was expecting Dodi's child, a claim vigorously denied by Rosa Monckton who said that Diana had had her period while she was with her in Greece. The official coroner Dr John Burton was brutally emphatic. 'I have seen inside her womb. I know she wasn't pregnant.'

Others, including Burrell, are equally dismissive. Her friend Lana Marks claims that Diana telephoned to say Dodi would soon be 'a past chapter' of her life, while another friend, Gulu Lalvani, said he had joked with her about saving up for a wedding present only to be told by Diana that while she was having a lot of fun, no marriage was planned. Other friends were concerned that she may be making the wrong choice – again. Her former boyfriend Teddy Forstmann phoned her on the Fayed boat and asked her 'what the hell she was playing at'. As a friend of Forstmann explained: 'He is very protective of those people he cares about and he thought that Diana could do much better for herself than Dodi.' The Princess placated him by saying that the romance was simply a 'summer fling'. It appears that the Princess was telling her friends what they wanted to hear, depending on their take on the romance.

The most intriguing testimony comes from her local parish priest Father Gelli, the curate of St Mary Abbott's Church in Kensington, whom she met after she was criticized for taking William and Harry to see the movie, *The Devil's Own*, a film about IRA terrorists, in May 1997. He wrote her a letter of support and as a result she invited him for tea where their conversation ranged over many spiritual issues, including exorcism, the Devil and Sufism. She was most concerned to know about marriage between Christians and Muslims and whether they would be allowed to marry in church.

Later she talked to him about another parishioner, Dodi Fayed, sharing with him her hopes and dreams. She felt Dodi could take care of her and offer her the love and security she had never really known. In the last week of her life she called the priest again, this time from the deck of the *Jonikal*. She asked him about marriage and a church wedding. 'Diana was so very happy and very much in love,' Gelli said. 'I honestly believe if they were alive today, they would be married.'

While the controversy over her feelings for Dodi will never be resolved, one area of agreement is that Diana had made considerable strides, emotionally, physically and spiritually. In the first year of her new life as a free woman she gave full expression to the real Diana, no longer inhibited by or afraid of those who had tried to shackle her during her royal life. 'I had never seen her so happy, particularly over those last three months,' recollected designer Jacques Azagury. 'I was dealing with her a lot, seeing her almost every day. You could tell she was a happy woman.'

Those friends who had seen her wayward, disheartened and, at times, stumbling on her journey of self-discovery sensed that at last she was savouring a true taste of happiness and contentment. The woman who just a few years before was a nail-biting, round-shouldered, diffident creature was now confident in body, mind and heart. 'I'm so strong now, I fear nothing, nothing,' she told a friend. Higher heels and shorter skirts were a semaphore of the positive woman she was becoming. Her astrologer, Debbie Frank, who had counselled her since her separation, spoke of the transformation: 'She was happy all the time – something that was unique. For Diana happiness usually lasted for just a day. I don't think she'd ever known that before. Her life had never been quite so fulfilled. She was loving her work and she was so proud of her boys.'

The Diana whom Rita Rogers saw in August 1997, just a few days before her death, was, she felt, much more spiritual than at any time she had known her: 'She was radiantly happy, loving life and full of it. Her conversations were all joy and laughter and full of excitement about everything that was going on.' For a woman with a religious outlook on life, the most hurtful decision during her divorce had been the decision by the Queen to have her name omitted from public prayers. Until then, Diana, like the other senior members of the royal family, was formally mentioned in Church of England services. Ultimately, however, it was a price she was willing to pay as she viewed the expanse of opportunity before her.

[237]

In a way that would have been unthinkable during her royal career, Diana felt more able to act on her own instincts. She spoke at a private therapy session for women suffering from eating disorders at the Priory clinic in May 1997 and made several private visits to the children's eating disorders unit at Great Ormond Street Hospital in London. A few days after her divorce was finalized, in September 1996 she flew to Limni outside Athens in Greece for the funeral of a young lawyer, Yannis Kaliviotis, a cystic fibrosis sufferer, whom she had befriended during her frequent visits to the Royal Brompton Hospital. At the funeral of the fashion designer, Gianni Versace, in July 1997 she impulsively placed a consoling arm around a sobbing Elton John.

These incidents are illustrative of the natural, spontaneous and human behaviour that was at the heart of the Princess but which had been stifled during her royal career. The girl who got 'smacked wrists' from courtiers for wearing leather trousers to a rock concert was also prevented by royal protocol from sitting with Angela Serota at the funeral of Adrian Ward-Jackson whom they had nursed together until his death in 1991. As for attending the funeral of a stranger, six years before that, Prince Charles had privately rebuked her for behaving like a 'martyr' for helping a pensioner who had collapsed with an angina attack during her visit to a hospital in Marlow.

During her royal career Diana had recognized that she was an outsider, wearing her difference like a secret badge of honour. Now she accepted and welcomed that role, her self-knowledge reflected in the certainty of her chosen path in life. She no longer felt any need for outside advisers – 'I left because she pretty much felt in control,' explained Stephen Twigg – and now saw mystics like the spiritual medium Rita Rogers less for sympathy, more to help her understand her work and her life. Rita recognized this, writing of the Princess in *From One World to Another*, 'She was a very strong person, wilful and capable of making her own mind up about life. The readings I gave her interested her, but she did not come to me to know which path she should take.'

In Diana's last interview, with the French *Le Monde* newspaper, published in August, she returned to the theme that crowded her thoughts, talking earnestly about her 'destiny' to help 'vulnerable people'. She had often spoken about her sense of destiny or her 'spiritual pathway', as she called it, seeing hers as a life ordained to help the sick, the disenfranchised and the dispossessed. That inner spirit, the essence of Diana, was now on permanent display through her passionate embrace of the landmine campaign and her work with the dying, as well as in her symbolic farewell to her royal gowns and hence her royal life. Diana was striding out on her journey.

A beach-front home in Malibu. A union between a Muslim commoner and a Christian princess. A string of Diana, Princess of Wales hospices established across the globe. A successful campaign against landmines. It all seems too far-fetched to be true; almost as ludicrous as the story of a woman destined one day to be queen who walked out of her marriage and away from her royal future. A princess who made her own fairy tale.

CHAPTER ELEVEN

The Final Odyssey

H E PURSUED HER, he wooed her, lavishing her with extravagant compliments and expensive jewellery. The wealthy tycoon collected people like others saved stamps and she was a trophy, a social prize of incomparable value. Their wedding shocked the world, the union of a modern-day princess and the buccaneering millionaire meeting with universal disapproval. 'The reaction here is anger, shock and dismay,' noted the *New York Times* critically, as the newspaper reported the marriage of America's former First Lady, Jackie Kennedy-Bouvier, to the Greek shipping magnate, Aristotle Onassis, in October 1968. Her neighbour Larry Newman reflected popular incredulity: 'How in God's name could she love that guy?' Their union touched a raw nerve in the national psyche, still living the dream that the First Lady, widowed in tragedy, would remain aloof, chaste and regal, a living symbol of the Camelot ideal. That her new husband was a rough-hewn Greek of coarse tastes and even coarser language was an affront to national pride, ensuring that the backlash was crude and unrelenting.

It was a scenario Diana, Princess of Wales now saw unfolding before her eyes on the last day of her holiday in the sun. 'I understand why Jackie married Onassis. She felt alone and in need of protection – I often feel like that,' she said during her romance with Dodi Fayed. Little did they realize how much protection she would need as she and Dodi left the calm waters of the

Mediterranean to face a ferocious storm on dry land. As the *Jonikal* nosed into the berth at the Cala di Volpe Hotel in Sardinia on Saturday 30 August 1997, they knew that their sunshine odyssey was coming to a close. Nothing could have prepared them for what lay ahead. Within a matter of hours they would be transported from the idyllic, pampered repose of his yacht, an island of blissful calm and safety detached from the real world, to a Dantesque frenzy of contorted faces, blazing flashlights and revving engines. They went from a life where their every whim was catered for, to a world where they were the prey, hunted, harassed and hemmed in. The contrast could not have been more violent or distressing.

They flew from Olbia airport in Dodi's private jet to Paris, where they were due to spend the night before Diana returned home to be with her sons whom she had not seen for a month. After the peace they had enjoyed adrift at sea, they were plunged into the frenzy their arrival had created. They landed at Paris's Le Bourget airport where they were greeted by a crowd of paparazzi, and were whisked away by a driver from the Ritz Hotel, owned by Mohamed Fayed. They stopped for a twenty-minute visit to the Windsor château before returning to the car and moving on to the Ritz. During the journey they were surrounded by motorbike riders, with cameramen on board desperately trying to get shots of the couple. As Diana, a veteran of paparazzi lunacy, remarked, 'Someone is going to get themselves hurt.'

The photographers' behaviour reflected the febrile excitement that had been brewing like a summer thunderstorm over the last few days. Even as Diana and Dodi wandered round the echoing rooms where a royal couple had spent their days in voluntary exile years before, newspapers in London were about to print stories that suggested a kind of collective derangement. In the *Independent* Diana was described as 'a woman with fundamentally nothing to say about anything'. She was 'suffering from a form of arrested development'. 'Isn't it time she started using her head?' asked the *Mail on Sunday*; the *Sunday Mirror* printed a special supplement entitled 'A Story of Love', the *News of the World* claimed that William had demanded that Diana should split from Dodi: 'William can't help it, he just doesn't like the man.' William was reportedly 'horrified' and 'doesn't think Mr Fayed is good for his mother' – or was that just the press projecting their own prejudices? The upmarket *Sunday Times* newspaper, which had first serialized my biography of the Princess, now put her in the psychiatrist's chair for daring to be wooed by a Muslim. The pop-psychologist Oliver James put Diana 'On the Couch', asking why she was so 'depressed' and desperate for love. Other tabloids piled in with dire prognostications – about Prince Philip's hostility to the relationship, Diana's prospect of exile, and the social ostracism she would face if she married Dodi. The reaction of the British media mirrored that of her butler Paul Burrell – anxious and possessive, consumed with an impotent desire to capture and control her once again. As she had done with the royal family, slowly but surely, finger by finger, Diana had been releasing herself from the constraining grip of the British media who had claimed ersatz ownership of her life and soul. Her attempt to assert herself had merely urged them on. She and her boyfriend were to die that day because a posse of men, spearheaded by the Nazgul of the mass media, the paparazzi, would stop at nothing. Even as she lay dying, they would not take no for an answer.

A day that began sedately and serenely, rapidly began to unravel. It would doubtless have been disconcerting for a woman like Diana, who liked order and routine in her life. From the array of bottles in her bathroom to her immaculately pressed clothes, she liked everything to be neat and tidy, just so. Before royal engage-ments, her private secretary Patrick Jephson had always been careful to warn her of any last-minute changes of plan, knowing that she did not like surprises. Yet on this day, there seemed to be no plan, the couple zig-zagging across Paris in a manner that was confusing and, surely, for Diana, deeply irritating. They were on Dodi time – improvised and chaotic.

After their brief tour of the Villa Windsor they went on to the Ritz Hotel where they pulled up at the rear service entrance to avoid the media mob waiting at the front. Once installed in the Imperial Suite, Dodi and Diana spent some time on the telephone, calling friends and relations to catch up on all the latest news – and to be asked about their relationship. The Princess made it clear that while she was very happy, marriage was not on her mind. She was more concerned about William who had called her from Balmoral, worried that he had been asked to appear at a photocall at Eton to mark his third year at the exclusive fee-paying school. As Harry had been held back a year at Ludgrove School, he felt that the staged event would overshadow his brother. Diana promised to discuss it with his father when she returned the following day.

Later that afternoon, while Diana visited the hairdresser, Dodi slipped across Place Vendôme to pick up the £125,000 'Tell Me Yes' ring from Alberto Repossi's store which he had ordered while they were in Monaco. This gesture excited speculation that he was about to propose to the Princess, perhaps over dinner that evening. As the ring was ordered only a few days into their relationship this scenario seems unlikely, and a crucial witness who further undermines this romantic notion is Dodi's step-uncle Hassan Yassin. He had just arrived from Los Angeles and was shaving in his suite in the Ritz when Dodi called him and asked him to join him and the Princess for dinner. The urbane Mr Yassin, who has rubbed shoulders with Nelson Mandela, the Sultan of Brunei and various Middle Eastern potentates, politely declined a chance to spend an evening with the world's most talked about couple, pleading a prior engagement. As he finished shaving he teased his nephew about his new relationship and told him that Diana was a 'jewel' that he should not lose. Dodi was emphatic that he was taking the relationship seriously and while the word marriage was never part of the conversation, the notion was there by insinuation.

It is hardly likely, however, that Dodi would have invited his uncle to join them for dinner if he was planning to pop the question. Indeed, Dodi even called Hassan Yassin again later in the evening to insist that if he changed his mind he was welcome to join them. As Hassan Yassin's plans had not changed, he once again declined but promised to meet them for breakfast – which suggests that it was his understanding that Dodi and Diana had intended to make the Ritz their overnight base. Later, he said sombrely, 'Of course, now I regret it. I might have been in the car too and I would have told him to slow down. I value life more than having some photographers following me.'

At seven in the evening, the couple left the hotel via the service entrance and drove to Dodi's luxurious ten-roomed apartment on the Rue Arsène-Houssaye, overlooking the Arc de Triomphe. Outside his apartment, half a dozen paparazzi lay in wait and the couple had to make a dash for the building while Dodi's bodyguards kept them at bay. At half-past nine, after they had changed, the couple left the apartment for the chic but casual Chez Benoît restaurant, only to discover that the place was overrun with excited paparazzi, some of whom had followed them from the apartment. They hastily changed their plans, heading back to the Ritz where they ran the gauntlet of twenty or so photographers waiting outside the front entrance. Some shoved their cameras just a few inches from Diana's face, an indignity which infuriated her companion. 'Dodi was more than upset,' recalled Kes Wingfield, one of Dodi's bodyguards. It was now ten o'clock and the girl whose idea of a fun Saturday night was to settle down with a garnished baked potato in front of the TV to watch the hospital soap, *Casualty*, was tired and famished. They entered the hotel's L'Espadon restaurant and ordered grilled fish and a bottle of Tattinger champagne. Within minutes of sitting down they were on the move again, security guards having identified two fellow diners as possible paparazzi. They turned out to be English tourists, but by then the couple were ensconced in the Imperial Suite enjoying room service.

For a time it seemed that the couple were settled for the evening. Dodi's bodyguards believed that they had managed to dissuade their anxious boss from running the gauntlet of paparazzi once more, especially as by now around thirty photographers and a swelling crowd of curious onlookers were waiting outside. But, in yet another unexpected change, Dodi consulted with the Princess and decided that they should return to his apartment as their belongings were there. The plan, one which had worked well enough before, was to leave by the back entrance accompanied by one of Dodi's bodyguards, Trevor Rees-Jones, with the hotel's acting security chief, Henri Paul, as chauffeur. A decoy vehicle, containing other bodyguards would leave from the front. Shortly before midnight Dodi called his father in London to obtain his approval for their great escape. Fayed agreed the ruse, telling his son to be careful.

A day that began in a bay of tranquillity was to end in mayhem, the last reel of Diana's life out of her hands and her control. Later, her friends and her freelance team of drivers-cum-bodyguards independently watched the CCTV footage of her departure from the rear of the Ritz Hotel to glean some clue as to her mood. To the professional watchers, men who had driven her for the last three years, the signs were clear and unambiguous. She was agitated, anxious and on the point of tears. It had been a long day, she had been drinking champagne and she was tired. Her hands and body were tense and she seemed on edge. As one of her drivers said, 'If this had been us we'd have parked at the end of the street, let her have a cry and dry her eyes, then moved on.' Her friend Lucia Flecha de Lima agreed with the professional assessment: 'To me, that film footage of her leaving the Ritz Hotel for the last time says it all; she looks cross and fed up.'

At 12.20 a.m. on 31 August 1997, just before Dodi and Diana slid into the powerful Mercedes S280 for their last journey, Henri Paul, who was not licensed to drive the limousine, taunted photographers: 'Don't bother following – you won't catch us.' By then he had consumed a lethal cocktail of prescription drugs and alcohol and was three times over France's legal drink-drive limit. He barrelled out of the Rue Chambron with a posse of photographers in pursuit. Five minutes later, the hired Mercedes hurtled into the thirteenth pillar of the Alma underpass, travelling at between 118 and 155 kilometres per hour (74–97 mph). The horrendous crash was witnessed by Mohamed Medjahdi, a forklift-truck driver, and his horrified girlfriend Souad Moufakkir, who were driving home in his grey Citroën. At first the couple thought the Mercedes was going to smash into them. 'A murderous piece of junk was coming closer and closer at high speed,' said Medjahdi, who accelerated hard to escape a collision. Its tyres squealing, the sound magnified in the concrete tunnel, the Mercedes ploughed into the pillar, the front of the car exploding on impact, with pieces of metal flying in all directions. 'It was like a bomb going off,' Medjahdi recalled. He has been interviewed several times by police for an as yet unpublished statement and is adamant that there was no other car or paparazzi involved: 'I am absolutely convinced, clear and certain that this was a tragedy – but it was an accident.'

Inside the wreckage, Dodi lay dead on the back seat, his blue jeans shredded by metal shards, and his legs at a grotesque angle. In the front, Henri Paul was slumped dead over the steering column, his body pressed against the horn that blared mournfully in the otherwise silent underpass. By his side Trevor Rees-Jones was unconscious, his jaw nearly ripped off and his face crushed by the impact. Only Diana seemed relatively unscathed. The Princess, who, like Dodi, was not wearing a seat belt, had been propelled forward by the force of the impact, coming to rest on the floor with her back to the car door, her body jammed between the front and back seats. She appeared to be semi-conscious, and although a trickle of blood ran out of her left ear and from her nose, she did not seem badly injured. The smear of blood in her hair made it look as though she had tried to brush it from her face with her bloody right hand. While there has long been dispute about her 'final words', in her damaged state they will have been brief and incoherent. The first policeman on the scene, Stéphane Dorzée, claims Diana moaned and mumbled 'My God', while a fireman said she mumbled, 'What happened?' Whatever fragments of speech she uttered, she was certainly not conscious for long.

Within minutes the photographer Romuald Rat and his driver Stéphane Darmon arrived at the scene. Rat pulled open the door and felt Diana's pulse to see if she was alive. 'I'm here,' he said in English, 'be cool.' Moments later an off-duty doctor, Frédéric Maillez, stopped to help – it was the third time that he had been the first doctor at the scene of a serious car smash. After surveying the four passengers he raced back to his white Ford Fiesta and pulled out the only piece of medical equipment he had with him, an Ambu – a mask attached to a portable self-inflating oxygen bottle – which he tried to place over Diana's nose and mouth. By now her head was slumped forward, her eyes open but glassy. The signs looked bad, but as her external injuries appeared slight, Maillez thought she would survive.

But internally Diana had suffered from 'grave haemorrhagic shock', which meant, in layman's terms, that her chest and lung cavity were rapidly filling with blood. The force of the impact had ripped the vital pulmonary artery from her heart – a common cause of fatalities in aircraft crashes. This injury caused her heart to spasm and she suffered several huge heart attacks.

Diana's life began to ebb away the still-smoking Mercedes was by now surrounded by photographers, the doctor's frantic efforts to resuscitate the Princess illuminated by an explosion of flash-lights. 'It was like a scene out of the annals of Hell,' recollected Dorzée. By now, in London, newspaper executives, with the first pictures of the stricken Princess on their desks, were waiting for news of her condition. If she lived, the shots went on the front page. If she died these last pictures would never be spoken of again. Or, at least, that is what they hoped.

For the next three hours, a medical team strove to save the Princess and Trevor Rees-Jones. It took until 1.30 a.m. for the fire service to carefully cut both victims from the crushed car. Diana was on artificial respiration, her blood pressure very low and she had already suffered major cardiac arrest. The ambulance, surrounded by a police escort, crawled the 3.8 kilometres to the Pitié-Salpétrière hospital, stopping once while the doctor tried to prevent a second cardiac arrest. It was not until two in the morning that the Princess arrived at the hospital, where two surgeons, Bruno Riou and Dr Alain Pavie, and their team were waiting.

As the team worked frantically to save her, using electric paddles and manual resuscitation to shock her heart back to life, the British Ambassador, Sir Michael Jay, and the French Interior Minister, Jean-Pierre Chevènement, stood outside the operating theatre, anxious to relay any news to Balmoral, where the Queen and the rest of the royal family, including Prince Charles and his sons, were staying.

When Sir Michael first contacted the Queen's Scottish retreat, her deputy private secretary, Sir Robin Janvrin, was uncompre-hending; he had not even been aware that the Princess was in Paris. He quickly threw on some clothes and went up to the 'big house' to confer with the Queen and the Prince of Wales. The

Queen and Charles, still in their dressing gowns and slippers, held a brief meeting in the Prince's sitting room. They decided to let the boys sleep until the situation became clearer, although they took the precaution of quietly removing the radios from their bedrooms and the television from the nursery in case they inadvertently woke. Then Prince Charles telephoned Camilla Parker Bowles in Gloucestershire to let her know about the accident, after which he rang his deputy private secretary, Mark Bolland, in London to glean more news. For once, Bolland, who was now being contacted by national newspaper editors, was as much in the dark as his royal boss.

Meanwhile, the police at Balmoral contacted Diana's driver, Colin Tebbutt, at his home, having heard that Diana's chauffeur had died in the accident and being concerned that he was the victim. After Tebbutt had reassured them of his safety, he raced to Kensington Palace where he joined the chain-smoking comptroller Michael Gibbins, Diana's secretary, Jackie Allen, and Paul Burrell in the office. Diana's butler had earlier been woken by Lucia Flecha de Lima who had called from Washington, where, having seen the CNN report on the accident, she had been frantically and unsuccessfully calling the Princess's mobile phone, as had Sarah, Duchess of York, who was on holiday in Italy. While Lucia gave up and phoned the butler, Fergie considered hiring a private aircraft and heading for Paris.

At that stage, news reports were still saying that the Princess was alive, and Tebbutt began looking into hiring an air ambulance to fly her home. The first news reports, flashed around the world at two o'clock in the morning British Summer Time, were relatively optimistic as to the condition of the Princess, though they revealed that Dodi had died. In the initial confusion, it was stated that Diana had only sustained minor injuries, probably a broken arm; one eyewitness account was quoted as saying that she had walked unaided from the scene of the crash.

This gave short-lived hope to her mother, Frances Shand Kydd, sitting alone in front of the television, smoking cigarette after cigarette and desperately praying that her youngest daughter was safe. She had been woken by her friend, Janey Milne, who had telephoned her at her cottage on the isle of Seil after seeing a news flash on Sky Television. After she had made herself a cup of tea, Mrs Shand Kydd packed what she hoped were 'dignified clothes' into a suitcase in preparation for a hospital visit to see a daughter with whom she had not spoken for six months. 'It seemed natural to go to my wounded child,' she said later. All the while, she tried to contact her other daughters, Jane, who was on holiday in Norfolk, and Sarah, at home in Lincolnshire. Both phones were continually engaged. After speaking briefly to her son, Charles, in South Africa, Mrs Shand Kydd eventually heard from Jane. The news was not good. It seemed that Diana was severely brain-damaged and Dodi was dead. A few minutes later she received the dreadful news that her daughter was dead. 'I knew of her death an hour before the news was given out. Protocol was such that heads of state had to be informed before it was made public. So I was left in an amazing, stunning situation of having an hour to wait, knowing she was dead and unable to transmit this news or ask for help of a friend.'

For hours she waited for a phone call or fax from Prince Charles. 'Why hasn't he rung? What is going on?' she asked aloud, ready and willing to fly to Paris if she was asked. According to her, that call never came. She added, 'I didn't go to Paris to bring Diana home to London because I wasn't asked.' It reawoke an enduring pain for her – that she had never seen or held her son John, the child born before Diana, who had died when only a few hours old: 'It really seems ironic to me that having buried two children, for entirely different reasons, I did not see or touch or hold them when they were dead.' Since her daughters flew to Paris, it seems odd that they, rather than the royal family, did not make arrangements for their mother to be with them.

The only fragment of solace at this anguished time was that before Diana was pronounced dead at 3 a.m. British time, the British Ambassador had requested the services of a French priest to deliver the last rites, known as extreme unction, to her daughter. Father Yves Clochard-Bossuet, who lived nearby, was escorted to the hospital where he was taken to the Princess's side: 'I prayed for her soul. All I could think of was the sadness of this young woman dying when she had everything to live for.' For the next four hours he sat with her so that she would not be alone. It was a gesture from a stranger that the Princess, who had held the hands of so many as they made their last journey, would have appreciated.

She would have appreciated too the confusion that reigned at Balmoral. As a grief-stricken Mohamed Fayed, who had flown to Paris in his private jet, entered a Paris mortuary to identify and claim his son, the royal family remained in Scotland, considering how to proceed. Apart from the link with her boys, as far as the royal family was concerned Diana was a figure from the past. She had not been present at any family gatherings, at Windsor Castle, Sandringham or Balmoral, for several years and had last seen the Queen at William's confirmation in March, some five months before. By a supreme and tragic irony, the family that cast her out just as she was washing her hands of them were now obliged to repossess her. As Dave Griffin, Princess Margaret's chauffeur, absorbed the news of Diana's death he could not help but reflect on the portentous words of his employer a few months before: 'Poor Lilibet and Charles have done everything they can to get rid of the wretched girl, but she just won't go.'

Even before dawn had broken, the full seriousness of the situation was beginning to sink in. 'They're all going to blame me, aren't they?' Prince Charles said to anyone who would listen. 'What do I do, what does this mean?' The Prime Minister, Tony Blair, at home in his Sedgefield constituency in County Durham, saw far beyond his personal feelings, telling his aide, Alastair Campbell, 'This is going to unleash grief like no one has ever seen anywhere in the world.'

While Blair had been party to the decision to let the boys sleep through the night, it was their father who had the task of breaking the news that their mother was dead. At 7.15 in the morning, a haggard Prince Charles, who had spent some time walking around the Balmoral grounds alone with his thoughts, went with a heavy heart to tell his sons about their mother. 'I knew something was wrong,' William reportedly said. 'I kept waking up all night.' His father explained that he had to fly to Paris and that the boys would stay at Balmoral with their grandparents. 'Thank goodness we're all together, we can look after them,' was the immediate response of the Queen Mother when she was told the news.

A symbol of stoicism and imperturbable calm, the Queen Mother, like the rest of the royal family, instinctively responded to the tragedy by maintaining the rhythm and routine of everyday life. Her mood, according to a courtier, was 'steely'. The Sunday service at Crathie church was scheduled for later that morning and no one saw any good reason to cancel it. The boys were persuaded that, if they attended, they might find it more consoling to be with the rest of the family than inside Balmoral Castle. However, the service, conducted by a Church of Scotland minister, was remarkable for the fact that no mention was made of the Princess, causing Prince Harry to ask, 'Are you sure Mummy is dead?' Apart from black ties, the royal family gave no outward sign that this was anything other than a routine church service, while the minister stuck to his prepared sermon about moving house, including jokes about the Scottish comedian, Billy Connolly. Even *The Times* was moved to remark 'No Mention of Accident'. It was the start of a growing chorus of criticism.

Buckingham Palace issued a bleak eight-word statement expressing 'shock' at the news, and it was left to the Prime Minister to reflect on what Diana meant to the nation. 'They liked her, they loved her, they regarded her as one of the people. She was the People's Princess and that is how she will stay, how she will remain in all our hearts and memories for ever,' he said that morning.

While the Prince worried about how Diana's death would reflect upon him, and the rest of the royal family maintained their traditional reserve in the face of disaster, Diana's butler, Paul Burrell, was inconsolable. 'I must go to her, I must go to her,' he repeated, barely able to speak coherently. Diana's comptroller, Michael Gibbins, agreed to let him travel to Paris but on the proviso that he was accompanied by the Princess's driver, Colin Tebbutt. 'I want you to be my eyes and ears,' Gibbins told Tebbutt, not only to watch over the rapidly disintegrating Burrell, but also any manoeuvrings by the other royal households.

They managed to catch the 6.30 a.m. British Airways flight to Paris, the plane so full that Prince Charles's bodyguard, Ian von Heinz, had to sit in the jump seat. On their arrival in Paris, Colin Tebbutt, Paul Burrell and Ian von Heinz were met by the British Ambassador, Sir Michael Jay, on the Embassy steps. 'Am I glad to see you,' he said in greeting, aware that this unlikely trio were the first representatives of the royal family to arrive on French soil. After a brief meeting in the Embassy boardroom, Tebbutt headed for the Ritz Hotel to pick up Diana's belongings only to discover to his consternation that Mohamed Fayed had taken Diana's luggage back to London with him in his private jet. When he returned to the Embassy with the news that they had none of her clothes to dress her in, the Ambassador's wife, Sylvia Jay, who was roughly the same size as Diana, came to the rescue and popped next door to the ambassadorial residence to pick out some clothes from her wardrobe. Together they chose a black cocktail dress with a shawl-collar and a pair of black shoes for the Princess.

Finally they arrived at the hospital to find a scene of controlled chaos. Outside, dozens of media and public milled around, while in the first-floor corridor of the freshly painted Gaston Cordier wing, the British Consul-General, Keith Moss, was valiantly manning a specially installed bank of phones. As Moss fielded the calls, Tebbutt, von Heinz and Burrell were led to the hospital room set aside for the Princess. When they entered they saw Diana. She was lying on a hospital bed under a white sheet. It simply looked as though she was asleep. Paul Burrell broke down, sobbing and crying, 'Get up! Get up!' Years of police work had taught Tebbutt and von Heinz to be more detached, to focus on the practical rather than emotional, but Burrell was so overwrought that Tebbutt feared that if he saw the scratches on one side of her face he would collapse completely.

A fan in the room turned slowly and a light breeze stirred a wisp of hair lying across her forehead as though wafted by a breath from Diana's lips. It seemed almost like a shiver of life. At this unnerving sight, Paul Burrell crumbled completely and was escorted outside for counselling by Martin Draper, an English clergyman who had arrived to relieve Father Clochard-Bossuet.

With the day promising to be warm and humid, and with photographers already looking for vantage points to take pictures of the morbid scene, Tebbutt ordered blankets to be draped over the windows and an air-conditioning unit to keep the room cool.

While Burrell composed himself, before fetching Mrs Jay's black dress and shoes for the Princess, Tebbutt and von Heinz put Diana in the care of two gowned and masked French undertakers who worked efficiently and discreetly to make the Princess ready for her journey home. While the undertakers were doing this, Prince Charles telephoned the hospital from Balmoral to find out the latest situation and to pass on his condolences to the distraught butler. 'What is happening? What is going on?' he wanted to know.

Meanwhile in Paris, there came the most bizarre sight of the day – the entrance of the men from the royal funeral directors, Levertons, who marched down the corridor in full frock-coats carrying a special lead-lined custom coffin and a royal standard, which Burrell and the others had not thought to bring with them. There was concern that the British undertakers, distinguished by their royal appointment and their more than two centuries of business (the firm was established in 1789, the year the French Revolution broke out) would be aggrieved at not having prepared the Princess's body themselves. But they examined the handiwork of their French counterparts and gave their approval. The only doubt concerned Diana's hair. No one quite knew what had been her latest style so Burrell went into the room to help with the final arrangements before the Prince of Wales and Diana's sisters, Jane and Sarah, arrived. A picture of the boys found in her purse was carefully placed in her hands, as too were rosary beads, a much treasured gift from Mother Teresa of Calcutta who died less than a week later.

By now most of the Princess's jewellery had been recovered from the crash site and brought to the hospital, and her necklace, bracelet and watch were put on her, which helped make her look less stark. Only one earring had been found – the second was discovered later, embedded in the dashboard of the Mercedes.

Late in the afternoon, Prince Charles arrived at the hospital with Diana's sisters, to be met by the French President, Jacques

Chirac, and other dignitaries, who escorted the royal party to pay their respects to the Princess. Outside her room, Sarah and Jane gave Paul Burrell a hug, while the Prince of Wales shook Colin Tebbutt's hand and thanked him for 'looking after the fort'. They spent some minutes privately with the Princess, calling for the priest to lead them in prayer. Then the trio emerged, visibly distressed, to take Diana home. Before leaving they thanked the medical staff who had worked in vain to save the Princess. 'You sensed Prince Charles had the weight of the world on his shoulders,' Thierry Meresse, the director of communications, remarked later. 'He was very, very, very upset.'

The nurse who was present there, however, was disconcerted by the fact that when Prince Charles talked to her, he seemed curiously obsessive about the missing earring. 'It is absolutely essential that she is wearing both earrings. She can't leave like that,' he insisted. It was the second time that day that hospital staff had noticed the royal family's concern about detail and jewellery. Earlier they had received a telephone call from the Queen's senior courtiers on the special 'Balmoral hotline' enquiring as to the whereabouts of Diana's jewellery and asking for its safe return. After discussions with the Consul-General, Meresse explained that medical staff at the crash site had been more concerned about the Princess's condition than her jewellery. (When the Queen's sister, Princess Margaret, died in 2002, the Queen visited Kensington Palace herself to pick up her jewellery.)

The preoccupation with the protocol surrounding her jewellery was matched by concern about the form her funeral should take, discussions that foreshadowed and exposed the future battles for Diana's memory that would end in Number One Court at the Old Bailey five years later. At first glance, the plan to repatriate Diana was coherent, considered and uncontroversial. Once Diana's death had been confirmed and announced at 5.45 a.m. British time by the French doctors and the British Ambassador, Operation Overlord, a scheme drawn up in the 1980s to bring back a royal body from abroad, went into action. Under the plan every member of the royal family has a codename, taken from a bridge – for the Queen Mother it was Tay Bridge, for the Queen it is London Bridge,

Prince Philip is Forth Bridge and Prince Charles Menai Bridge. For an organization so reliant on protocol, these codenames, according to Dickie Arbiter, have an elegiac explanation – the 'bridge between life and death'. Diana, however, being young and disengaged from the royal family, had no codename.

When Diana's death was officially confirmed, a number of procedures were put in place that had previously been discussed and agreed by the Lord Chamberlain. The order went out from Buckingham Palace to lower to half-mast the Union flags at Holyrood House and Windsor Castle. At Buckingham Palace, which only flies the Royal Standard when the Queen is in residence, no flag flew at all. This was to become a cause of considerable public anger.

The attention to detail was so careful that when BA 146 of the Queen's flight landed at RAF Northolt, the plane was taken away from the gaze of the watching media and the coffin carrying Diana's body unloaded and turned around so that when she formally came home, she would be taken off the plane head first. After an RAF guard of honour placed her in the hearse, the Princess was driven to a mortuary in Fulham where she was formally identified by her sisters and her body fully examined by the royal coroner Dr John Burton. It is likely that it was here that she was dressed in her own clothes. Then, as Operation Overlord anticipated, she was taken to the Chapel Royal at St James's Palace and her coffin, with a white cloth on which were laid white lilies, was placed on a catafalque surrounded by tall candles. For that week the wood-panelled chapel was treated and dressed as a shrine, a constant stream of members of the royal family and their staff paying their last respects. Apart from minor adjustments on the day – Prince Charles, for example, insisted that Diana's body be taken from the Paris hospital to the airport in a hearse rather than a helicopter – Operation Overlord worked smoothly.

In the coming weeks and months, however, the impression was given by Prince Charles's staff and his literary apologists, notably Penny Junor, that it was only his decisive intervention in the critical first few hours, and his subsequent mastery of the funeral details, that saved the monarchy. While the Queen and her courtiers dithered about whether Prince Charles should go to Paris in the first place and, if he did, whether he should be authorized to use the royal flight, Charles, it was said, showed a steely resolve, determined that he should go to France to bring his ex-wife home. If a royal flight were not forthcoming, his assistant private secretary and spin doctor, Mark Bolland, declared, the Prince would get a scheduled flight from Aberdeen. Again, when they returned to Britain, the Prince was so horrified that Diana was going to the mortuary in Fulham – a strict legal requirement – that he insisted she should be laid to rest in the Chapel Royal at St James's Palace. Using the vernacular of an East End gangster, the Prince, according to Junor, told a hapless aide: 'Sort it. I don't care who has made this decision.' In touch, compassionate and strong-minded, the busy Prince was subsequently credited with virtually every innovation during the funeral week, from lengthening the route to include Kensington Palace to installing video screens in the park. In doing so, he apparently fought head-on with the Queen and the Old Guard at Buckingham Palace, their stuffiness and over-reliance on protocol contrasting with his imaginative and sensitive handling of the event.

This, however, was not the way senior courtiers remembered the funeral week. Not only were there existing plans in place to bring home a royal body from abroad, but many innovations of that momentous week came from the notorious 'men in grey', at both Kensington Palace and Buckingham Palace. Even the Downing Street spin doctor Alastair Campbell was impressed. 'Charles was like a wet weekend at Balmoral,' commented one of the Queen's staff, perhaps a little unkindly. 'He was poleaxed with guilt, and any suggestion that he was taking charge is ridiculous.' It was, though, a foretaste of the tussles to come and a reminder to courtiers just what Diana had endured for so many years. As the Queen's biographer Robert Lacey observed:

> A simple way of making Charles look good was to make Diana look bad. After Diana's death other figures in the royal family and in Buckingham Palace proved easy targets. The Queen herself was supposed to be off limits but that didn't stop an easy sneering at the

ancien régime and the big house. In fact after recent reforms, Buckingham Palace was a model of modern management practice compared to the feudalism and favourites surrounding the Prince.

While Charles's supporters were eager to place their royal master centre stage, Paul Burrell, far from the sobbing creature remembered by those who were with him in Paris and London, portrayed himself in his memoirs as a forceful royal Zelig, like Woody Allen's screen character, at the heart of every major decision concerning the Princess's welfare. One story is typical. He claimed that when he and Lucia Flecha de Lima visited Diana's coffin in the Chapel Royal there were no flowers and it was only their stern intervention that forced the uncaring authorities to make good this omission. Lucia is said to have warned the Queen's chaplain, the Reverend Willie Booth, in a moment of melodrama, that if there were no flowers by the time she returned then she would go outside and tell the people, the implication being that they would rise against the monarchy in disgust. As already mentioned, however, when the Princess's coffin arrived at the Chapel Royal it was treated with the reverence and dignity befitting the mother of the future king. Candles surrounded the coffin, which was decked with white lilies and a simple, plain white cloth. To commemorate the historic event, an illustrator from *The Times* newspaper was invited to sketch the scene.

Then there was the funeral itself. The Spencer family entered the fray early on. While the royal family's Operation Overlord was put into effect to bring Diana home, when she arrived at the Chapel Royal that Sunday evening, there was still uncertainty about which family would take ultimate charge of the funeral arrangements, the Spencers or the Windsors. In the first hours, the collective reaction of the Spencer family was that Diana should be buried quietly on the estate at Althorp, followed some weeks later by a memorial service, in keeping with the traditional farewells to the great and the good. Earl Spencer, who was in South Africa, recalled that his sister had expressed a desire to have any service centred upon her favourite piece of choral music, Fauré's Requiem. Initially, it seems that the Queen agreed with this proposal, and the

Spencer family were scheduled to take over arrangements once the Princess's coffin had been installed, with full royal honours, at the Chapel Royal.

Indeed, the Queen's press secretary Geoff Crawford, on holiday in Australia at the time, was told by Sir Robert Fellowes, who naturally was in constant discussion with his wife Jane and other Spencer family members, that, under these circumstances, it was not necessary for him to fly back to Britain immediately. That evening when the royal party arrived at RAF Northolt, the Lord Chamberlain Lord Airlie informed the Prime Minister, Tony Blair, and his press secretary, Alastair Campbell, that it was still not clear which family was going to organize the funeral. 'We are going to need help to respond to this,' Lord Airlie told them.

Any thoughts Sarah McCorquodale and her sister, Jane Fellowes, might have harboured that the Spencers could say goodbye to their royal sister in private evaporated when they saw the crowds standing by the side of the dual carriageway as they drove into central London in the convoy carrying her body. Diana's comptroller, Michael Gibbins, who was in the procession, saw the sea of faces and observed, 'There is no way this can be a private funeral.' In her isolated cottage on the isle of Seil, Frances Shand Kydd took rather more persuading, unhappily agreeing to the unpalatable fact that her daughter's funeral, like her life, would become a public spectacle. It irked her that Westminster Abbey was the venue chosen for the funeral, the place where, in 1954, she had married Diana's father, the late Earl Spencer – 'That was something I had to grasp, digest and get on with.'

Like so many others at the centre of this emotional vortex, she had not appreciated the sheer scale of the public response to the Princess's death. 'I expect you will get one or two bringing flowers to the gates,' the duty police inspector at Kensington Palace remarked, with blithe unconcern, on the morning of Diana's death. By that evening the Palace gardens had been transformed into a makeshift place of worship, the flickering glow from a sea of candles casting an ethereal light over the growing carpet of flowers.

When Earl Spencer arrived back in Britain from Cape Town, he, like his mother, was irritated that the funeral seemed to have been wrenched away from his family and was now being orchestrated by the House of Windsor. There were personal reasons for his annoyance. During the last year of her life Charles and Diana had restored their fond familial bond, the years of distantness, sparked off by the row over the cottage on the Althorp estate, seemingly behind them. Before her visit to South Africa in March 1997, she had told friends that she was looking forward to being reunited with her brother as much as she was to meeting Nelson Mandela.

With his sister's possible feelings in mind, Charles Spencer expressed strong opposition to the suggestion that, in keeping with royal tradition, the boys should walk behind the coffin. He felt that Diana would not have wanted it on the grounds that her sons would find it a painful ordeal. 'I thought that was where tradition and duty went too far against human nature,' he told Ian Katz of the *Guardian*. During one acrimonious conversation with Prince Charles he reportedly slammed down the phone. While the final decision was left to William and Harry themselves, in the end it was the intervention of their grandfather, Prince Philip, that proved decisive. 'If I walk, will you walk?' he asked. William agreed. 'The boys are very close to their grandparents, adore them,' observed Dickie Arbiter. 'Significantly, they walked for their grandfather, not their father or uncle.'

In a week redolent with symbolism, this decision was probably the most telling, the sight of these two young princes walking behind their mother's coffin an enduring and potent image of loss and grief. 'I have never been in such a nightmarish place in my life,' recalled Charles Spencer of that long walk. Paradoxically, it was the fact that the boys displayed the traditional royal virtues of stoicism and fortitude amidst a sea of tears that lent the tableau such an emotional resonance. They adhered impeccably to the maxim of Princess Alice, Countess of Athlone: 'You don't wear private grief on a public sleeve.'

Yet it was these very attributes that came under fierce and anguished attack during the week. If the service at Crathie church had reinforced the royal family's image as emotionally cold, then the reluctance to fly the flag at half-mast above Buckingham Palace and the decision to remain at Balmoral represented their apparent indifference, not just to Diana but to a nation in mourning. 'Where is the Queen when the country needs her?' asked the *Sun* newspaper plaintively. In this highly charged atmosphere, which came to be characterized as 'floral fascism', the decision by the Queen to return from Scotland early and broadcast her own tribute to Diana from Buckingham Palace helped defuse the evident dislocation between the monarchy and the people. But while the Queen praised Diana's maternal devotion, kindness, warmth and sense of humour, the feeling remained that it was too little, too late. Certainly Frances Shand Kydd was upset that the Queen had not personally contacted her to offer her condolences or to talk about the grandsons they shared. As Mrs Shand Kydd's friend and biographer Max Riddington commented, 'It remains almost inexplicable that the Queen did not even telephone Frances to express her sorrow that Diana had died.'

Whatever the machinations behind the scenes, the dramatic funeral was testimony, ironically, to the work of the 'men in grey', proving to be a 'unique day for a unique woman', which neatly meshed the ancient and modern, the traditional and innovative. As he walked past the motley moist-eyed mass of mourners on his way to Westminster Abbey, the lawyer Richard Greene, one of only eight Americans in the congregation, reflected on Diana's impact: 'She wanted to expand the capacity for people to feel and show emotion. And she succeeded. The police were in tears, everywhere there were flowers, London was like another planet. I looked up at the sky and said: "You did it." What an impact for a nursery school teacher. Even in death she was orchestrating the whole thing.'

For the last few years of her life, she had, without truly acknowledging it, achieved her ambition. She had reached out, over the heads of the Palace and the mass media, and made a genuine connection with the people. In their turn, they had witnessed and watched her journey of self-discovery, seeing in her victories and defeats, her strengths and frailties, her loves and losses, something of their own lives.

While the collective reaction to her death has been characterized as a retreat from reason into mawkish sentimentality, the underlying mood of dislocation and unease reflected a wider disenchantment with the great institutions of State, not only the monarchy, but the mass media and political Establishment. Since Diana's death this scepticism has become firmly entrenched in the national consciousness, reflected not just in the cynicism surrounding her accident – illustrated by the variety of conspiracy theories that abound – but also with regard to day-to-day political discourse, notably opposition in 2003 to the Iraq war. On the day of the funeral this sense of alienation found articulate and biting expression in Earl Spencer's speech.

He threw down the gauntlet to the Sovereign and her family, revealing the hurt felt by Spencer towards Windsor as he implicitly rebuked the Queen for stripping Diana of her title 'Her Royal Highness', as well as, for good measure, chiding the royal family for the way they had brought up their children: 'On behalf of your mother and sisters, I pledge that we, your blood family, will do all we can to continue the imaginative and loving way in which you were steering these two exceptional young men, so that their souls are not simply immersed by duty and tradition, but can sing openly as you planned.'

Having cloaked the young princes in the Spencer standard, he proceeded to tear a strip off the mass media who had made his sister's life such a daily torment: 'My own and only explanation is that genuine goodness is threatening to those at the opposite end of the moral spectrum. It is a point to remember that of all the ironies about Diana, perhaps the greatest was this – a girl given the name of the ancient goddess of hunting was, in the end, the most hunted person of the modern age.'

As he finished his peroration, praising his sister as the 'unique, the complex, the extraordinary and irreplaceable Diana, whose beauty, both internal and external, will never be extinguished from our minds', applause rippled from outside the open doors of the Abbey as the crowds watching on the giant screens gestured their support. Inside the Abbey the congregation took their own cue, in turn applauding an electrifying address that somehow typified the Spencer clan – reckless, brave, intemperate, yet capturing the popular mood.

There were many, however, particularly supporters of the royal family, who thought the Earl's words ill-judged and inappropriate. As with much of Diana's behaviour, the speech took the royal family and their households completely by surprise. 'The mood inside the royal family was very angry about what he said and the courtiers were apoplectic, shell-shocked,' recollected Dickie Arbiter. 'But then if you look into the history of the Spencer family they have tended to go off half-cocked and on the wrong occasions.'

The rout was complete, however, when the Queen's private secretary, Sir Robert Fellowes, suggested to the Earl that the Sovereign might be willing to reinstate Diana's title. Their informal conversation, on the royal train heading to Althorp where Diana was to be buried, had only one result – her brother turned it down flat. He had no real choice, especially just having told a worldwide audience that Diana 'needed no royal title to continue to generate her particular brand of magic'. As one member of the family said, 'It was a gesture far too late, which perhaps should have been made during her life.'

On her last journey to the island on the Althorp estate, chosen by her mother and brother for her grave, Diana had come full circle. In a final and fittingly symbolic gesture, the royal standard that had covered her coffin during her journey from Kensington Palace to Westminster Abbey, and thence to Althorp, was replaced by the white, red, black and gold of the Spencer flag. It was a decision that had been mutually agreed and prearranged.

During the private thirty-minute ceremony attended only by her immediate family, Colin Tebbutt and Paul Burrell, there was a palpable feeling that she had returned home. As her mother later noted, 'Diana had become a Spencer, independent and herself again.'

CHAPTER TWELVE

Trials of the Torch Bearers

HISTORY HAS NOT BEEN KIND to Princesses of Wales. Ignored, betrayed, evicted and abused, they have suffered harshly for marrying the heir to the throne. It is a title written in tears. During the fifteenth century, the Spanish princess, Catherine of Aragon was engaged to be married to Arthur Tudor, heir to the mighty dynasty, when she was just two and he only one. Married and publicly bedded at fifteen, they could not even speak each other's language and had to converse through bishops who translated for them. When he died a year later, Catherine, lonely and unhappy in a strange country, was passed on, like so much luggage, to his younger brother, Henry, becoming the first of his six wives.

While there are parallels between Catherine and Diana, Princess of Wales, in that both were chosen as potential brides because of their dynastic pedigree, the figure Diana most closely resembles is Princess Caroline of Brunswick, the sorrowful but spirited wife of the Prince of Wales who, in 1820, became King George IV. Like Diana, she married a Prince who had a long-term lover, an issue which became a source of hot dispute and unhappiness. Like Diana, Princess Caroline was cast out of court and, being forced to make her own way in life, was determined to go down fighting. Seen as a victim of a cold, devious and calculating Establishment, she was a hugely popular figure, loved by the common people for her pluck.

'She symbolized, as Diana did, the revolt of the outsiders, the excluded, against the insiders, the ruling powers,' the historian Dr David Starkey wrote. When the wronged Queen was barred from attending King George IV's coronation in 1821 many supported her when she rode to the ceremony uninvited. Sternly the king had ordered every door to be guarded by prizefighters and she left the scene, humiliated. Three weeks later she died, the new king ordering her body to be returned to Germany lest her grave become a rallying point for opposition to his rule. Yet, as her coffin was taken to the coast, thousands flocked to the 'ramshackle cavalcade' in a gesture of popular support for the first 'people's princess'. Within months the Carolinian movement, an audacious attempt to capture her spirit, was over and the Princess, now buried in a foreign land, consigned to the position of an entertaining footnote in history.

After the death of Diana, Princess of Wales, her former husband, like his forebear George IV, attempted to define himself apart from his wife and mistress, to be valued for his public achievements rather than his messy private life. As a strategy it was entirely understandable if ultimately unrealistic, the Prince's followers seeking to diminish Diana's memory by their indifference, quietly sniping from the sidelines. It was, however, the vacuum created by the withdrawal of the Prince and the royal family from any involvement in defining her legacy and memory that would ultimately diminish the institution. Diana's influence on the royal family was to be far more potent from beyond the grave than when she lived.

In the void left by the Windsors' apparent lack of concern, it was, paradoxically, among her erstwhile supporters and allies that the cruellest infighting took place as they attempted to define, burnish and control her memory. In the process, the self-appointed keepers of her flame were severely burnt. As the commentator Michael Ignatieff observed, 'At the centre of it all, three great families – the Spencers, the Windsors and the Fayeds – duelled in public over the ownership of her symbolic remains.' One name missing from his roll call was that of Diana's butler, Paul Burrell, who went from walk-on part to centre stage, the battle for her legacy ending in a raucous trial in No. 1 Court at the Old Bailey, as well as a formal police investigation into her last hours led by Britain's most senior police officer.

Within a few months of her death it was as though Diana had never existed. Her apartment at Kensington Palace had been completely stripped bare; the furniture was taken to St James's Palace for the boys or the Royal Collection, her clothes burnt or taken to Althorp, and her papers sent to the Royal Archives at Windsor Castle or to her family home. Everything, from the carpets, the silk wallpaper, the plants and even the light bulbs, was removed, leaving Apartments 8 and 9 empty and anonymous. It took six months to make a comprehensive inventory of the Princess's belongings. Every single item from nightshirts to robes to writing pads was logged and noted. Just before the first anniversary of her death the sign outside her former home was painted over. The only reminder of her luminous presence was a portrait by John Ward exhibited in the public rooms at Kensington Palace.

It was a process that began within hours of her death. The bloodied and torn clothes she wore that fateful night were kept in the fridge at Kensington Palace and then secretly burnt in a brazier in the back garden of Paul Burrell's Cheshire home. Diana's gymwear, knickers, swimming costumes, tights and stockings were also incinerated to stop them getting into the hands of misguided collectors. The Spencers were terrified of trophy hunters. In the first days Prince Charles suggested that her apartment be sealed, but the Princess's comptroller, Michael Gibbins, opposed the notion. He decided that it would be neither feasible nor appropriate – and he was concerned about what would happen if the suicidal Burrell was denied access to 'his' domain.

In the coming weeks it was left to Diana's mother and her sister Sarah McCorquodale, as well as her butler, to sift through the detritus of a life cut short. As her family sat in the now quiet apartment, her spirit seemed still to be present: in the smell of her perfume and scented candles, the wardrobe filled with her clothes, and the notes and cards on her desk that spoke of a life in full flood. They were also presented with four sacks of letters assembled by the butler, which they divided into bread-and-butter thank-you notes, letters for her boys and correspondence to friends, family and others. As they began the sad task of sorting through her belongings, they were helped by Meredith Etherington-Smith, who had catalogued Diana's dresses for the charity auction in New York. She now made a final inventory of the Princess's four giant wardrobes – Diana habitually gave away many of her clothes, to her sisters, friends and staff, including Maria Burrell – while David Thomas, the Crown jeweller, compiled details of her jewellery. Burrell himself went through the twenty rooms labelling, describing and noting their contents. Every night the rooms they were working in would be sealed with masking tape.

As the family sifted through her life, they could see at first hand the impact Diana's death had had on her butler. Before the funeral, Mrs Shand Kydd was so concerned about Paul Burrell's mental state that she handed the grieving butler a necklace with a gold cross to give him spiritual sustenance. Afterwards, when they went through the Princess's belongings, the three of them, as well as other visitors like Diana's hairdresser Sam McKnight, were able to reminisce about Diana's foibles and fads, vices and virtues with the ease of those who knew the character concerned intimately. With Burrell they didn't have to pretend. He was considered part of the family. Often when they had finished their work for the day, Mrs Shand Kydd would join Paul and his wife Maria in their grace-and-favour apartment in Kensington Palace, a home that was something of a shrine, every surface covered in framed photographs and other memorabilia of their life with the royal family. Taking pride of place on the wall was a bullwhip given to Diana when she attended the première of an Indiana Jones movie. Knowing his love of films – he is a collector of cells from Disney movies – she had passed it on to her butler with the joking proviso, 'As long as you don't use it on Maria.'

Relations between the Spencers and Burrells could have been very different. In those first months, the Spencers found Burrell's intimate knowledge of her affairs invaluable. On one occasion when Lady Sarah asked about the significance of a rosary amongst

Diana's belongings, Burrell told her, to her evident surprise, that it was a gift from the Pope. And it was he who retrieved the key, from the bottom of a tennis racket case, which opened the now notorious mahogany box containing Diana's 'crown jewels' – notably a signet ring from James Hewitt; letters from Prince Philip to the Princess following the publication of *Diana: Her True Story* in 1992; the resignation letter from her private secretary Patrick Jephson; and a tape recording of her conversation with Prince Charles's orderly George Smith in which Smith alleged that he had been raped by a member of the Prince's staff.

So helpful was he that, if they were at all aware of any of his curious behaviour, they turned a blind eye to it. A few days after the Princess's death he was caught by a patrolling policeman at 3.30 in the morning loading his estate car with two of Diana's designer evening dresses and a mahogany-topped box. Was this the box containing the crown jewels? Burrell has always denied it. Burrell told the officer that he was working 'discreetly' at the specific request of Sarah McCorquodale. When the incident was followed up, however, Sarah denied ever giving him such instructions. Further suspicions were aroused when Earl Spencer's estate manager, David Horton-Fawkes, went to collect some of Diana's clothes from Kensington Palace. When he observed that she only had four hats, yet countless shoes and handbags, Burrell told him that she gave many of her clothes away. On another occasion, the Princess's chef, Darren McGrady, who claimed that he was offered a pair of Diana's diamond earrings by Burrell as a keepsake for his daughter, also witnessed the butler loading his car late at night.

Far from being suspicious of Burrell's nocturnal activities, Sarah and her mother were grateful for his loyalty and discretion at a difficult time. Indeed, in appreciation of his endeavours, they, as executors of the estate, altered Diana's will to include a bequest to him of £50,000 in recognition of his service. Their largesse continued. In December 1997, as he was no longer employed by the royal household, he and his family were given notice to quit their grace-and-favour apartment in Kensington Palace. In a gesture which Burrell described as 'incredibly kind', Mrs Shand Kydd offered him £120,000 towards a London base on condition that she held the lease and had a room for her own use when she came to London.

Before Diana's death, the Spencers were aware that Burrell was on the point of leaving. Earl Spencer knew that he was registered with several domestic agencies. Now, in 1997, Diana's sister, Jane Fellowes, knowing that the royal family were not going to offer him alternative employment, petitioned her brother vigorously to give him a job as butler at Althorp. Earl Spencer, however, refused, telling Burrell that he would find life 'boring' on his Northamptonshire estate, adding that he already had a full staff complement. The Earl was to pay dearly for that rejection.

With a £50,000 cheque, the offer of £120,000 for a home and members of the Spencer family trying to find him work, Burrell repaid his benefactors by seeking an audience with the Queen on 19 December 1997 to pour bile and vitriol into her ear about the family, especially Diana's mother, who were trying to support him. By his own account he spent three hours with the Sovereign – although courtiers dispute this – outlining his grievances against Dodi Fayed, who had threatened to take his Princess away; his concerns about the Memorial Fund, and most particularly his complaints with regard to Mrs Shand Kydd's unilateral decision to shred some of the Princess's correspondence. She had even shredded the ink blotter on Diana's desk. 'I was not shredding history,' Mrs Shand Kydd declared four years later at the Old Bailey, asserting that what she had shredded had been mundane invitations or routine correspondence. That was not the case as far as the butler or her friends were concerned. Both Rosa Monckton and Lucia Flecha de Lima knew that their correspondence had been shredded and when Richard Greene called from California to ask for the return of his letters, Burrell told him that it was too late as they had been shredded. At least that is the butler's version of events.

Crucially, Burrell told the Queen that he intended to keep Diana's secrets safe and hold on to the documents and artefacts she had given him. His audience with the Queen raises many more questions than it answers. He has given no convincing explanation as to why the meeting took place in the first place. Certainly, as far as the Spencer family are concerned, he went to see the Queen in order to return Prince Philip's letters that were in the famous mahogany box. The Queen's courtiers, on the other hand, have suggested that Burrell, still agitated and emotional after Diana's death, had sought an audience with the Queen to ask for advice on how he should comport himself after being asked in November 1997 to be a member of Chancellor Gordon Brown's memorial committee to select a suitable memorial to commemorate Diana's life. Her now famous words about 'powers at work in this country about which we have no knowledge' were, they aver, nothing more than a warning to him about the strong and important characters, who included Rosa Monckton, Lynda Chalker and Lord Attenborough, on the committee. Burrell reflected that she might have been referring to media barons, the Establishment or the intelligence services.

At the same time, for a man who had complained endlessly to his lawyer friend, Richard Greene, 'How am I going to take care of my family?' when he was made redundant, it seems remarkable that, in the very month that he was given notice, he did not use the opportunity of a royal audience to plead for another job in the world that he loved and knew so well. Or perhaps he did and the Queen was not forthcoming.

The subtext of this extraordinary meeting, though, as his memoirs make clear, is that her butler felt that he was losing his grip on a woman over whom he felt he had power during her lifetime. The erstwhile puppeteer had lost his puppet. 'After being in charge of the Princess's entire life when she was alive, I suddenly found myself on the periphery,' he recalled. 'I felt I was losing control over a world the princess expected me to control for so long. I had never felt so helpless.' Ultimately then, his audience with the Queen was a *cri de cœur*, a last-ditch attempt to gain dominion over Diana's life, an ersatz control that, realistically, during the last months of her life he knew was slipping away.

Just as he had jealously ousted those who came too close during her lifetime – whether bodyguard, chef or boyfriend – so in her death he strove to diminish those whose position threatened his own. While her family were the official keepers of her flame, in his eyes he was the one true believer, Diana's self-appointed representative on earth. The Spencers then were a threat not just to his position but his very identity. Thus at the time of their greatest largesse towards him, he worked assiduously to undermine them. 'All the time they were creating a monster and they never saw it coming,' said the Princess's friend Vivienne Parry.

Of all the ironies of Diana's life, this is one of the more poignant. If she was anything, Diana was a woman who courageously struggled to take control of her body, her heart and her life. She endeavoured to make her own choices in spite of her querulous heart and outside hostility. Yet in death her memory was massaged by a man whose protestations of loyalty and duty masked, it seemed to me, a profound need to manipulate, manage and monitor. In his memoir the word 'control' seems to appear more often than 'duty'.

But whatever delusions and illusions he harboured away from the limelight, Paul Burrell cut a rather forlorn and pathetic figure – out of a job, facing eviction and unable to let go of his Princess.

The Diana Memorial Fund was a remarkable charity, founded from the spontaneous public outpouring of grief, expectation and hope following her death. Within days of her fatal accident, thousands of pounds had been sent to Kensington Palace, the royal garages turned into a makeshift postal sorting office as her driver-cum-bodyguard Colin Tebbutt and two police officers attempted manfully to open and sift the 6,000 letters that arrived every day. 'The flood of tears that followed Diana's death has been matched by a tidal wave of cash,' noted one commentator. Cheques and cash were arriving in a flood. One had a £1 coin and was marked 'pocket money'. Another contained a letter which read 'I hope you are OK in heaven and Thomas' dad'll look after you.' It was accompanied by a note from the sender's teacher explaining that Thomas's father had died on the same day as Diana.

Born out of sentimental enthusiasm, the infant charity came to symbolize the Princess's life and spirit, inevitably becoming the hub of arguments, as her memory was fought over, and where so many matters unresolved in Diana's life would continue to unsettle after her death. The very existence of the Fund was seen as a provocation to those who had wanted Diana's voice curbed in life, and it became a focal point for the snipes and sneers of her enemies, notably at St James's Palace, Prince Charles's London base. Her brother, Charles Spencer, commented, 'I think there is a feeling among those who were never Diana supporters of "Let's try and marginalize her and tell people she never mattered."' That antagonism was obvious the moment the Fund came into being. 'Certainly, St James's Palace wanted the Diana Fund wrapped up as quickly as possible,' Vivienne Parry, one of the charity's first trustees, recalled.

Within a matter of weeks this embryonic charity, still without an office or full-time staff, became a commercial licensing organization, charged with the virtually impossible dual task of protecting the Princess's image while exploiting it for the greater good.

A critical and ultimately disastrous element of this legal burden was the fact that they had to police any perceived infringement of Diana's image. After taking extensive legal advice the trustees agreed on a course of action which would cost the charity dear. In April 1998 they sued Franklin Mint, an American company which produces porcelain dolls and other collectables, for manufacturing and marketing a Diana doll without their approval. After a four-year legal battle not only did they lose the case, but it cost the charity £4 million. Worse followed. Franklin Mint's billionaire owners, Stuart and Lynda Resnick, stung by accusations from the charity's agents that they behaved 'like vultures feeding on the dead', now sued the Diana Memorial Fund and its trustees for 'malicious prosecution'. The charity's assets were frozen and over a hundred charities found their projects put on ice during the bitter legal wrangle which, at the time of writing, has yet to be resolved. The only people who suffered were the disadvantaged and dispossessed, the very people to whom Diana spent her days reaching out.

Certainly those who called and wrote to the Fund in the months following her death would never have wanted her charity to go down this route. They saw it as much more than just a charity; it became also a conduit for grief counselling and an emotional lightning rod for much unresolved hurt and anguish, the public inundating the Fund with heartfelt poems, poignant letters and tearful phone calls. Dramatic, complicated, well-intentioned but prone to reckless errors, the Fund was to become a mirror image of Diana's complex character.

The figure who symbolized this emotional conflict was Diana's sister Lady Sarah McCorquodale, chairman of the trustees along with Diana's comptroller Michael Gibbins and her lawyer Anthony Julius. In the months after the funeral Lady Sarah, known for her biting wit and, like Diana, love of risqué jokes, cut a desolate figure. Painfully thin, emotionally tightly wrapped and tense, she sat in meetings with her arms folded across her chest or her hands clenched so tightly that her knuckles showed white. The wife of a wealthy Lincolnshire farmer, like many of her class she had little awareness of or interest in organizations or committee work. Inexperienced, arrogant and impulsive, she was a difficult team player but, as both executor and trustee, she was easily the most powerful figure in this brave new charity. On her slim, hunched shoulders rested much of Diana's legacy.

Like her mother and sister, Lady Sarah felt a sense of responsibility towards Diana's former right-hand man. Knowing that her brother had no intention of offering Paul Burrell a job and seeing that the butler's brave talk about working in America had come to naught, she was entirely instrumental in offering him, in March 1998, a full-time post as the Fund's events manager. In so doing she faced strong objections from a number of trustees, including Michael Gibbins, who believed that Burrell was 'nothing but trouble'. Others thought that he was a 'man on the edge' and 'would be in tears most of the time' and hardly able to function. He took to using the Princess's fountain pen because, he would say, 'it brings me closer to her'; he aped Diana's mannerisms and boasted how her mother considered him her 'second son'.

More than that, they had seen how, even before he was on the payroll, he and Lady Sarah had embroiled the charity in a controversial commercial deal. In February 1998 he agreed with Flora to use Diana's name on their tubs of margarine, a move that was greeted with 'an audible intake of breath' at a trustees' meeting.

Sarah curtly stilled criticism by saying that she too had signed off on the proposal.

Within weeks, the Fund, already on the ropes for spending £500,000 on legal fees, was blasted for 'tastelessness' by none other than the Spencer family themselves. Earl Spencer wrote to the Fund, calling for it to be wound up at the earliest opportunity. It was a spectacular blunder especially as Sarah had approved the arrangement and, as executors, she and her mother had the final right of veto over matters of taste and sensitivity – they were effectively complaining about themselves. Moreover, they played into the hands of St James's Palace, who leaked the Earl's confidential letter to the media. 'Their motive is clear,' noted Vivienne Parry. 'The Fund has filled a media vacuum left by her death and the quicker we are shut down, the quicker she will go away.'

In spite of the ill-feeling surrounding the Flora débâcle, Lady Sarah kept faith with Paul Burrell, insisting on his appointment as a £35,000-a-year fundraiser. She was to regret it bitterly. Enthusiastic but commercially inexperienced, it was clear he was better at glad-handing at public functions than trying to negotiate business deals on behalf of the charity. Very quickly he became the Fund's human face, Diana's rock in action, appearing at galas, village fêtes and carnivals, even spending a weekend in Glasgow to judge a bagpipe contest. He enjoyed his newfound celebrity, being interviewed on TV and appearing regularly in the social pages of celebrity magazines. In the past he had dealt with the media on behalf of the Princess. Now he found that he had become the story, and naively believed that journalists courted him out of a genuine interest in him, rather than to glean titbits from him about his life with Diana.

With rumours about his private life, notably his friendship with the gay entertainer Michael Barrymore, now beginning to surface in the media, there was concern that this fragile character was, to borrow a phrase used to describe Diana, a loose cannon who was a danger to himself and to the Fund. Indeed, Barrymore later claimed that Burrell had tried to seduce him just days after Diana's death. Burrell subsequently denied the allegations, calling them a 'vengeful pack of lies'.

When Burrell flew to Los Angeles in March 1998 to represent the charity at the Princess Ball fund-raiser event there was concern when he slipped away from his colleagues to spend time on private activities. At the time he considered himself untouchable and was mortally offended when he was told by the charity that he could not appear on a BBC religious broadcast to talk about family values. While other trustees voiced their concerns, Sarah McCorquodale would not hear a word said against him, staunchly defending him from his critics. 'In her eyes,' according to Vivienne Parry, 'Paul could do no wrong.'

With the Spencers staying out of the limelight and friends of the Princess remaining silent, Paul Burrell eagerly stepped into the publicity vacuum, believing that he and he alone was prepared defend Diana's memory and prevent her from disappearing from view. Slowly Lady Sarah came to see, like the other trustees, that the butler had lost sight of what the Memorial Fund was about and had become more interested in being a celebrity, using the charity to promote himself while ostensibly seeking new ways to raise funds. 'Remember where you are from,' a senior figure in the Spencer clan was said to have told Burrell, a snobbish reference to his lowly upbringing.

In June 1998 matters were not helped by the appointment, as chief executive, of Andrew Purkis, known as 'the vicar' by the Spencers because he had worked for the Archbishop of Canterbury. Not only had he never met the Princess but he also sought to focus the charity away from fund-raising to grant-giving, dispersing the existing millions of pounds quietly and effectively to the causes Diana espoused, such as landmines and care for the dying. While Burrell still felt he could 'bring a unique perspective to the table and inject the Princess's wishes into the Fund's work', the tide was running against him. That December, just nine months after he had started, an awkward lunch in a London wine bar with a typically silent Sarah McCorquodale and Anthony Julius made clear what Purkis had already told him: his job was redundant. Within minutes of the meeting he had told two journalists about his plight and the story of his abrupt departure made front-page headlines.

Later the new chief executive acknowledged, with laconic understatement, the dilemma that Burrell faced: working for the charity or promoting himself. 'There's bound to be tension,' Purkis observed, 'when someone who is a full-scale media personality, and who in many ways would dearly love to be even more of a media personality, is working as just one staff member in a charity.' Burrell was 'saddened and distressed' and the Fund was in even deeper trouble than before.

Burrell's departure – with his head held high but nursing a grievance against the Spencers and the Fund – from the charity marked a parting of the ways for other members of Diana's staff who resigned shortly afterwards. In a tearful statement, Diana's former assistant, Jackie Allen, said that Burrell's departure was 'tragic' and praised his contribution to the Fund. There was even more sympathy for the loyal butler when he signed on the dole. But he soon found himself an agent and made a lucrative living on the British and American lecture circuit and on cruise liners regaling his eager audiences with anodyne anecdotes about life with the royal family. A book on royal entertaining further established his celebrity status, the butler deftly revealing the secret of how to cut a banana while himself deftly avoiding the figurative banana skins by discussing any personal details of Diana's life. The image of the discreet royal servant was complete.

While Burrell's star, as the keeper of Diana's flame, was firmly in the ascendant, the moral high ground was rapidly slipping away from the Spencer family. Earl Spencer had been warned by the MP Alan Clark soon after the funeral that the fallout from his oration would be harmful. 'Just watch now,' he had written. 'The press and the Royal family are two of the most powerful institutions in this country and they will make sure your name is dragged through the dirt.' His warning evoked memories of similar advice Rupert Murdoch gave to *Sunday Times* editor Andrew Neil shortly before he serialized *Diana: Her True Story*. The fallout began with the gleeful coverage of Earl Spencer's messy divorce in December 1997, with merciless reporting of the legal tussle between him and the bizarre alliance of his wife Victoria and his former mistress Chantal Collopy. In court the

Earl was depicted as a cruel, arrogant adulterer who claimed to have bedded a dozen other women while his wife was recovering from an eating disorder. Neither did it escape notice that for all his brave words about letting the boys sing openly, their uncle had had little contact with William and Harry in the year after Diana's death. It was conveniently leaked, by royal courtiers, that the Princes had turned down an offer of a summer holiday with the Spencers in Cornwall, and it was also noted that they were in Balmoral for the first anniversary of their mother's death. A family friend remarked, 'They [St James's Palace] are keen for the Spencers to be portrayed as a squabbling, dysfunctional family.'

The Spencers' blemished image was further tarnished not only by the misguided Flora deal, but also by the way Earl Spencer was portrayed as rushing to exploit his sister's memory by building a memorial at Althorp which was variously described as 'vulgar' and 'tacky'. As the first visitors queued to visit the museum celebrating the Princess's life, Lady Sarah was storing up yet more trouble for the Spencer family. That summer she travelled the country in her estate car visiting the homes of Diana's seventeen godchildren, distributing trinkets, usually wrapped in newspaper, chosen by the executors (namely herself and her mother). They included a framed print, a gift to the Princess from the Argos catalogue company, a coffee set, a china cockerel, a porcelain bunny, a decanter inscribed to the Princess from a Women's Institute in Wales, along with an incomplete tea set. Under the terms of her will, signed in June 1993, the Princess had agreed a letter of wishes which allocated 25 per cent of her 'goods and chattels' to her godchildren, the remainder to be given to her sons. Unknown to most of the parents of her godchildren, the executors had chosen to ignore her instructions, instead handing out items that they considered appropriate. The family, and Lady Sarah in particular, were to pay a heavy price for their high-handed actions.

A knock on the door of Paul Burrell's Cheshire home early on the morning of 18 January 2001 began a chain of events that was to expose the keepers of Diana's memory to the searing flame of public exposure, humiliation and disgrace. When Burrell, bleary-eyed and still in his dressing-gown, came to the door he was confronted by two officers and told that he was being arrested on suspicion of the theft of a golden dhow. The dhow, valued at anywhere between £30,000 and £500,000, had been given to the Prince and Princess of Wales by the Emir of Bahrain as a wedding present in 1981. For years the small jewel-encrusted ship had been on display in the hall at Kensington Palace. When it was sold to a Chelsea dealer for £1,200 by Princess Margaret's butler, Harold Brown, it was scratched and marked – probably because William and Harry had used it for marble-throwing practice when they were youngsters. The sale of this incongruous treasure ship, which, Brown claimed, had been effected on Burrell's instructions, had led to the police arriving on the doorstep of his Georgian home in Farndon.

'We've come for the Crown Jewels,' one officer reportedly said when they arrived in the first stage of what was codenamed Operation Plymouth. The police officers, who had a search warrant, were taken aback by the Aladdin's Cave of royal memorabilia they uncovered, much of it stored in the loft. More than thirteen hours and dozens of plastic bags later, they had carefully noted hundreds of items belonging to the late Princess, Prince William and Prince Charles. Their haul was as varied as it was huge, and included an 1826 silver salver inscribed to the Duchess of Clarence, numerous photograph albums and negatives, signed CDs, designer bags, hats and dresses by Valentino and Versace, a presentation US bicentennial proof set of silver coins, a *Baywatch* card autographed to Prince William by the Hollywood star David Hasselhoff and three framed pictures of Prince William with supermodels Christy Turlington, Naomi Campbell and Claudia Schiffer, as well as the Indiana Jones bullwhip. While memorabilia, clothes and photographs comprised the majority of the 342 items, there were also numerous memos and letters – including some from Earl Spencer, the former Prime Minister, John Major, and Mother Teresa of Calcutta – and a floppy disk containing Diana's personal accounts. During the course of the search, Burrell was asked if he was writing a memoir and whether he had removed a mahogany box from Kensington Palace – the storage place for her sensitive items, the so-called 'crown jewels'.

The whereabouts of the mahogany box is still a mystery. By the end of the search Burrell was too distressed to attend a black-tie dinner, organized, as fate would have it, by the Cheshire police, at which he was guest speaker.

While Burrell's prospects looked bleak he wrote, in April 2001, to Prince William to try to explain the misunderstanding. He argued (as his defence was to do at his trial) that he was merely acting as the custodian of the Princess's world: 'I know that you realize that I would never betray the trust and confidence which your mother placed in me and that I remain the person you have always known.'

He was helped by the fact that Prince Charles felt that if Burrell apologized, confirmed that he had only taken the property for safe-keeping and promised that he would not reveal confidential information that might hurt the boys, then there would be no prosecution. But then, in August 2001, the police came to High-grove for a critical meeting with Prince Charles and others, at which they outlined a damning case against Burrell. They informed the Prince that they had 'compelling' evidence to show that Burrell's bank balance had soared, presumably from the sale of Diana's belongings to wealthy American collectors. (As a sign of their intention of 'catching him in the act', Burrell had been fol-lowed by plain-clothes Scotland Yard officers when he gave lectures on board the *QE2* cruise ship, and teams of officers had also been sent to Italy, Australia and America to seek Diana's belongings.) Moreover, they said that they had photographic evi-dence showing male servants dressed in the Princess's clothes before they were packaged up and sent abroad. (It later transpired that the servants had been photographed at a fancy-dress party.) Not only did it seem that her 'rock' was profiting from her death, he was mocking the woman he so strenuously sought to champion.

Plans to meet with Burrell and sort out the matter were dropped and both the Prince and the Spencer family agreed to follow police advice, which ultimately proved to be grossly misleading. The runaway train was gathering speed.

In August 2001, Burrell was charged with the theft of items valued at £6 million from Diana, Princess of Wales, Prince

William and Prince Charles. For a serious breach of trust, he would face a minimum of five years in jail if found guilty. In spite of various manoeuvrings beforehand, the trial assumed a grim inevitability for all concerned. Just days before the trial began, Burrell's defence counsel privately warned the Prince of Wales's legal adviser that, as the essence of the defence was the butler's close and unique relationship with Diana, the case was 'a disaster waiting to happen for the royal family'. He could have also included the Spencer family in this dire prediction.

All sides were struggling with the tension surrounding the trial of the year at Number One Court at the Old Bailey, the scene of so many sensational dramas through the years. The son of a truck driver and canteen worker, Burrell was on medication as he prepared to face two of the mightiest families in the land. His skin had started to flake with the stress, he was drinking too much and at one point considered suicide. It was little easier for the Spencer family, particularly Mrs Shand Kydd. Not only was she suffering from a degenerative illness, but she had taken a nasty fall at her island home not long before the trial started. 'Can't say I want to be there but she was my daughter and so I'll be giving it my best shot even though my insides are like a tumble dryer,' she revealed in a letter to Princess Margaret's chauffeur, Dave Griffin. He – formerly Diana's immediate neighbour as well as a friend of Paul Burrell – was also due to be called as a prosecution witness. Diana's mother knew what she faced even before she took the stand. 'I'm sweating a bit over Paul's do,' she wrote to Griffin later. 'I'm portrayed by him as a dysfunctional mother – perhaps I am but it's not great to be in open court with that sort of thing.' In another note she wrote: 'What a wretched business it is. I'm glad she and her dad aren't around to witness such total abuse of trust.'

Yet it was the question of trust that went to the heart of the case, just as the issue of taste went to the core of the Memorial Fund. In a way these values, indefinable, imperceptible, and imprecise, highlighted the difficulty of describing Diana's legacy. What she stood for, who she was and where she was going were open to endless interpretation and debate, just like the character of the woman herself. If the trial at the Old Bailey was to prove anything it was that those who sought to claim dominion over her soul, spirit and legend were chasing shadows.

Stripped of its legal flummery, the Old Bailey trial was the equivalent of a domestic row about who was Diana's best friend – her family or a one-time honorary family member. So when Diana's mother told the court that Paul Burrell, the man she had called her 'second son', was not her daughter's 'rock', she was promptly reminded that she had not spoken to Diana for six months before her death and then had drunkenly accused her of consorting with Muslim men. 'There were normal up-and-downs but it was normal family behaviour,' she said, hotly denying that she would ever have criticized the men in her daughter's life. If she was skewered as a bad mother and a snob, then Lady Sarah McCorquodale was diminished as arrogant and unfeeling, arbitrarily ignoring Diana's letter of wishes in her will to give her godchildren a quarter of her goods and chattels. When questioned about the bequests that the godchildren had never received, Lady Sarah replied blithely that there were 'not too many paupers there'. She never explained why she and her mother ignored Diana's instructions, especially as they did not stand to gain personally by altering the will and her letter of wishes. When details emerged about Earl Spencer's letters to Diana rejecting her plea for a house on the Althorp estate, it added to the impression of a superior and condescending family who had little time for, or true understanding of, their sister and daughter.

Just before Burrell himself was due to take the stand, the trial was halted. As in many family feuds, it was the mother-in-law who played a crucial role. On 25 October 2002, just before the memorial service at St Paul's Cathedral for victims of the Bali bombing, the Duke of Edinburgh apparently mentioned to Prince Charles that the Queen had had a conversation with Paul Burrell in which he had referred to safekeeping documents. She had not considered this relevant as they formed only a small proportion of a large quantity of property allegedly stolen. This revelation fatally undermined the prosecution's contention that Burrell had never told anyone that he was taking Diana's property for safekeeping. Now it seemed he had. When the Queen was further questioned by Prince

Charles's private secretary, Sir Michael Peat, she confirmed that Burrell was going to look after Diana's papers as he was concerned what might happen to them. During this conversation, the Queen was non-committal about his actions but assumed that Burrell was not going to keep these items for ever.

Earlier, Diana's mother had denied such wholesale destruction of her daughter's papers, refuting the suggestion that she had sat on the sofa in Diana's sitting room, glass of red wine in hand, shredding documents day after day. As she pointed out, the cable from the shredder, which was on the desk, about nine feet away, was not long enough to allow the machine to be operated from the sofa. It begs the question also of Burrell – if he were so concerned, why did he not stop her, or at least make his disapproval clear? They were at that time still good friends, after all.

While the Queen's intervention added to the surreal domestic nature of the trial, equally bizarre is the fact that Paul Burrell, in the two years since his arrest, had not once mentioned this vital three-hour conversation with the Queen to his legal team. This is all the more remarkable given the fact that the thrust of the prosecution's case, namely that before his arrest Burrell had never told anyone he was acting as a custodian of Diana's property, had been known to the defence for months. Just to add to the sense of bafflement is the fact that, in his memoirs, he claims that his motive for the meeting with the Queen hinged on his concerns about Mrs Shand Kydd shredding documents. He went on to say in his witness statement that, because of his worries about this wanton destruction, he was going to keep some documents secure. But was this really the case?

Take, for example, the case of the famous letters from Prince Philip. In his subsequent memoir, which he wrote after the trial, Burrell reprints extracts from these letters, or copies of letters, to which he has access. These letters were kept in the notorious mahogany box. In his police statement Burrell said that he had never seen the box or its contents, which included the Duke's letters, after he and Sarah McCorquodale had opened it in the days after Diana's death. If that is the case, how did he apparently come to have the Prince Philip letters in his possession, unless he copied them before Diana's death and, therefore, before the shredding of historic documents allegedly took place? If he had copied them his motive for doing so could not have been to protect them from the shredding, which he subsequently complained about to the Queen. He already had them, or had access to them. So what was his motive? As he was never questioned about this matter in court under oath, the full picture may never be known. One clue to his motives was later provided by the Kensington Palace chef Darren McGrady, who often saw Burrell sending copies of royal documents to his friends in America, boasting 'They are for later on.'

As a result of the Queen's intervention, the trial was not only halted but, after two days' debate, abandoned, Judge Anne Rafferty directing that Burrell was free to go. The butler, who promptly broke down in tears, walked smiling out of court to tell the media scrum: 'The Queen's come through for me.' In the stampede, the finger of blame for the collapse of the trial was pointed firmly in the direction of Buckingham Palace. It was widely believed that the Queen was so worried about what Burrell might say when he entered the witness box that it prompted her last-minute recall of that now famous meeting. Now both the monarchy and the justice system were called into disrepute.

With the flame of Diana's memory spluttering in the Spencers' torch, Paul Burrell eagerly stepped forth to tell the world about the Diana he knew and loved.

His legal trial was over. Now he faced trial by media when he decided to sell his story to the *Daily Mirror*. As he shredded the last vestiges of the Spencers' dignity by his revelations, rival newspapers printed lurid details about what they claimed were his promiscuous homosexuality and seedy lifestyle. The reputation of Diana's rock crumbled along with that of the family he had once loved and now loathed.

In the coming months, the one man who had never wanted the case to come to court in the first place now found himself in the dock. The ordeal of Paul Burrell may have ended. The trial of Prince Charles was about to begin.

CHAPTER THIRTEEN

The Curse of the Lost Princess

S HE IS OUT OF SIGHT NOW, but rarely out of mind. While his heart belongs to another, Charles still wears her ring and prays for her each night. Even though his country home at Highgrove has been redecorated he continues to list the guest room as 'Her Royal Highness's bedroom' and the study as 'Her Royal Highness's sitting room'. He signs his correspondence with a pen which the Princess gave him, still wears the gold and enamel cufflinks from her and has an assortment of monogrammed slippers, cashmere sweaters and cotton shirts she chose. After more than thirty years in the company of Camilla Parker Bowles there are still, as commentators never tire of observing, three people in the relationship. After all, Diana, Princess of Wales, is the mother of his children, the mother of the future king. It is her ineluctable legacy.

Yet while the Prince may still think fondly of his former wife, may perhaps, in his own way, still love her, Diana has returned from beyond the grave to haunt and torment him in ways that even she never dreamed possible. As the writer Dominick Dunne observed, 'It's hard to resist thinking that, beneath her celestial tiara, Diana has a plan. My theory is that she's not going to rest until her son William becomes King of England in place of her ex-husband.' Her legacy has shredded his dignity, questioned his integrity and provoked doubts about his sexuality.

At first the Prince attracted overwhelming public sympathy not just for the dignified manner in which he handled the tragedy of her sudden death, but also as a bereaved single parent trying to bring up two boys during their difficult teenage years. In many ways the slow, subtle introduction of Camilla Parker Bowles into the public arena became the litmus test of his rehabilitation. That Camilla was to be a permanent fixture in his life was, as far as the Prince was concerned, 'non negotiable'. In the months following Diana's death, she stayed out of sight, allowing the man the boys called 'Lord Blackadder', the Prince's spin doctor Mark Bolland, to handle her public profile. As acid-tongued and scheming as the nobleman from the BBC TV comedy, Bolland, one of the so-called 'gay mafia' who surrounded the Prince, worked on the simple but effective carrot-and-stick approach, giving favoured journalists tit-bits of information about Prince William in return for favourable coverage about his master and his mistress. So when Camilla met Prince William at St James's Palace in 1998, an encounter which went well but had the nervous 'Mrs Wales' calling for a stiff drink afterwards, the overall media impression was positive.

The Prince and his paramour were even able to fly to Greece on board a friend's private plane that summer for their first ever holiday together without attracting unduly hostile headlines. This policy of stealth culminated in a photocall at the Ritz Hotel in London where the couple entered the building in January 1999. In September, Bolland was on hand to guide her through her launch into New York society, meeting TV doyenne Barbara Walters, media mogul Michael Bloomberg and designer Oscar de la Renta. By the end of what was to all intents and purposes a royal trip – even though it was a private holiday – photographers were calling Camilla 'ma'am'. When she and the Prince hosted King Constantine of Greece's sixtieth birthday party at Highgrove in June 2000, which was attended by the Queen, there was carefully choreographed talk about Camilla as a future consort. The idea of Queen Camilla was, however, a spin too far, the lady herself apparently preferring a supportive rather than starring role. When she was invited to join the Queen for the Golden Jubilee service at Westminster Abbey in June 2002, her acceptance in royal circles was complete. Her excitable biographer, Christopher Wilson, even went so far as to predict a royal marriage in early 2004. While Camilla now has her own suite of rooms at Clarence House, into which the Prince has moved, following the death of the Queen Mother, and is the mistress of Highgrove, there is still no sign of a ring.

A year after Charles and Camilla had taken their seats at the Queen's Golden Jubilee service, however, the heir to the throne was under attack and Camilla back in the shadows. 'Positive coverage of the Prince has, frankly, disappeared, while acres of newsprint are devoted to what is wrongly depicted as the cranky Prince, the spendthrift Prince, the hunting and shooting Prince and the meddling Prince,' lamented Mark Bolland, who is now a newspaper columnist.

The unravelling of this carefully composed tapestry of parental devotion, civic dedication and connubial decorum began during the appearance of Paul Burrell at the Old Bailey. As Burrell's solicitor warned, the royal family, particularly Prince Charles, were on trial as much as the butler. The revelations about the practice of gifting – where servants were given unwanted royal items; the allegations of male rape contained in the tape held in Diana's mahogany box, and the activities of the Prince's valet Michael Fawcett, relentlessly demolished years of duty and dependability. The resulting furore, which rumbled on for nearly two years, ensured that Diana's voice was heard from beyond the grave. She would not, as she herself had said, go quietly.

Following the ignominious collapse of the Burrell trial, the Prince asked his new private secretary, Sir Michael Peat, to investigate the now notorious allegations, the first ever inquiry into a member of the royal family. While his report, published in March 2003, cleared the Prince and, for that matter, Michael Fawcett of any wrongdoing, the impression was left of a self-indulgent heir and a louche, sycophantic and chaotically organized royal household. It emerged that capital gains tax was not paid on the sale of gifts; that unwanted presents were sold or exchanged, while some were burnt or otherwise destroyed, and that proper records not kept. 'If the Prince of Wales were a government minister he would have spent last week drafting his resignation letter,' commented one observer. Even Prince Charles admitted that the report made for 'uncomfortable' reading.

After the Peat Report and during the summer of 2003, a whispering campaign began, hinting that the now notorious rape tape contained even more sensational allegations, namely that a member of the royal family had been witnessed in a compromising position with a servant. After weeks of circling round the issue, which involved Michael Fawcett obtaining several court injunctions, it emerged that orderly George Smith's central claim was that he had witnessed an 'incident' involving Prince Charles and a member of staff after taking the Prince breakfast in bed.

That these allegations, made by someone who was, as even the newspaper concerned admitted, 'hardly a reliable witness', were even printed showed the cynicism with which the media and the public now viewed the monarchy. A *Sunday Times* leader went to the heart of the malaise: 'The problem for Charles is that an environment has been created in which people can believe almost anything. A dysfunctional family is attended upon by an oddball collection of servants, many of whom are only too ready to sell their accounts of life with the Windsors. Others profit in different ways.'

Even after the Prince's former valet Simon Solari, who worked with Smith at the time of the alleged incident, had said that Smith simply could not have witnessed what he claimed because his position as an orderly would never have allowed him access to the royal bedroom, the gossip still continued. Eventually, in a bid to calm the media hysteria, the Prince's private secretary, Sir Michael Peat, made a televised statement in which he dismissed the claims as 'risible', adding, 'Anyone who knows the Prince of Wales at all would appreciate that the allegation is totally ludicrous.'

After the Prince's private secretary's high-risk and high-profile intervention, the only sound that could be heard was of knives being sharpened. For the sub-text of this whole affair was about palace politics as much as it was about personal peccadilloes.

When Peat – a successful accountant who had effected dramatic cost savings and administrative reforms at Buckingham Palace – was given the job of guiding the Prince, it was widely viewed as an attempt by the Queen, Prince Philip and senior courtiers to bring Charles to heel and his office into the twenty-first century, ending the culture of feuding, feudalism and favourites.

Top of the hit list were Michael Fawcett, who was felt to be too close to the heir, 'too flaky and too extravagant', and Mark Bolland, whose spin-doctoring in the Prince's favour had left other members of the royal family, including the Queen, as collateral jetsam. In the fallout from these scandals, Bolland and Fawcett, both enthusiastic supporters of Camilla Parker Bowles, were ousted, though Peat himself was not immune from bitchy criticism. Bolland, in his newspaper column, took the opportunity to score points against his nemesis, claiming in the *News of the World* that, after the collapse of the Burrell trial, Sir Michael had telephoned him and asked if Prince Charles was bisexual. 'I was astonished at Sir Michael's question. I told him emphatically that the Prince was *not* gay or bisexual,' Bolland insisted. 'It is astonishing that even he . . . wanted to check the various allegations with as many people as possible.'

If the fallout from the Burrell trial had caused even those closest to the Prince to question his attitudes and behaviour, fate had not finished toying with him. In October 2003, Paul Burrell, now running a flower shop in Cheshire, published his memoir. *A Royal Duty* was not just an act of vengeance on the Spencer family, whom he blamed for his two-year ordeal from the day the police raided his home in January 2001 till the collapse of his trial in November 2002; it was also to prove a further torment for Diana's husband. Much as Burrell tried to paint a portrait of Charles and Diana as affectionately reconciled following their divorce, William and Harry, in an unprecedented public attack, called it a 'cold and overt betrayal'.

At the same time the book contained a secret that even the butler refused to reveal, a secret that went to the bitter heart of their marriage, the tragedy of her death, and was manna from Heaven for conspiracy theorists the world over. In the handwritten letter, allegedly given to the butler in October 1996, just ten months before her death, the Princess had written about her suspicions of a plot to kill her. When the book was published, the name behind this plot was blacked out.

However, the *Daily Mirror*, who serialized the book, eventually named Prince Charles following the formal announcement of an inquest into her death in January 2004. 'My husband is planning "an accident" in my car, brake failure and serious head injury in order to make the path clear for Charles to marry,' she wrote. As previously discussed, it is more likely that this was written a year earlier, in 1995, not long before her famous television interview – certainly these thoughts haunted her then. This extraordinary turn of events was propelled by the decision of the official coroner, Michael Burgess, to instruct Sir John Stevens, the Metropolitan Police Commissioner, to open his own investigation into Diana's death, rather than simply rubber-stamping the findings of the exhaustive two-year French inquiry. In announcing his decision, the coroner said that he wanted to 'separate fact from fiction and speculation' and indicated that he was aware of 'speculation that their deaths were not the result of a sad, but relatively straightforward, road traffic accident in Paris'. It meant that, with ten officers assigned to go over the ground again, it will probably take until mid-2005 before a full inquest is completed.

The release of further details from Diana's letter to coincide with the inquest announcement caused further anguish for Prince Charles. Headlines stating, 'Charles: How much more can I take?' accompanied stories saying that the heir to the throne was expected to be interviewed by Britain's top policeman who was formally assigned to investigate her death. Diana's letter, which spoke of her husband's cruelty and her own anguish, now formed a vital part of the inquiry. During a visit to the Pont de l'Alma crash site in April 2004, Sir John emphasized his determination to 'draw a line' under the affair, while interviewing all concerned, including Prince Charles.

For the first time since her funeral, the Spencers and Windsors were united, dismayed that the coroner had seen fit to leave open the Pandora's box of rumour and speculation once again. 'As far as my family is concerned, the sooner the legal technicalities surrounding Diana's death are finalized, the happier we will all be,' declared Earl Spencer. 'I have never seen a shred of evidence that it was anything other than an accident.' A friend of the shell-shocked Prince of Wales admitted: 'We just never saw this coming,' while Princes William and Harry, who had, in 1998, urged the nation to stop grieving and move on, were 'hurt and upset' when their mother's letter accusing their father of plotting against her was published.

It was also a slap in the face for the French investigation which had used thirty detectives and interviewed 300 witnesses. They condemned the British media for creating an 'atmosphere of controversy' which in turn fed 'hypotheses, theories and allegations' which they had already investigated. The only torchbearer of Diana's memory who was delighted by the inquiry was Mohamed Fayed, who had spent £5 million and hundreds of thousands of man-hours attempting to prove that his son and the Princess were murdered. 'Absolutely black-and-white, horrendous murder,' he stated, a view which resonated deeply with the public, particularly in the Arab world where it is widely believed that the couple were killed because the royal family did not want a Muslim to marry a princess. *Who Killed Diana? Order From the Palace* was the title of one best-selling book in Egypt, while the Libyan leader, Colonel Gaddafi, joined in, broadcasting his view that British and French secret services arranged 'the assassination of the Princess of Wales and the Arab citizen who were planning to get married'.

Many went along with Fayed's conspiracy theories – one British newspaper survey revealed that 43 per cent of the public believed that Diana was murdered. Fayed, however, was a largely discredited figure as so much of what he had previously contended had been found to be untrue. Even though many of his assertions, notably that the paparazzi had caused the crash, that she had said last words to a nurse which he had passed on to Lady Sarah McCorquodale, and that she was pregnant, proved to be demonstrably false, he doggedly continued to pile up theory upon conjecture upon allegation. Every official conclusion was contested, every avenue explored. He offered a £1 million reward for information leading to the discovery of the driver of the mysterious white Fiat Uno that he believed had forced the Mercedes to crash, while his lawyers even strong-armed the American National Security Agency to produce 1,056 pages of documentation they possessed which related to Diana for the period surrounding the accident. As 124 pages were classified as 'Top Secret' this further encouraged the belief that her telephone calls were being tapped by a security agency.

The private investigation conducted by Fayed also zeroed in on other unexplained occurrences: the fact that surveillance cameras in the tunnel were switched off; that the Mercedes may have been deliberately forced into the tunnel; the roadworthiness of the car, which had been stolen and tampered with three months before; and that just before the accident a blinding flash was seen by certain witnesses aimed at the driver. Much conjecture surrounded the driver, Henri Paul, who was fingered as a possible secret-service informer based on his freelance work as a tipster and the large and unexplained amount of cash in his many bank accounts. There was speculation too that his blood sample, which showed his high level of alcohol and drugs, had been, accidentally or deliberately, switched. Evidence for his apparent sobriety was the fact that CCTV footage showed him tying his shoelaces in the lobby of the Ritz Hotel without any evident problem. After carefully reviewing all the available evidence, Mohamed Fayed's firmly held view that it was Prince Philip – rather than Prince Charles – who had ordered the British secret service to murder Diana and Dodi.

While the supposed mastermind behind her 'murder' was a matter of debate, certainly the most popular conspiracy theory concerned the involvement of Britain's secret services in Diana's death. This was given extra weight by maverick former British intelligence agents, Richard Tomlinson and David Shayler, who cited a plan to kill the former Serbian President Slobodan Milosevic in a fake car crash in Geneva. Even the KGB, the Russian secret service, found this hard to swallow. The espionage writer Philip Knightley quoted a KGB agent as saying, 'It takes a genius to make murder by car look like an accident.'

Yet the car crash theory seemed utterly plausible when ranged against the 36,000 conspiracy theory websites devoted to Diana's death. Hypotheses ranged from claims that she was killed by international arms dealers because of her support for a ban on landmines, to those that say Osama bin Laden had her murdered as she was a bad role model for Muslim women, to some that insist that she was murdered by the royal family. On the wilder shores of credibility is a theory that she was killed by the shadowy Babylonian Brotherhood as she was named after the moon goddess and Pont de l'Alma, the underpass where the crash occurred, means passage of the moon goddess.

The truth is that, at heart, people find it difficult to believe that a modern-day goddess could meet her maker in the banality of a car accident where a drunk driver simply drove too fast. It seems that psychologically, individuals need conspiracy theories to make the chaotic, inexplicable universe more ordered and bearable. As Dr Patrick Leman of Royal Holloway College, University of London, who has conducted research into mental attitudes, observed: 'When a big event happens we prefer to have a big cause. It upsets our view of the world if there isn't a significant powerful explanation.' So the assassination of John F. Kennedy, the death of Elvis and even the attack on the World Trade Center are surrounded by a multitude of competing and ever more elaborate hypotheses. In times gone by, the Jews and Freemasons were at the centre of every conspiracy. These days, given the increasing disrespect for and disbelief in authority, it is the secret service, the hidden agents of a malign Establishment, who are held responsible. 'The new irrationalism,' remarked the writer Francis Wheen, 'is an expression of despair by people who feel impotent to improve their lives and suspect that they are at the mercy of secretive, impersonal forces, whether these be the Pentagon or invaders from Mars.' We may be less deferential but we seem to be more gullible.

The plain fact of the matter, as a correspondent to the *Daily Telegraph* pointed out, was that if Diana truly believed that she might die in a pre-arranged car accident then why did she not wear a seat belt? The world-weary comment of former royal coroner Dr John Burton captured the official exasperation with the continued focus on secret plots. 'When it's all over,' he commented, 'ninety-five per cent of the people will still disregard the facts and want to go back to their conspiracies.'

While the maelstrom of scandal swirling around the Prince of Wales has diminished his standing, it has done little to enhance the reputation of Diana, Princess of Wales either. Her letter of foreboding, which was both pathetic and comic, served to seal the growing perception that she was, as *The Times* noted, either a 'drama queen or a tragic princess'. The witty, self-deprecating, courageous, caring and humane woman who her friends knew, and to whom the world responded when she died, was becoming lost in the riot of lurid allegations and theories. In life she had always feared that she would be dismissed as mentally unstable. Now, in death, she was described at best as flawed, by many as mad, a woman who had preserved her reputation by dying young. The commentator David Aaronovitch figuratively shook his head in despair at the confluence of conspiracy theories and Diana's volatile personality. Writing in the *Guardian* he opined: 'The polls show me to be in a minority. They suggest that Diana was indeed the people's princess. She, it turns out, was barking – and so are we.'

With the passing of the years her critics felt more able to speak out. Her behaviour, particularly her seemingly ill-judged relationship with Dodi Fayed, concerned many commentators. The Queen's biographer Robert Lacey told talk-show host Larry King in March 2004: 'I think she was out of control and that it would have got worse. And I think – this is a tragic and maybe cynical thing to say – her death was the best possible thing that could have happened to her reputation.' Others, like royal writer Hugo Vickers, joined the growing chorus of condemnation: 'I still think she was spiralling into chaos. I don't think it was going to get any better. It might have been a very sad middle age for her.'

Even before the release of Diana's damning letter, supporters of the royal family had given occasional glimpses of how Britain's First Family felt about the lost princess. A television documentary by William Shawcross, now the Queen Mother's official biographer, which was broadcast during the Golden Jubilee weekend, featured two of the Queen's close friends, Countess Mountbatten and Lady Penn, a lady-in-waiting, casting doubt on Diana's character. 'The Queen found Diana's ill health or mental instability very hard to understand because she's a very matter-of-fact person,' was the damning verdict of Lady Penn.

Charles's biographer Penny Junor twisted the knife further when she wrote a laudatory book about the Prince of Wales, arguing that the late Princess suffered from Borderline Personality Syndrome, a recognized medical condition. She had been briefed by St James's Palace which had read the final manuscript. The profile of Diana by American writer Sally Bedell Smith reached a similar conclusion, presumably influenced by off-the-record sources. As Diana's former private secretary, Patrick Jephson, noted, 'It passed into the public consciousness that the Princess of Wales was mentally ill in some way.'

Mad and, like Princess Caroline before her, seemingly soon forgotten. The fact that there were only a handful of bouquets outside Kensington Palace on the sixth anniversary of her death was seized upon as a sign of her wilting legacy and fading memory. It gave ammunition to those eager to dismiss the cult of Diana, the primacy of feeling over reason, of the personal over the political, as nothing more than a disguised version of self-love, a fad as ephemeral as the Carolinian movement. Intellectuals who had viewed with alarm the outpouring of public grief at her death now regarded this phenomenon as a symbol of society's general retreat from reason and rationality, the death knell of the Age of Enlightenment.

At the same time, many of the grandiose plans to honour Diana's memory had petered out. Senior politicians, who in the immediate aftermath of her death had suggested renaming Heathrow airport and the August Bank Holiday in her name, fell silent. Even those schemes that were launched were mired in endless controversy and acrimony. For a woman who considered herself a healer, her legacy was smothered in rancour and bitterness. A £3 million water feature in Kensington Gardens to commemorate her life symbolized the difficulties. During her life she had always sought out water, either by the riverbank or sea shore, as a soothing source of solace and reflection. Yet when the Memorial Committee, chaired by the strong-minded Rosa Monckton, came to select the final design, they were so divided that the Culture Secretary Tessa Jowell was called in to make the final decision. She chose the design by American landscape artist Kathryn Gustafson in preference to one submitted by the Indian-born British sculptor Anish Kapoor. No sooner had she made her choice, than the critics piped up, Diana's mother saying that the fountain 'lacked grandeur'. A place of contemplation and deliberation was turned into an unseemly but all too predictable wrestling match about what she would have wanted. In the face of sustained criticism of the royal family and of their treatment of the late Princess, the Queen agreed to unveil the principal memorial to her at a ceremony in the summer of 2004, attended by Spencers and Windsors. The move was seen as a long-overdue attempt at reconciliation between the two families.

A children's playground and a memorial walkway in Kensington Gardens fared better and are both now enjoyed by the public. Noticeably no member of the royal family attended the opening of these projects, much to the 'sadness' of Rosa Monckton, who, accompanied by Earl Spencer, opened the playground, and the 'irritation' of Chancellor Gordon Brown who inaugurated the walk. For the royal family seem all too happy to let Diana rest in peace, her memory unobserved and all but forgotten. They are conspicuous by their absence at any event relating to the late Princess. So a hospice outside Cardiff, a hospital in Grimsby, a community-nursing scheme for sick children and other projects, all named after the late Princess, have been dedicated without remark or support from the royal family.

They took no part in discussions about a memorial and left the Memorial Fund charity to fend for itself (although unnamed courtiers were always quick to express 'dismay' at its many and varied difficulties). Even Prince Charles's former spin doctor Mark Bolland was moved to suggest, 'If the royal family want to learn lessons from Diana it is still not too late. Why don't they build their own memorial to her? Encourage William in some way to honour his mother's memory in a public way?'

The response was a collective shrug of the shoulders. After all, the huge turnout for the Queen Mother's funeral – the controversy over the fact that BBC newsreader Peter Sissons wore a lilac, rather than black, tie showed that knee-jerk deference was not dead – and the affectionate popular response to the Queen's Golden Jubilee confirmed the monarchy *sans* Diana in people's hearts. At a parade which formed the centrepiece of the Jubilee celebrations, the late Princess was relegated to a drive-on part, appearing as a cut-out figure on one of a convoy of floats that paraded down the Mall past the royal party, which included Mrs Parker Bowles. The irony would not have been lost on the late Princess. As the writer Robert Harris was moved to point out, 'Not since Trotsky was expelled from the Soviet Union in 1929 has a prominent public figure been so comprehensively airbrushed out of a nation's public life.' When the royal yacht *Britannia* was decommissioned in December 1997, it was noticeable the Queen and the rest of her family shed more tears for their floating palace than they had for the late Princess. 'Diana is never mentioned, it was as though she never existed,' commented a friend of the royal family.

Forlorn, foolish and forgotten, seven years after her death the impression is now given that the Princess inhabits a nether world where the flames of her memory are stoked only by scandal, her celebrity enduring by virtue of the latest sensation, be it voyeuristic TV shows revealing tantalizing glimpses of her dying in the underpass in Paris or titbits of gossip from former servants. It seems that the woman known to those in her circle, the irrepressible, kind, emotional, vulnerable yet sophisticated individual, never really walked on this earth and that her legacy is a chimera, a splendid firework that exploded dramatically and faded as rapidly. This one-dimensional portrait is now equally as misleading as the saccharine caricature that she was a saint in designer clothes. Her life, like her legacy, is much more complex and elusive, a journey of endless twists and turns. Ironically it is a journey to one of the world's most remote and unknown regions which yields important clues to one of the century's most famous women.

Epilogue

Passport to Parachinar

P ARACHINAR IS NOT A PLACE for the unwary. This remote town lies in the notorious mountains of the North-West Frontier, the crossroads between Afghanistan and Pakistan. For centuries it has been an anarchic haven for drug smugglers, gun runners and refugees. In the local bazaar, hashish, opium, and Russian and homemade rifles are sold alongside mixed fruit and cattle. There is no civil law, only *Pashtunwali*, a tribal code of honour and conduct. Levels of literacy are among the lowest and those of child mortality among the highest in the world. Curfews are a regular feature of life, gun battles between feuding tribes not uncommon. One vicious firefight in September 1996 left 200 dead and scores of women and children raped and kidnapped. Bullet holes still scar the minarets of the local mosques. 'The atrocities were out of the Stone Age,' according to a paramilitary official.

Over the years these fierce mountain warriors, the Pashtuns, or Pathans, have fiercely defied attempts by the Moguls, the Sikhs, the British, the Soviets and the Pakistanis to control them. They have paid a high price; during the Russian invasion of Afghanistan, helicopters and planes indiscriminately dropped thousands of landmines and booby traps that have killed untold thousands and left many, mainly women and children, brutally scarred and maimed. The impoverished North-West Frontier adds significantly to the annual tally of 26,000 victims of landmines around the world.

In this backward country it is now the turn of the United States to attempt control. Just a few miles north, the Americans and their allies unleashed their full military fury at the Tora Bora caves, the hideout for Osama bin Laden and his Taliban and al-Qaeda followers. Today American intelligence reckons that bin Laden, who escaped the pummelling, is hiding within a ten-square-mile radius of the town of Parachinar which is the capital of the Kurram tribal agency. Slogans on the walls proclaiming LONG LIVE OSAMA BIN LADEN reveal where local sympathies lie. These days it is a not a place where Westerners are welcome.

Yet, in the local general hospital, an enlarged photograph of Diana, Princess of Wales dominates the entrance to one ward, where men and women wait for artificial limbs to be fitted. In this region where suspicion and defensiveness are ingrained, her image is a passport, a guarantee of safe passage for the handful of Western aid workers. For the last year, a British charity, Response International, has been one of the few outside aid organizations allowed to work in this lawless land. Not only are its workers organizing the fitting of artificial limbs for landmine victims in the hospital, they are travelling around forts and villages teaching landmine awareness, first aid and trauma care. Everywhere they go musicians, children dancing and armfuls of flowers greet them. The reception is all the more extraordinary as the very idea of charitable organizations is alien to this proud, self-reliant people. Just one word guarantees a warm welcome and an assurance of security: 'Diana'. The charity, which focuses on the forgotten victims of conflict in remote parts of the globe, has been financed in its work by the Memorial Fund set up in the Princess's name, a tangible and practical legacy of her humanitarian work. The charity's chief executive, Philip Garvin, was genuinely astonished by the impact Diana has had on the people in this remote region: 'I was treated like a king because I had the image of Diana hanging over my head. We used her name ruthlessly to get things organized and make contact with local people.' Her appeal lies in the fact that she is not seen as English or a typical Westerner, but as an apolitical humanitarian who worked for the removal of the landmines that were killing or maiming so many of their people.

In a world where assassination is a way of life, the widespread belief that she was murdered by the royal family merely adds to her kudos. There is too a curious cultural symmetry about her appeal in this forbidding land; she is a heroine in a world where Osama bin Laden is a hero. At the beginning of the new millennium they are iconic bookends, one strove to bring East and West together, both in her relationships and her humanitarian mission and vision; the other is now violently and fanatically attempting to divide the world on religious lines.

So, much as the royal family and her critics would like not to imagine otherwise, Diana's work does continue, unacknowledged and unremarked, helping the dispossessed, the unpopular and the forgotten, the very people that in her life she so fulsomely embraced. Since its rocky inception the Memorial Fund in her name has handed out more than £50 million in grants for 300 or so projects, ranging from assisting refugees to helping youngsters with learning difficulties in Britain and abroad. While it can never take the place of the Princess – 'No one has come close to her since she died,' in the words of David Puttnam – it has the money to make a genuine and continuing difference to people's lives.

Mired in controversy from the moment the first one-pound coin stuck to the back of a postcard arrived at Kensington Palace, the Fund has been seen as a bastard child by the royal establishment, unwanted and unloved. It has never been visited by a member of the royal family, nor have Diana's children, William and Harry, ever taken part in any of its work, either in private meetings or public events. This is one of many ticklish challenges facing Diana's sons.

For in three years' time, when Prince William is twenty-five, he will be entitled not only to the money she bequeathed him and his brother in her will, but also to take a substantial role at the helm of her charity, at some stage presumably taking over the role of Diana's sister, Sarah McCorquodale. His brother has already spoken publicly about his desire to follow in her footsteps. On his eighteenth birthday Prince Harry, now destined for a career in the Armed Forces, talked for the first time about his mother and her legacy: 'She had more guts than anyone else. I want to carry on the things she didn't quite finish. I've always wanted to – but before I was too young. She got close to people and went for the sort of charities and organizations that everybody else was scared to go near, such as landmines.'

Besides the rhetoric, the litmus test of the boys' determination to carry on her work will be the extent of their involvement with the Memorial Fund. There are many powerful voices, not just inside the palace, who would like to see the charity wound up, adding to the pressure on Prince William, who is already concerned about finding a role that does not compete with his father. That conflict may be inevitable, as Mark Bolland pointed out: 'The real worry is for Prince Charles, who can't seem to get in the papers now without standing next to his son. That was always one of his nightmares. It's clearly coming true.' Yet it is the vulnerable and voiceless, like the crippled children waiting patiently for artificial limbs in Parachinar general hospital, who will be the ones who suffer if the young Princes walk on by.

During her lifetime the Princess gambled everything on her boys. They, particularly Prince William, are her living legacy. 'All my hopes are on William now,' she told Tina Brown, then editor of the *New Yorker*, in June 1997. 'It's too late for the rest of the family. But I think he has it.' For the next decade at least, this good-looking prince will be the pin-up of the royal family, the flag bearer of the future, not just of the monarchy but of his mother's memory. That is important. For while courtiers believe that he is far more of a Mountbatten-Windsor than a Spencer in character, his public image is that he has the same diffident appeal as his late mother. In an age where image is everything his casual good looks and unstudied easy charm guarantees the similar glamorous appeal as Diana. 'As a modern young royal, William has been fortunate in having much more freedom than any previous member of the family,' observes his biographer Brian Hoey. 'He is undoubtedly the star of the future, the one on whom the royal family's hopes rest.'

The time Diana spent taking her sons to hostels for the homeless and to hospitals so that they could understand real life more clearly seems to have paid off. 'I was influenced a lot by my visits to hostels with my mother when I was younger,' said Prince William, during an interview for his twenty-first birthday. 'I learned a lot from it, more so now than I did at the time.'

In many respects, though, if Queen Victoria came back today, she would be unsurprised by his upbringing. Like many children of the aristocracy he was sent away from home to boarding school, he attended Eton, still seen as the most elitist school in the land, and is now at St Andrew's university, which has among the highest proportion of privately educated school pupils in the country.

Again, like his forebears, the Prince's pastimes are predominantly upper class, fox-hunting with fashionable meets near his father's Gloucestershire home and joining shooting parties at Sandringham and other country houses. 'I do think I'm a country boy at heart,' he said unsurprisingly. A country boy who, when he is at his father's house at Highgrove, will have the services of one of three valets to lay out his clothes in the morning. A country boy who will inherit a £700-million fortune one day, maybe even becoming the first billionaire Prince of Wales.

Yet by royal standards he has led a much more relaxed and informal lifestyle than his father ever enjoyed. The very fact that he appeared barefoot and in a torn sweater at the photocall for his first ever interview is testament to a more casual style. If nothing else, as a result of his mother's tragic life, William will, as Earl Spencer observed, be able to choose the bride he wants rather than having her chosen for him. That though has not stopped British TV shows trying to pick a bride for him, albeit tongue-in-cheek. The experience of his college friend Kate Middleton, who hit the headlines when she accompanied the Prince and the rest of the royal party on a skiing holiday to Klosters in Switzerland in 2004, shows that the media's fascination with his love life will be as intense as during his father's days.

He will though inherit an organization more in tune with today's world, modernizing work having been undertaken by Buckingham Palace and now, belatedly, by Prince Charles. As Earl Spencer told Ian Katz, 'One of Diana's greater legacies to her sons and their successors is that she has made many more things acceptable in a royal context and showed the old guard at

Buckingham Palace that, in fact, a lot of that stuff is wanted by the people as a whole.' Indeed a YouGov poll said that 'humanizing the royal family' was Diana's greatest achievement, ahead of her landmine campaign.

For all the attempts to diminish and dismiss her, the Princess still looms large in the popular imagination. In a BBC poll in 2002 she ranked third, behind Winston Churchill and Isambard Kingdom Brunel, as the greatest Briton, easily outstripping any other member of the royal family, dead or alive. Her death, according to those who responded to a poll for the History Channel, was perceived as the most significant event of the twentieth century – ahead of the beginning of the Second World War.

People responded to her death precisely because her life had so much meaning. As a woman, a mother, a daughter and a public figure, she reflected many of the dilemmas and conflicts of our own lives as she tried to discover who she really was. Her courage in defying a powerful family, her decision to live by her own lights, her haphazard, sometimes foolhardy, search for love, as well as the way she challenged and embraced her past are windows into a complex personality that struggled to face up to and overcome her demons, be they related to her body, her self-belief, her self-esteem or her ambitions. She was never standing still, always looking to assert herself, through her speeches, her humanitarian work or her lifestyle. Diana was a woman who was growing and developing rather than sitting on her laurels.

Yet the prevailing orthodoxy is that she was out of control and pretty well out of her mind. The evidence for that contention centres largely around the paranoia that infected her life at the time of her infamous BBC television interview. In this book I have tried to demonstrate that, given the way her fears were being cleverly fed by reporter Martin Bashir, as well as hearing other alarming information relating to the boys' nanny Tiggy Legge-Bourke and Prince Charles's orderly George Smith, she had every right to feel physically afraid as indeed would any other person under those pressures at that time. Perhaps this re-evaluation of the facts of her life will lead to a fresh look at who she was and where she was heading, a richer appreciation of a woman striving to make sense of a multifaceted lifestyle, rather than a mournful individual on the fringe of sanity. That she learned so much and travelled so far is testament to her strength of character and indomitable spirit. The truth is, as I have argued, that the Princess was leaving her demons behind and using her great gifts of empathy and communication in a worthwhile, satisfying work.

Perhaps the last word about this extraordinary woman should go to the woman she once reviled and then came to admire, her stepmother Countess Raine Spencer: 'She managed to get through very difficult parts of life with enormous courage and turned herself from being a very shy, insecure girl, not nearly as pretty as her other two sisters, into a world-class beauty, world-class fashion model who had a world-class heart. She loved people and helping people. It gave her a tremendous boost, the feeling that she could make a difference. She was a very remarkable, unusual and extraordinary person. Truly an icon of our time.'

Timeline

1961

1 July   The Hon. Diana Spencer born at Park House, on the Sandringham Estate, Norfolk.

1978

September   Earl Spencer, Diana's father, collapses after a massive brain haemorrhage.

1981

6 February   Prince Charles proposes to Lady Diana Spencer.
29 July   Marriage of Prince Charles and Lady Diana.

1982

21 June   Prince William is born.

1984

15 September   Prince Henry (Harry) is born.

1991

Diana secretly undertakes interviews with Dr James Colthurst for what will eventually become *Diana: Her True Story.*

1992

29 March	Earl Spencer dies of a heart attack.
7 & 14 June	Serialization of *Diana: Her True Story* in the *Sunday Times*.
16 June	*Diana: Her True Story* published.
25 August	'Squidgygate' tapes published.
9 December	Prime Minister John Major announces royal separation.

1993

17 January	'Camillagate' tapes published.
3 December	Diana announces her withdrawal from public life.

1994

June	TV documentary, in which Charles admits adultery, broadcast.
August	Diana accused of making nuisance phone calls to Oliver Hoare.

1995

January	Andrew and Camilla Parker Bowles announce they are to divorce.
September	Julia and Will Carling announce their separation.
20 November	*Panorama* interview broadcast.
	Diana flies to Argentina.
11 December	Given the 'Humanitarian of the Year' award by Henry Kissinger in New York.
December	Diana receives a handwritten request from the Queen to divorce.
	Diana makes a comment to Tiggy Legge-Bourke at the Royal Household's Christmas party.

1996

12 July	Charles and Diana announce agreement to divorce.
July	Diana resigns as patron of a majority of her charities.

1996 (*cont'd*)

28 August	Charles and Diana are officially divorced.
October	Diana collects a humanitarian award in Rimini, Italy.
November	Diana's romance with Hasnat Khan is publicized.

1997

January	Trip to Angola, where she walks through a minefield.
March	Charles and Diana are together for William's confirmation.
May	Visit to Pakistan; also sees Hasnat Khan's family. Foreign Secretary Robin Cook announces ban on landmine sales.
June	Charity auction of Diana's royal wardrobe at Christie's, New York.
July	Holiday in the South of France with the Fayed family and William and Harry.
31 August	Diana dies in a car crash in the tunnel beneath the Pont de l'Alma in Paris; also killed are Dodi Fayed and driver Henri Paul.
6 September	Diana's funeral takes place at Westminster Abbey. Later the same day she is buried at Althorp, the Spencers' estate in Northamptonshire.

1998

July	William and Harry organize a play to celebrate Charles's fiftieth birthday. Camilla Parker Bowles is welcomed.
November	Camilla hosts a fiftieth birthday party for Charles.

1999

April	The first building to take Diana's name, Princess of Wales House, Bournemouth – a centre for those living with AIDS and HIV – is opened by her mother, the Hon. Mrs Frances Shand Kydd.

2000

February	Commemorative walkway through the London parks opened.
July	Diana Memorial Gardens opened.

2001

January	Diana's former butler, Paul Burrell, arrested on charges of theft.

2002

November	The case against Paul Burrell at the Old Bailey collapses.

2003

13 March	Publication of the Peat Report.
October	Publication of *A Royal Duty* by Paul Burrell.
November	Publication of the so-called 'rape tape' and its contents.

2004

January	British inquest into the deaths of Diana and Dodi is opened and adjourned.
March	Extracts from the Diana–Morton tapes broadcast in America in a two-part NBC documentary.

BIBLIOGRAPHY

ANDERSEN, CHRISTOPHER, *The Day Diana Died* (Blake: London) 2002

BEDELL SMITH, SALLY, *Diana: The Life of a Troubled Princess* (Random House: London) 1999

BOWER, TOM, *Fayed: The Unauthorised Biography* (Macmillan: London) 1998

BRADFORD, SARAH, *Elizabeth* (Mandarin: London) 1996

BURRELL, PAUL, *A Royal Duty* (Michael Joseph: London) 2003

CAMPBELL, BEATRIX, *Diana: How Sexual Politics Shook the Monarchy* (Women's Press: London) 1998

CANNADINE, DAVID, *The Decline & Fall of the British Aristocracy* (Picador: London) 1992

CARPENTER, HUMPHREY, *Robert Runcie: The Reluctant Archbishop* (Sceptre: London) 1997

CLAYTON, TIM & CRAIG, PHIL, *Diana: Story of a Princess* (Coronet: London) 2001

DELORM, RENE, *Diana & Dodi: A Love Story* (Pocket: London) 1998

GREGORY, MARTYN, *The Diana Conspiracy Exposed* (Olmstead Press: London) 1999

HASTINGS, MAX, *Editor* (Pan Macmillan: London) 2002

HURD, DOUGLAS, *Memoirs* (Little, Brown: London) 2003

JEPHSON, PATRICK, *Shadows of a Princess* (HarperCollins: London) 2000

JUNOR, PENNY, *Charles: Victim or Villain?* (HarperCollins: London) 1998

KEIRSEY, DAVID, *Please Understand Me* (Prometheus Nemesis: California) 1998

LACEY, ROBERT, *Royal: Her Majesty Queen Elizabeth II* (Little, Brown: London) 2002

LEAMER, LAURENCE, *The Kennedy Women* (Bantam: London) 1994

LINDLEY, RICHARD, *Panorama: 50 Years of Pride and Paranoia* (Politico's: London) 2002

MACARTHUR, BRIAN (Ed.), *Requiem* (Pavilion: London) 1997

ORBACH, SUSIE, *The Impossibility of Sex* (Penguin: London) 1999

PAXMAN, JEREMY, *The English* (Penguin: London) 1999

PIMLOTT, BEN, *The Queen* (HarperCollins: London) 2002

PONTAUT, JEAN-MARIE, & DUPUIS, JEROME, *Enquête sur la mort de Diana* (Éditions Stock: Paris) 1998

REES-JONES, TREVOR, *The Bodyguard's Story* (Warner Books: London) 2000

RIDDINGTON, MAX & NADEN, GAVAN, *Frances* (Michael O'Mara: London) 2003

ROBERTSON, GEOFFREY, *The Justice Game* (Chatto & Windus: London) 1998

ROGERS, RITA, *From One World to Another* (Pan Macmillan: London) 1998

SANCTON, THOMAS. & MACLEOD, SCOTT, *Death of a Princess* (Orion: London) 1998

SEITZ, RAYMOND, *Over Here* (Weidenfeld & Nicolson: London) 1998

SHANLEY-TOFFOLO, OONAGH, *The Voice of Silence* (Random House: London) 2002

SIMMONS, SIMONE, *Diana: The Secret Years* (Michael O'Mara: London) 1998

SNELL, KATE, *Diana: Her Last Love* (Granada: London) 2000

THORNTON, PENNY, *With Love From Diana* (Pocket: New York) 1995

WHARFE, KEN, *Diana: Closely Guarded Secret* (Michael O'Mara: London) 2002

WILSON, CHRISTOPHER, *The Windsor Knot* (Pinnacle: New York) 2002

INDEX

_____